Man in a Hurry

Royal Asiatic Society Hong Kong Studies Series

Royal Asiatic Society Hong Kong Studies Series is designed to make widely available important contributions on the local history, culture and society of Hong Kong and the surrounding region. Generous support from the Sir Lindsay and Lady May Ride Memorial Fund makes it possible to publish high-quality works that will be of lasting appeal and value to all, both scholars and informed general readers, who share a deeper interest in and enthusiasm for the area.

Recent titles in the series

Grounded at Kai Tak: Chinese Aircraft Impounded in Hong Kong, 1949–1952
Malcolm Merry

Hong Kong Public and Squatter Housing: Geopolitics and Informality, 1963–1985
Alan Smart and Fung Chi Keung Charles

More than 1001 Days and Nights of Hong Kong Internment: A Personal Narrative
Chaloner Grenville Alabaster; edited by David St Maur Sheil, Kwong Chi Man, and Tony Banham

War and Revolution in South China: The Story of a Transnational Biracial Family, 1936–1951
Edward J. M. Rhoads

Man in a Hurry

Murray MacLehose and Colonial Autonomy in Hong Kong

Ray Yep

Hong Kong University Press
The University of Hong Kong
Pok Fu Lam Road
Hong Kong
https://hkupress.hku.hk

© 2024 Hong Kong University Press

ISBN 978-988-8842-92-6 (*Hardback*)

All rights reserved. No portion of this publication may be reproduced or transmitted in any form or by any means, electronic or mechanical, including photocopying, recording, or any information storage or retrieval system, without prior permission in writing from the publisher.

British Library Cataloguing-in-Publication Data
A catalogue record for this book is available from the British Library.

Digitally printed

For my friends in Hong Kong

Contents

List of Figure and Tables	viii
Acknowledgements	ix
1. Introduction	1
2. The Restive 1960s	22
3. Pre-empting the Sovereign: The Creation of ICAC and the Police Mutiny	45
4. Pushing Back: Social Reforms and the Hong Kong Planning Paper	78
5. Humanitarianism Outsourced: The Vietnamese Refugee Crisis, 1975–1979	108
6. Asserting Local Concern: Land Leases in the New Territories and the Future of Hong Kong	138
7. Final Remarks	170
Bibliography	187
Index	195

List of Figure and Tables

Figure

Figure 7.1: Patterns of London's involvement — 176

Tables

Table 2.1: Crime statistics 1961–1966 — 26
Table 3.1: Complaints of corruption and investigation proceeded by ICAC 1974–1976 — 66
Table 3.2: Complaints, prosecution, and disciplinary action against police officers 1974–1976 — 68
Table 3.3: Investigation of corruption cases by ICAC — 75
Table 4.1: Estimated public expenditure on social services 1978–1983 — 103
Table 5.1: Vietnamese refugees situation in Southeast Asia by 1 May 1979 — 124
Table 5.2: Quota of extra intake for Indochinese refugees agreed at Geneva Conference 1979 — 134

Acknowledgements

I grew up in the MacLehose era. He is probably the first colonial governor I had ever paid attention to. This is however not much to do with his policies or benevolent rule. As a teenager, I had no knowledge or interest in the fact that my home in a public housing estate or my study in a local school both had something to do with his reform programmes. I remember vividly, though, my bus ride to Kowloon with my father on the first day of Cross-Harbour Tunnel operation, a few hours after MacLehose announced its opening. Kowloon was regarded as rough and unsafe in those days and crossing the harbour was something really special for me. My interest in this Scot only grew after my parents finally afforded to buy a TV in the mid-1970s. I watched TV whenever possible and he was on the news all the time. His height and well-combed hair somehow always gave me a sense of assurance. The way a kid saw the world did not always make sense. In fact, our 'bonding' almost elevated to another level as I was supposed to have a chance to meet him in person. As a committed boy scout, I was chosen to represent the Victoria District in St. George's Day parade. As the Queen was the patron of boy scouts all over the world, the Governor was expected to inspect the parade on her behalf. But he didn't show up, as he apparently had other more important events to officiate. We never got a chance to renew our bonding, as he left Hong Kong a few months afterward, after a long twelve-year tenure.

MacLehose has of course made a major impact on the development of Hong Kong. There were substantial progress in public service provisions and infrastructure development during his years and many people regard the creation of the Independent Commission Against Corruption (ICAC) as a pivotal moment in Hong Kong's history. I always wonder why there is no book-length study of his governorship. This book is, however, driven by my other (misguided) observation of colonial rule. I recall growing up under colonial rule without noticing the presence of the British sovereign. This is of course not true, as the image of the Queen was everywhere. Yet in policy terms, until the commencement of the Sino-British negotiations in the early 1980s, I could not find much evidence of the involvement of London in domestic affairs. 'Where is London?', this question has always been at the back of my mind even since I started more serious inquiry into the history of Hong Kong ten, fifteen years ago. And the drive has been accelerated by what I regard as a stark contrast after 1997. Visits and directives of top Chinese leaders have become more and more frequent over the last two decades, and it is almost impossible to find a speech or announcement of Hong Kong Special Administrative Region Government officials without reference to Central People's Government after 2019. How did the colonial governor actually interact with London? How did Hong Kong government work with the sovereign before? What has changed in this relationship since 1997? Or more fundamentally, how could local autonomy be defined? These are the questions I would like to address in this volume. The eventful governorship of MacLehose could be a window for understanding these puzzles.

The final version of this book was written in Bristol, UK. I joined Bristol University's newly created Hong Kong History Centre in 2023. I am grateful for my colleagues, Robert Bickers and Vivian Kong in particular, for making me felt very welcomed. They have provided me a new home, both professionally and emotionally. I am also indebted to many friends who have commented on the different aspects of the project over the years. I am thankful to Tak Wing Ngo, Tai Lok Lui, Anthony Cheung, John Darwin, John Carroll, Angelina Chin, John Wong, Michael Ng, Chi Man Kwong, Maurice Yip, Florence Mok, Alan Smart, Su Lin Lewis, Simon Porter, Simeon Koole, Tom Larkin, Jonathan Howlett, and Lu Yan. I am particularly grateful for the support of David Clayton who has read and commented on the full draft of the book. I also benefited from the outstanding and reliable research support of Lily Bickers, Jason Chan, Matt Lui, Yiu Wa Chung and Tim Tang. Michael Duckworth and Kenneth Yung of Hong Kong University Press have been instrumental to the publication of this manuscript and I appreciate the constructive comments and support of the two anonymous reviewers. The City University of Hong Kong, the Hong Kong History Centre at the University of Bristol, and Hong Kong Research Grant Council (Project No. 9042302) have provided financial support for this project. Part of Chapter 3 was published previously in my articles 'The Crusade against Corruption in Hong Kong in the 1970s: Governor MacLehose as a Zealous Reformer or Reluctant Hero?', *China Information* 27 (July 2013): 197–221, and 'Beyond the "Great Man" Narrative: Scandals, Cumulative Reforms and the Trajectory of Anti-Corruption Efforts in Colonial Era before MacLehose Years', *Social Transformation in Chinese Societies* 18, no. 2 (2021): 154–170, and I also reproduced some of the materials from my article 'Revisiting the Golden Era of MacLehose and the Dynamics of Social Reforms', *China Information* 24, no. 3 (2010): 249–272, in Chapter 4. I would like to express my gratitude to the publishers SAGE and Emerald Publishing for allowing me to reuse some of the materials in this book.

I must thank my family. I thank Carolin for her love, sacrifices, and support over the years. Without her understanding and devotion, I will remain stuck in my miserable space in Tat Chee Avenue. Charlie, Chelsea, and Paul are my guardian angels who always manage to brighten up my cold and lonely days during Britain's winters. Last but not least, I am most grateful for my extended family: my friends in Hong Kong, for their warmth and courage. They are the reason why I somehow managed to survive the adversities over the last few years. They continue to show me how to live in truth and push me to solider on during trying times. We hold on to each other as we endure the traumas and dislocation. Hong Kong remains my home though I choose to continue my professional life elsewhere. It is a privilege to be able to continue writing on Hong Kong's history. It is a pleasure that hurts. This book is dedicated to them.

1
Introduction

The Challenge of Running a Colony

> An executive is sent out to take charge of a sensitive operation with full authority to sort things out and run the business on the ground. After a while, when one or two problems arise, the board starts to wonder whether its executive out there has got it quite right. 'I wonder whether this and that have been considered quite as fully as they might have been? Has everyone on the spot been properly consulted? Why didn't such and such get done?' Imperceptibly at first, and then more openly, head office succumbs to the temptation and starts to second-guess and micro-manage from the centre. Meanwhile the people on the ground become extremely frustrated. Should they make a fuss? Doesn't it all look rather petty if they do? If they appeal to the chairman, won't the chairman regard that as a distraction from more important issue?[1]

This may sound familiar to a senior executive of a local branch of a multinational corporation. However, the author of this quote is not a business professional. This is a reflection by Chris Patten, the last Governor of Hong Kong, whose tenure was arguably one of the most eventful governorships in terms of relations with China. Not only did his proposal of constitutional reform for the colony anger Communist officials in Beijing, it also attracted severe criticism from 'old China hands' in the Foreign Office. His friendship with top officials in high places such as Douglas Hurd and John Major certainly enabled him to withstand the turbulence. Yet his authority waned during the last few months of his term after the Labour Party returned to power in the UK.

Running a colony is a colossal task. Stephanie Williams' accounts of colonial administrations across the British Empire between 1857 and

---

1. Chris Patten, *East and West: The Last Governor of Hong Kong on Power, Freedom and the Future* (London: Pan Macmillan, 1998), 107–108.

1912 depict challenging conditions of governorship: colonies were mostly regarded as backwaters beyond the pale of civilization, and a governor 'was usually seen as someone who had been passed over at home, relegated to a small provincial society of second-raters abroad'.[2] Patten's reflection uncovers essential aspects of a governor's job. Firstly, the relationship between the governor and the British government was hierarchical in nature. Colonial governors were held accountable to the Colonial Secretary, and then to the Foreign Secretary after 1968. Formally speaking, the governor was expected to be subordinate. Nevertheless, colonial administration also implies a process of delegation of power under which the governor could adapt and improvise in response to local situations. Consequently, the actual scope of the autonomy of colonial administrations was hardly preordained; both the interests of their superiors in London and their confidence in the ability of these colonial officials would determine the degree of freedom enjoyed by the governors. The fate of these governors hinged thus upon their success in placating two constituencies simultaneously, both the British side and the colonial community. It is, however, not always easy to decipher who this 'British side' was and what they really wanted. The perception of British empire as a coherent entity is misguided, for it represented not only the interests of kings and queens, politicians or career civil servants, but it was also shaped by the multitudinous and frequently conflicting concerns and activities of individuals in Britain: merchants, missionaries, soldiers, scientists, scholars, bankers, businessmen, and idealists. Governors were obliged to respond and attend to the fiats and directives issued by officials in Whitehall, but the latter were in turn pulled and pressured by a multitude of interests and lobbying efforts at home and abroad. The quarrels and bargaining of these 'imperialists' in diverse guises rendered the expectation of a British Empire with a unified centre unrealistic.

Even within the government, fights and altercations between departments were permanent features of bureaucratic life. Each department looked at the colonial problem through a different lens. The Treasury, a powerful state agency, was fixated on the financial implications of any development in colonies. It may not be fair to paint these financial officials as merely hyper-conservative and negative-minded, but the question of whether local administrations could address their domestic issues without financial contribution from the United Kingdom was their primary, if not their only, concern. The Foreign Office, on the other hand, took great pride in overseeing and managing the global interests of Britain as a whole. The parochial concerns of colonies were not always within their reckoning

---

2. Stephanie Williams, *Running the Show: Governors of the British Empire* (London: Penguin, 2011), 10.

and the situation of any British overseas possession was seldom viewed in isolation. Most importantly, neither of these departments had to bother with the task of administering the colonies, the primary responsibility of the Colonial Office.

Interdepartmental wrangles and clashes were simply integral parts of the policy process. For the colonies, the situation was further compounded by the relatively low status of the Colonial Office, the champion of their interests in the British bureaucracy. The miserable physical conditions endured by this unit in its early days may be illustrative of its low esteem. The old Colonial Office in Downing Street in the 1830s was situated in an unsuitable building that was declared inadequate, unsafe, and unworthy of substantial repair. This was matched with a lack of equipment for proper office operations. As a young officer complained, 'we have no maps that are fit to be consulted . . . we have no furniture—carpets, chairs, tables are all decrepit'.[3] The situation certainly changed with the arrival of Joseph Chamberlain in 1895, and the Office expanded further in the 1930s with the development of specialist departments complementing those handling the general affairs of a subgroup of colonies. Yet a general perception of the Foreign Office as unhelpful remained by and large intact until their merger into the Foreign & Commonwealth Office (FCO) in 1968.[4]

The incoherence and intermingling of private and public interests within the British establishment bred a certain degree of ambiguity which in turn offered some space that the colonies could exploit to pursue local interests. Their endeavours were further helped by the general character of the British Empire, which was primarily a commercial project. As pointed out by John Darwin, British imperial ambition was mostly confined to the capture of profits and commerce via control over the terms of trade with slight interest in raising a direct local revenue to invest in public goals limited.[5] There was thus little incentive to rule closely and oppressively once the challenge of rival imperialists was excluded, and it made no financial sense to install a huge British administrative machinery on the spot. The history of British Empire also reveals a certain degree of hesitation with regards to imperial expansion, which was particularly prevalent during the mid-nineteenth century. The American Revolution was one of several catalysts for growing concerns about the emergence of colonial nationalism, and later developments in South Africa, India, and Rhodesia further ignited

---

3. John Cell, *British Colonial Administration in the Mid-Nineteenth Century* (London: Yale University Press, 1970), 4.
4. Ronald Hyam, *Understanding the British Empire* (Cambridge: Cambridge University Press, 2010), chapter 7.
5. John Darwin, *The Empire Project: The Rise and Fall of British World-System 1830–1970* (Cambridge: Cambridge University Press, 2009).

the debate on how ties with the Empire's vast overseas possessions could be maintained. Anti-imperialists argued that as colonies grew and matured, they would drop off the vine when they ripened just as the American territories had. Free-trade advocates, on the other hand, contended that if favourable trading ties could be maintained, there was no reason to hold overseas possessions against their will. The notion of responsible government was the compromise. First introduced in Nova Scotia in 1846, it gradually expanded to Western Australia, Africa, and other parts of the British Empire.

Both the anti-imperialist and the free-trade positions undermined the propensity of British imperialists to adopt a highly interventionist approach to running the empire. Instead they believed in 'respecting the man on the spot', or, as Sir Cosmo Parkinson succinctly summarized, the general philosophy of overseeing the colonies was that 'it was not for Whitehall to usurp functions which could, or at any rate should, be adequately performed in the colonies themselves'.[6] Such laid-back attitudes underlined the need for colonies to have a degree of autonomy in colonial rule, with several characteristics discernible. Given the general lack of enthusiasm from the centre for meddling in the governing of colonial society and its reluctance to invest in the development of colonial administrative structures, British bureaucracy on the ground was small in relation to the size of colonial population or territories. On the eve of the Second World War, the administrative division of the colonial service in Africa numbered slightly more than 1,200 persons, who were responsible for governing over 43 million locals and 2 million square miles. Even India, 'the jewel in the crown of the British Empire', for a population of 353 million, the maximum number of covenanted members of the Indian Civil Service was capped at 1,250.[7]

The limit of bureaucratic capacity contributed to distinctive governing styles within British colonial rule. With their capacity to reach out to indigenous societies hamstrung by this scarcity, colonial authorities tended to rely on local institutions of governance. The use of intermediaries between the colonial rulers and local population was common, and respect for traditional practices and values was upheld as a social contract under alien rule. The British rule of Weihaiwei between 1898 and 1930 is exemplary. Even since the beginning of British administration of this leasehold, the British government decided to maintain good relationships with village headmen. These were lineage leaders chosen by the villagers a result of their wealth, personality, and social position, and they were responsible for

---
6. Sir Cosmo Parkinson, *The Colonial Office from Within* (London: Faber & Faber, 1947), 25.
7. John Cell, 'Colonial Rule', in *The Oxford History of the British Empire: Volume IV, The Twentieth Century*, ed. Judith Brown and W. M. Roger Louis (Oxford: Oxford University Press, 1999), 232.

the maintenance of order and peace in their villages. In addition, headmen were required to collect land tax and keep records of land deals, and to relay official notices to the villagers. Not only did the British administration continue to respect their role as intermediaries, it made further efforts to institutionalize their responsibilities. A new position of district headman was introduced, who was responsible for twelve villages on average. The headmen were still chosen by the villagers, but the appointment was now formally confirmed by the British authority and rewarded with a monthly allowance.[8] This call to respect traditional institutions was echoed by Frederick Lugard, whose famous thesis of the 'dual mandate' was seen by many as a major reference point for colonial rule. He warned against the dangers of ignoring indigenous authorities:

> It becomes impossible to maintain the old order—the urgent need is to adapt to the new—to build up a tribal authority with a recognized and legal standing, which may avert social chaos. It cannot be accomplished by superseding—by the direct rule of the white man—such ideas of discipline and organization as exist, nor yet by "stereotyping customs and institutions among backward races which are not consistent with progress.[9]

The institutionalized use of intermediaries was more than simply a pragmatic measure to meet the challenge of the paucity of resources; it was also imperative to the legitimation of colonial rule. Prasenjit Duara's notion of a cultural nexus of power is relevant here. In his seminal work on the failure of state-building efforts by the Nationalist government in rural north China between the 1920s and the 1940s, he offered important insights on the significance of cultural symbols and norms embedded in traditional organizations. These moral values, he argued, define status, prestige, honour, reciprocity, and, most importantly, social and political responsibility. The Qing government had skilfully exploited these symbolic assets by making use of the traditional brokerage system in rural China—such as gate association and the *baojia* system, under which respected leaders and chosen by local communities could continue to play a role in assisting the county government in implementing arduous tasks, particularly tax collection. Via this process, the cultural affiliation lent the Qing state respectability and legitimacy and this, in turn, further motivated those aspiring locals to seek out positions and influence within the formal institutions of power. The Nationalist government, however, failed to achieve a similar a rapport with local communities, breaking with traditions by replacing

---

8. Pamela Atwell, *British Mandarin and Chinese Reformers* (Hong Kong: Oxford University Press, 1985).
9. Frederick Lugard, *The Dual Mandate in British Tropical Africa* (London: Forgotten Books, 2012), 217.

brokers with more reform-minded outsiders or entrepreneurial tax collectors. Such moves alienated rather than engaged the local community and undermined its legitimacy. Duara contends that the lack of moral alignment between these state agents and the local population accounted for the widening rift between state and society in Republican China.[10] This was, in fact, exactly the case in Weihaiwei. The return of Weihaiwei to China in 1930 brought about a fundamental change in the philosophy of its governance. Respect for traditional organization was seen as a hindrance to the modernization project of the Nanjing government. The Nationalist officials now expected the locals to see themselves not as members of lineages or villages, but as Chinese nationals and citizens. A more proactive and intrusive approach in governance was evident in extensive efforts by local government to introduce surveillance of the landscape and the documentation of land deals and tax payments. Consequently, the scope for adaptations at the grass-roots level lessened, and local officials were deprived of their own discretion. The size of the national state expanded, but there was a parallel rise in local complaints and resentment. There was a glaringly obvious chasm between state and society.

Serving the Sovereign and the Indigenous

While the previous discussion underlines the ideal conditions for and necessity of colonial autonomy, one should not lose sight of the other side of the equation that the sovereign still mattered. Governors, after all, acted under a general metropolitan supervision. The trust of their superiors in London was of great consequence to the personal careers of these governors. They were expected to govern, and the tradition of respecting the man on the ground did not excuse these royal agents from blame and castigation if the home government found the situation in the colonies undesirable and uncomfortable. Isolation from the metropole and insulation from the rigour of parliamentary affairs may have brought tranquillity and peace to some colonial officials, but it could also herald professional uncertainty and the marginalization of aspiring talents. Minimal attention from London could be damaging for an ambitious official aiming at an eventual return to the homeland departments or a reassignment away from the backwater which was under their care. At the very least, London had to be accurately informed whenever a response from the colony was warranted. Maintaining the confidence of London was thus essential for the survival of governors, and this confidence took considerable effort to nurture.

---

10. Prasenjit Duara, *Culture, Power, and the State: Rural North China 1900–1942* (Stanford, CA: Stanford University Press, 1988).

Governors deployed a wide array of strategies in maintaining a 'comfortable distance' from the metropolitan government, with a bottom line of not arousing attention from London. Written communications were the major ways of presenting the local situation in the best possible light in the colony's favour, and the outward dispatches carefully crafted by governors and other senior colonial officials were intended to shape and structure home officials' understandings of local developments. These were usually supplemented by unofficial communications like private letters, in which more personal and candid reflections were included. The latter probably also offered a façade of intimacy or even friendship with superiors in London, and may even have made governors feel more like insiders than isolated subordinates. Among governors, there was a general concern over the lack of understanding of colonial reality in London, with Frederick Lugard observing that 'it is naturally galling to high officials in the colonies to know that their suggestions are criticized by youth almost free from school or college, and their mature and well-weighted advice possibility rejected on the recommendation of these embryo statesmen'.[11]

Face-to-face engagement was perhaps a more effective mode of communication and persuasion. Advancement in aviation technology made regular duty visits to London possible for governors. These were opportunities to explain queries, pass on information, publicize colonial development, put pressure on MPs and officials, and collect gossip and updates on British politics. Traffic went in the other direction as well, and visiting MPs and ministers could serve similar functions. Fed with detailed policy briefings, elaborate meetings with colonial officials, selective presentation of highlights in local development, and generous hospitality, these politicians and career civil servants were expected to go home with empathy towards the colonies, transformed into informed participants in policy discussion concerning these remote parts of the world.

Some colonies were further determined to make their case with more elaborate metropolitan connections. There were colonial governors who found it useful to send an envoy with colonial experience back to London. These were, in most cases, the private staff of governors, although they were usually sent at the expense of colonial finance. Their role was to inform and persuade London the colony was in good shape. By the 1830s, most of the American and West Indian colonies had made similar arrangements in London. Meanwhile, it was also common to find senior colonial officials making serious efforts to cultivate or maintain their ties with the metropolitan society. Global networks connecting veterans with common military experience, university and school alumni, members of extended

---

11. Lugard, *The Dual Mandate*, 159.

aristocratic families, enthusiasts of shared interest in scientific matters, and activists of religious or civic causes in Britain and the colonies were businesses taken seriously by all involved.[12] These were platforms where patronage and influence were nurtured, and networks through which accessibility to metropolitan policy makers was enabled.

Engagement with the colonies could also be initiated by London. A Royal Commission of inquiry could be set up if politicians in the homeland decided to dig into unfortunate developments in the colonies, in order to allocate blame and responsibility and inflict punishment. The disgraceful downfall and political and financial ruin of Warren Hastings in India was a powerful reminder of the repercussions of London's wrath for all colonial officials.[13] In most cases, however, attention from metropolitan government was more mundane and routine, reflecting a rising demand for facts and statistics. The Board of Trade founded the first statistical unit in Britain in 1832, and the passage of the Registration Act of 1836 led to both the creation of the General Registry Office and the registration of births, marriages, and deaths from 1837 onward. This drive towards scientific administration naturally spread to the colonial order across the globe. More detailed requirements for quantitative reporting were introduced, with landscape surveys becoming routine. The joint auspices of the Indian Survey and the British Museum in the late nineteenth century, for example, represented one of the major efforts to produce and classify knowledge about the empire.[14] Oversight of colonial finances also became an integral part of metropolitan supervision, and this was further reinforced in the early post–Second World War years by London's strategy of subsidizing welfare development as a method of leverage for maintaining ties with overseas possessions.[15]

Running a colony was thus a precarious business. Colonial governors struggled with the tension inherent in their roles as local administrators and royal agents. They were neither independent autocrats who could do whatever they wanted under royal prerogatives, nor were they puppets of metropolitan officials. Colonial administrations were mostly undemocratic until after the Second World War, yet electoral politics in Westminster interacted with colonial affairs when the British public perceived developments

---

12. Zoe Laidlaw, *Colonial Connections, 1815–45: Patronage, the Information Revolution and Colonial Government* (Manchester: Manchester University Press, 2005).
13. Michael Cullen, *The Statistical Movement in Early Victorian Britain: The Foundations of Empirical Social Research* (Brighton: Edward Everett Root, 2017).
14. Thomas Richards, *The Imperial Archive: Knowledge and the Fantasy of Empire* (London and New York: Verso, 1993).
15. Michael Havinden and David Meredith, *Colonialism and Development: Britain and Its Tropic Colonies, 1850–1960* (London: Routledge, 1993).

in overseas possessions overlapping with their interests and concerns. Respect for Indigenous values, customs, and practices was crucial for effective local administration, but colonial practices still had to be reconciled with the traditions of freedom and legality of the British polity. Ultimately, colonial government was created to serve British interests, but this was hardly tenable if local community felt that it was being abandoned and exploited.

How to get the balance right? When and how could colonial administrators make their case to London when colonial officials perceived metropolitan assessment inadequate or unfair and felt compelled to stand up for local interests? What were the motivations for the sovereign to meddle and intervene in colonial administration? What were the limits and leverages of the colony in its pursuit of local interests? These are the fundamental issues related to the running of the British Empire, as well as for the understanding of the legitimation of colonial rule, and these are the questions this book seeks to answer.

The Long 1970s

Hong Kong in the 1970s is a good lens for understanding the intricacies of colony-sovereign relationships. It was a period of transition, during which the colony made a major stride towards becoming a modern city and set out on its trajectory of reunification with China. It was also during this decade that a fundamental reconfiguration of the socio-economic outlook of the city and a major shift in the approach to its governance took place. All these developments were propelled by vicissitudes within domestic conditions as well as changes in global geopolitics. It was a time when the colonial governor was presented with opportunities for and challenges in defending the local interests, and it was also a key moment for London to reconsider its commitments to the colony and reassess Britain's strategic priorities.

Hong Kong's origin as an 'enclave colony'[16] engendered favourable conditions for colonial autonomy. That is, the colony was valued not for its natural resources, as in the case of Spanish conquest of South America in search of silver and gold, or for the climate's ability to sustain lucrative cash crops as with British Malaya. Hong Kong was colonized in order to act as a gateway to China, a haven of British laws and security which could facilitate penetration into the mainland.[17] With Hong Kong merely a component of a larger British informal empire in China, there was a limited

---

16. Jurgen Osterhammel, *Colonialism* (Princeton, NJ: Markus Wiener Publishers, 2005).
17. John Carroll, *Canton Days: British Life and Death in China* (Lanham, MD: Rowman & Littlefield Publishers, 2020).

incentive to foster a strong British presence in the colony. The cultural gap between expatriates and the local community and the lack of numbers in British personnel on the ground moreover generated a persistent sense of insecurity despite Britian's political and social domination. The small tax base of the administration and the resultant paucity of administrative capacities further reduced the colonial rulers' ability to engage with locals. All these rendered the general approach of relying on customary practices and intermediaries even more important in the case of Hong Kong. The first hundred years of British rule in Hong Kong was thus characterized by social segregation,[18] intermediation of the Chinese elites,[19] and general indifference towards the governed population.[20]

However, the environment of colonial governance fundamentally changed during the post-war years. Local people became more assertive in demanding proactive engagement from the government in local affairs. The trauma of the Japanese Occupation of 1941–1945 had several consequences for the relationship between colonial rulers and the governed. The image of British invincibility was gone, and the feeble defence that the British force put up against the Japanese invaders was seen as a betrayal by considerable number of locals. There was an urgent need for the colonial government to recapture the trust and respect of disillusioned local communities.[21] This marked the beginning of a more engaged style of governance, with gradual increases in public expenditure and infrastructure. This was fortunately made possible by Hong Kong's strong economic growth from the 1940s. The industrialization process prompted by the trade embargo against China during the Korean War had laid a solid financial basis for public sector growth. Meanwhile, the emergence of the baby boomer generation in the post-war years and the demographic change which resulted from the increased local birth rate contributed to discernible changes in feelings of belonging within the local community. Together with the steady expansion of public services, especially housing, education, and healthcare, and the resulting increase in interaction with the colonial administration, a new sense of citizenship and a nascent civil society was on the horizon by the 1970s.[22] Popular acquiescence with social ills like general filthiness, cor-

---

18. John Carroll, *A Concise History of Hong Kong* (Lanham, MD: Rowman & Littlefield Publishers, 2007).
19. Wing Sang Law, *Collaborative Colonial Power: The Making of the Hong Kong Chinese* (Hong Kong: Hong Kong University Press, 2009).
20. Elizabeth Sinn, *Power and Charity: A Chinese Merchant Elite in Colonial Hong Kong* (Hong Kong: Hong Kong University Press, 2003).
21. Philip Snow, *The Fall of Hong Kong: Britain, China and the Japanese Occupation* (New Haven, CT: Yale University Press, 2004).
22. Agnes Ku and Pan Ngai, eds., *Remaking Citizenship in Hong Kong: Community, Nation and the Global City* (New York: Routledge, 2006).

ruption, or exclusion of Chinese residents from the policy-making process could no longer be assumed.

Post-war Hong Kong also witnessed another seismic change in the global political landscape: the rise of Communist China. For the first time in almost a hundred years since the commencement of colonial administration in Hong Kong, there was a powerful and united regime reigning in the mainland. The ideological outlook of the People's Republic further complicated the picture. Its socialist stance entailed fundamental tension with Britain, which China regarded as a core member of the wicked capitalist-imperialist band led by America and denied the unequal treaties signed between the Qing government and the British authorities. Fortunately, the Communist leaders were shrewd in their calculations, helping to contain these tensions to generally manageable levels. This pragmatism prevailed, with Chinese Communist policy towards Hong Kong phrased as the principles of 'long-term planning and full utilization', a code message for paying lip service towards sovereignty concerns and its continuous use of the colony as a platform for foreign trade and outward engagement. The realism was however mutual. Britain was persistent in engaging the new regime despite their ideological differences and territorial dispute. Britain was among the first batch of Western governments to acknowledge the People's Republic of China as a sovereign state.[23] Persistent efforts to bolster Britain's diplomatic relationship with Beijing also illustrated London's positive approach towards the new power in Asia. British businesses, such as Jardine, were also keen to maintain their presence in the mainland despite the anti-capitalist stance of the Communist Party. Both sides adopted restraint, caution, and flexibility when navigating this maze of conflicting ideologies, diplomatic loss and gain, and tangible economic growth. The metropolitan government's strategic investment in this game with China always prompted London to advise, instruct and intervene in Hong Kong's handling of its powerful neighbour.

Colonial Hong Kong's cardinal principle for survival was thus not to provoke Communist China. This strategy worked most of the time, with local Communists mostly content with propaganda and networking building in local community. Yet the turbulence of Cultural Revolution was overwhelming, and Hong Kong was not immune to this tsunami of violent radicalism. The 1967 Riots, largely an extension of political fanaticism in the mainland, caused the most serious disruption in the territory during the post-war years. The leftists took most of the blame for the mayhem, but the saga uncovered various structural problems, such as the gap in social

---

23. Chi-Kwan Mark, *The Everyday Cold War: Britain and China, 1950–1972* (London: Bloomsbury Academic, 2017).

services and public provisions, limited opportunities for public participation, and general frustration under colonial rule. The 1970s was the time to make amends.

However, Cold War politics was not confined to the issue of managing China. It also concerned Britain's obligations to the Western allies—or more specifically the necessity of indulging America. Maintaining its 'special relationship' with the United States was Britain's dominant strategy for preserving its waning global relevance in post-war years. Yet this further complicated its relationship with Communist China. On the one hand, the British needed the American presence in Hong Kong as a deterrent against the possible aggression of China. The Americans saw the value of the colony's strategic position in the region. Hong Kong was an ideal location for observing the authoritarian regime in the mainland as well as a good platform for counteracting Communist propaganda and infiltration. On the other hand, the American presence in the territory had, in turn, emboldened the Nationalist elements. Taiwanese agents found the colony's proximity to the mainland made it a perfect base from which to launch 'attacks' and sabotage against the Chinese authorities.[24] Unfortunately, Hong Kong was the collateral damage in this conflict, since violence against the Communists often led to aggression and confrontation in the territory more widely. During the 1950s, Hong Kong witnessed waves of Kuomintang (KMT)-related violence. There was a failed assassination attempt against Premier Zhou Enlai in 1955, and vehement attacks on Beijing sympathizers during the Double-Tenth Festival confrontation in 1956. Both incidents were believed to have been orchestrated by the Nationalists. The colonial administration was on constant alert to avoid a total fallout between the Communists and Nationalists in Hong Kong, while strenuously trying to maintain its façade of 'neutrality'.[25]

American interest in Asia, however, extended beyond China and the cross-strait relationship. The US strategic priority was to avoid the domino effect of communist expansion in the region, that is, stopping the potential chain reaction after any single country fell under Soviet control. This prompted ceaseless US military commitments in Asia, first in the Korean Peninsula, and then in Indochina in the post-war period. One of the consequences of direct military confrontation during the Korean War was the

---

24. Nancy Tucker, *China Confidential: American Diplomats and Sino-American Relations, 1945–1996* (New York: Columbia University Press, 2001); Angelina Chin, *Unsettling Exiles: Chinese Migrants in Hong Kong and the Southern Periphery During the Cold War* (New York: Columbia University Press, 2023).
25. Steve Tsang, 'Strategy for Survival: The Cold War and Hong Kong's Policy towards Kuomintang and Chinese Communist Activities in the 1950s', *The Journal of Imperial and Commonwealth History* 25, no. 2 (1997): 294–317.

imposition of the United Nations' trade embargo against China, which severely affected Hong Kong. At the start, protracted US involvement in Vietnam were of some benefit to the colony. Hong Kong was visited by American soldiers on leave, and the local hospitality business thrived on this regular influx of personnel.[26] The mooring of American battleships in the harbour was also comforting for the local community during the height of the conflict of the 1967 Riots. However, the creation of the Communist regime in Vietnam and the deterioration of the situation in Indochina did have severe repercussion for the colony. The consequent exodus of millions of refugees was a global humanitarian crisis. Britain, as a loyal ally of the United States, was expected to make a substantial contribution to the situation. The obligations of the British government to the global community, and the United States in particular, always translated into pressure for interventions in Hong Kong.

The British 'decolonization' process was another important backdrop for post-war developments in Hong Kong. The colony was an outlier in the grand scheme of decolonization in the post-war period. Whereas almost all British possessions were given the option of self-government or independence, no route to self-determination was offered to Hong Kong. As Chi-Kwan Mark said, Hong Kong was too valuable a colony for Britain to abandon voluntarily, even though it was militarily indefensible and constitutionally 'awkward'.[27] Beijing refused to acknowledge the validity of the treaties signed between the former Qing government and Britain in the nineteenth century and maintained her claims of sovereignty over Hong Kong. For London, the political future of the colony beyond 1997 was always a key part of the Hong Kong question, and British officials were fully aware of the prospect of an eventual retreat from the territory. In a governmental long-term study of Hong Kong's future which was completed in 1969, it was concluded unequivocally that 'Hong Kong's future must eventually lie in China'.[28] Nevertheless, while attitudes of evasion and reticence over the political question prevailed, what was essentially a 'decolonization' process had commenced as early as the 1950s. Britain started to reexamine its military, economic, and political links and commitments to the colony, and how these could be accommodated and reconciled with the UK's role in larger geopolitical concerns. The process intensified when issues such

---

26. Peter Hamilton, '"A Haven for Tortured Souls": Hong Kong in the Vietnam War', *The International History Review* 73, no. 3 (June 2015): 565–581.
27. Chi-Kwan Mark, 'Crisis or Opportunity? Britain, China, and the Decolonization of Hong Kong in the Long 1970s', in *China, Hong Kong, and the Long 1970s: Global Perspectives*, ed. Priscilla Roberts and O. A. Westad (London: Palgrave Macmillan, 2017), chapter 11.
28. 'Hong Kong: Long Term Study', 28 March 1969, CAB134/2945, The National Archives (hereafter TNA).

as support for Chinese refugees, defence commitment, exports to Britain, and the value of the pound sterling arose. Whether intentional or not, this decoupling created the conditions for friction between the sovereign and the colony. All of these heralded a very eventful era for MacLehose as he steered the colony through countless negotiations with London in the 1970s.

A Decade of Reforms

Murray MacLehose was arguably the most popular colonial governor throughout the entire British rule in Hong Kong. Under his tenure between 1971 and 1982, the socio-economic and political outlook of the colony changed fundamentally. There were substantial increases in public expenditure with medical services, schooling opportunities, public housing, and safety networks expanding steadily during this period. Ground-breaking infrastructure was also introduced with the completion of the cross-harbour tunnel and the commencement of the Mass-Transit Railway project. Reforms allowing more room for public participation in community affairs were also evident, with the introduction of the district administration scheme towards the end of the 1970s. For many locals, however, all these achievements were dwarfed by the creation of the ICAC in 1974. Its contribution to the eradication of the cancer of corruption from the social fabric of colonial society and the promotion of social justice in the local community was monumental. With his nickname 'a man in a hurry', MacLehose's reign was fondly remembered by many as creating the pivotal moment when the colony began to become a fairer, better, and more modern society.

The reforms in the 1970s were the result of cumulative developments in the post-war years. The industrialization efforts which began in the late 1950s and the subsequent economic take-off provided the economic basis for the changes. The colonial administration had managed to maintain a fiscal surplus in almost all the financial years after 1945 and the availability of fiscal resources enabled the government to embark on its reform programs and rendered seeking of approval from London unnecessary in most cases, as the metropolitan officials were content with Hong Kong's multitude of initiatives as long as the colony could pay the bill. The drive for social reforms and the expansion of public services also illustrate London's willingness to respond to the changing political landscape in Hong Kong. As in in the mid-1940s, the local population was once again disillusioned with colonial rule in the aftermath of the 1967 Riots. MacLehose came into office with the task of restoring confidence in British rule in Hong Kong, and he wasted no time in responding to the call for change. By the 1970s, Hong Kong appeared to be on the road to modernization. Steady economic growth and prosperity, increasing access to public education, and the general rise in quality of life all bred a desire for participation and engagement. There was a nascent civil society in the colony with the emergence of student activism, the rise of pressure groups, and the budding social movement. Calls for electoral democracy remained muted, but a more vocal and expressive community which demanded from the government action was impossible to ignore. A virtuous cycle of reforms which would engender further change was on the horizon by the 1970s.

The momentum for change was, however, not entirely domestic in origin. The China factor had become even more pertinent during the 1970s. For the British, the major lesson of the 1967 Riots was that Beijing took the issue of nationalism very seriously and was not prepared to compromise on the matter of sovereignty over Hong Kong. For London, the issue of Hong Kong's future needed to be solved by the 1980s at the latest, and groundwork for prospective negotiations had to be done sooner rather than later. A stable and prosperous Hong Kong which Beijing would find useful for China's development would put the British in a good position at the negotiating table. These strategic considerations prompted a major rethinking of Hong Kong's development. Investment in social services and economic infrastructure was important for the progress and stability of the colony, but it was also deemed to be crucial for enhancing Britain's bargaining position with China. Meanwhile, China also had adopted a stark change in her diplomatic stance since the early 1970s as its engagement with the outside world accelerated feverishly. The success of replacing Taiwan as the only legitimate government of China in the United Nations in 1971 was a huge diplomatic victory for Beijing. It demonstrated Communist China's global diplomatic clout, but it also remitted Beijing's desire to engage in dialogue with the West. Richard Nixon's visit to Shanghai and Beijing in 1972 was an event of historic proportions. Beijing was ready and anxious to overcome ideological barriers and engage with the world. This new diplomatic posture of the People's Republic of China presented a different challenge to London. In 1972, Beijing finally agreed to reciprocate Britain's diplomatic recognition to the United Kingdom and allowed for exchange of ambassadors. The commencement of reform programs with the creation of Special Economic Zones in 1978 also denoted the pragmatism of the communist regime. As a poster boy for the free-market economy, the potential contribution of Hong Kong to China's modernization drive was tremendous. This posited a different problem for Hong Kong and London. More nuanced and skilled diplomacy was essential for handling a 'friendlier', more pragmatic, and engaging China, and increasing attention from London seemed inevitable. Consequently, MacLehose, a career diplomat, was appointed as the twenty-fifth governor of Hong Kong in 1971.

In short, the MacLehose era was a period of major change during which the colony was anxious to introduce reforms and the sovereign was concerned with the UK strategic handling of a different China and other seismic changes in global politics. During this decade of change, there was synergy and cooperation between London and Hong Kong, but there were also countless moments of altercation and heated debate. At times, Hong Kong and the UK government's priorities and diagnoses of the prevailing challenges aligned, yet differences and disagreement occurred. The MacLehose era is thus ideal for observing the relationship between London and Hong Kong.

Structure of the Book

This book does not intend to offer a comprehensive account of the governorship of MacLehose. Instead, it aims to uncover the dynamics and logics of engagement and bargaining between London and Hong Kong through an examination of four specific major episodes.

Anti-corruption Efforts

The cancer of corruption had been rife in the public life of the colony ever since its founding in 1842. MacLehose arrived at the time when the colonial administration finally decided to intensify its effort against corruption. His predecessor, David Trench, was determined to accelerate the fight against corruption and succeeded in passing the Prevention of Bribery Ordinance before he left office in 1971. This new legislation greatly facilitated prosecution against corruption since it laid the burden of proof on the suspect. Yet one last piece of the jigsaw was still missing: an independent body for the investigation of corruption. The colonial administration had stalled on the issue for more than a century and it was eventually the scandal of their failure to extradite Peter Godber from Britain that gave this change the push it needed. However, it was the potential intervention of the British Parliament that provoked the colony to further action. The creation of the ICAC was thus not just a response to the demand of the local community, but it was also a pre-emptive action to avoid parliamentary inquiry into the issue of corruption in the colony.

Social Reforms

Social reform seemed to be an obvious issue for the colonial administration. In the 1960s, there was limited regulation of working hours and child labour, and workers were exposed to the fluctuation of the markets with few statutory protection and scant state welfare. The dislocation caused by the confrontations in 1967 also helped convince the local business class that was necessary for change. Yet the call for social reforms was mostly reinforced by the UK interests. The return of a Labour government heralded the prevalence of leftist ideas in social policy thinking for the colony, and the 1997 factor certainly reinforced the concern of welfare provision in Hong Kong as well. However, the British industries also showed strong support for social reforms in Hong Kong. They were ill at ease with the massive inflow of Hong Kong products into the British economy and attributed this to the low production cost entailed by the 'blood and sweat workshops' in Hong Kong. While MacLehose had no objection to an expansion of welfare benefits and services, London had in fact planned to bestow a very comprehensive action plan on the colony. The metropolitan officials demanded drastic changes and swift action. A detailed plan for implementing social reforms was imposed, as well as a well-structured mechanism for monitoring the progress of the reforms was put in place. This was, however, beyond MacLehose's expectation, and the colonial administration's faith in fiscal discipline and low taxation was under severe test.

The Vietnamese Boat People Crisis

The Vietnam War and the subsequent dislocation triggered an unprecedented influx of refugees to the countries in South-East Asia. Hong Kong was especially vulnerable due to its proximity and geographical landscape. Between 1975 and 1982, more than 100,000 Vietnamese had arrived at the colony by boat and only Thailand, adjacent to Vietnam, received more. The strategic concerns of the sovereign were critical here. London felt obliged to honour the commitment inherent in its role as a major global power and was under constant pressure from Washington. Hong Kong was eventually designated as a port of first asylum for the refugees, a measure critical to the comprehensive American-engineered response to the situation. Britain's duty to address the humanitarian crisis was outsourced to the colony. The colonial administration was torn between obligations to the sovereign and ferocious opposition of the local population.

Land Lease in the New Territories beyond 1997

Towards the end of 1970s, there was growing unease among local business due to the uncertainty over Hong Kong's future. The legality of the land lease after its expiry in 1997 was a genuine concern for investors and property developers. MacLehose was under growing pressure from the local business sector and he came up with a creative idea to test the water. His initiative was the proposal to confine the discussions with China to the extension of the land lease in the New Territories beyond 1997, while leaving the matter of the legal status of the colony intact. While London shared MacLehose's judgement on the general good mood for initiating the dialogue on the future of Hong Kong with Beijing, the metropolitan government was indecisive and was not entirely convinced by MacLehose's sense of urgency of the matter.

These four episodes represent different configurations of interest and motivation within the London–Hong Kong relationship. London's interest in the colony varied across these episodes. Whereas the British government was very keen to impose a metropolitan vision of social reforms and anxious to designate a key role for the colony in the refugee resettlements, Britain's attention to the corruption issue in Hong Kong was mostly passive. In the case of the land lease issue, though both Hong Kong and London were aware of the importance of engaging with China to find a solution on the future of the colony, there were differences in pace and approach. These differences determined the scope and prospect of the colony's pursuit of local agenda, and it is through these interactions and exchanges that colonial autonomy is defined. Autonomy here can be understood in two senses: positive autonomy and negative autonomy. The former refers to the colony's success in proactively persuading the sovereign of the validity of its diagnoses and prescriptions as the best option for both handling local issues and in the pursuit of 'British interest'. The latter denotes the colony's accomplishment in delaying, derailing, or even resisting the rulings and directives imposed by London. These contrasting scenarios entail different strategies and rules of engagement which were likely to be determined by the parameter defined by the sovereign and the larger international context, yet common to these challenges was the colonial administration's concern to pursue its own agenda and maintain effective governance.

There is of course a rich body of literature on the relationship between London and Hong Kong. Ure made a bold attempt to offer an overview of the relationship between the colony and the Colonial Office during the first half of the twentieth century.[29] Tsang's work on the aborted attempts at constitutional reform in the plan to create a municipal council in the early post-war years uncovered how initiatives originating in Whitehall could be stalled by colonial administrators.[30] In a similar vein, Miners' account of the reformist move to abolish the *mui-tsai* practice, a disguised form of unfree labour, also shed light on the tension between the centre and the periphery.[31] Goodstadt also argued that 'remoteness from the United Kingdom not only gave the colonial administration considerable latitude to dispute London's recommendations and ignore its wishes, it also meant that Hong Kong officials had little fear of being found out if they occasionally resorted to obfuscation and outright prevarication to get rid of tiresome inquiries from London'.[32] Yet the story is not always 'Hong Kong versus London', as Smart's study on the evolution of public housing policy showed that the synergy between the two parties could also unleash the momentum for progressive change in the colony.[33] Nevertheless, one should not overlook the role of local players in colonial governance. Carroll's work on how local elites navigated between the parameters set by British and Chinese authorities provided illustrative examples from an early date.[34] A seminal work on Tung Wah Hospitals by Sinn also offered detailed case studies of how local leaders made themselves useful to the colonizers and got promoted in the colonial order through philanthropy, inserting themselves into public policy-making.[35]

The extant literature, however, suffers from several limitations. Firstly, most of these studies focus on the early colonial years or the immediate aftermath of the Second World War, failing therefore to investigate the transformed socio-economic and political landscape of 1970s and beyond. As previously discussed, the economic take-off and territory-wide confrontations in the 1960s induced major changes to the social and political outlook of the local community and catalysed the colonial administration's rethinking of its governing strategies. Bonds between the government and governed were now emphasized, and the expectations of the local community

---

29. Gavin Ure, *Governors, Politics and the Colonial Office: Public Policy in Hong Kong, 1918–58* (Hong Kong: Hong Kong University Press, 2012).
30. Steve Tsang, *Democracy Shelved: Great Britain, China and Attempts at Constitutional Reform in Hong Kong, 1945–1952* (Hong Kong: Oxford University Press, 1988).
31. Norman Miners, *Hong Kong under Imperial Rule, 1912–1941* (Hong Kong: Oxford University Press, 1988).
32. Leo Goodstadt, *Uneasy Partners: The Conflict between Public Interest and Private Profit in Hong Kong* (Hong Kong: Hong Kong University Press, 2005).
33. Alan Smart, *The Shek Kip Mei Myth: Squatters, Fires and Colonial Rule in Hong Kong, 1950–1963* (Hong Kong: Hong Kong University Press, 2006).
34. John Carroll, *Edge of Empires: Chinese Elites and British Colonials in Hong Kong* (Cambridge, MA: Harvard University Press, 2005).
35. Sinn, *Power and Charity*.

were changing. Civil society was growing more vibrant, and an unprecedented wave of protest movements for social reforms were on the horizon. These new sentiments were, for example, evident in the anti-corruption campaign of 'Arresting Peter Godber' and in the rise of student activism in the mid-1970s. Demand for social equality and greater public intervention had started to find more receptive ears among the new generation than those who had gone before. The new progressive mood was alarming for business interests. A new logic of interaction between the colonial administration and the local elites thus emerged during the 1970s.[36]

Secondly, although there are a few studies on the triangular interaction between the British government, Hong Kong colonial administration, and the local community, a more nuanced study of the coloniality of local governance is warranted. While domestic concerns were the driving force behind developments in Hong Kong, one should not lose sight of the role of the sovereign in this process. London did not dictate the trajectory of change, yet the twists and flows of policy-making and choices in the territories were mostly intentional or unintentional results of bargaining and negotiation between the colony and London. The sovereign mattered. For London, global diplomacy had always been more important than the parochial matter of colonial concerns. Its obligations to the international community, its special alliance with the United States, and its desire to maintain a viable working relationship with China were its top priority strategic interests. The colonial government's room for bargaining and resistance was certainly more circumscribed when Britain's geostrategic concerns were at stake.

Moreover, understanding Hong Kong in the 1970s and its pattern of engagement with the sovereign is of utmost importance for our understanding of contemporary Hong Kong. The post-1997 arrangement, endorsed by China, was modelled on Beijing's understanding of the prevailing socio-economic and political order in Hong Kong by the late 1970s. Meticulous reading of the Sino-British Joint Declaration and the Basic Law uncovers a preservation of the central-local relationship under colonial rule: the sovereign's right to make and repeal the laws of the territory, appointment of chief executives, and control of other key officials within the local administration, for example, were preserved beyond 1997. The 'transfer of best practices' of central regulation and control are evident. Yet the jury is still out on whether Beijing fully comprehends the true picture of the power relationship between Hong Kong and London under colonial rule. A nuanced analysis of the pattern and logic of the engagement between

---

36. Stephen Wing Kai Chiu and Tai Lok Lui, eds., *The Dynamics of Social Movement in Hong Kong* (Hong Kong: Hong Kong University Press, 2000).

London and Hong Kong could thus enhance our understanding of the relationship between Beijing and the Hong Kong Special Administrative Region beyond 1997. The gap between the actual pattern of interaction between the centre and the colony in the 1970s, and Beijing's understanding (or misunderstanding) of this reality, may account for the tension and political dislocation witnessed in the territory in the twenty-first century.

Lastly, the book chooses to focus on the role of a governor, Murray MacLehose. Margaret MacMillan once spoke of history as a rambling, messy, and eccentric house, where people could choose different angles to dissect in order to analyse its past. While some may focus on its design or interior structure, others may prefer to dig out bewildering stories and spectacular episodes which happened on the premises. Some think, however, that it is most important to focus on the most powerful and influential inhabitants of the house.[37] This stems from an eternal debate over whether events are moved by individuals or by objective forces and structural constraints imposed by socio-economic changes and technological developments. There is probably no right or wrong answer in this debate, but I believe that while structure matters, individual agency still plays its role. We may be products of our times, but our choices and decisions still help to make history. The governor was the face of the colonial administration, and he was the one who interpreted, articulated, and defended the interests of Hong Kong. As will be uncovered in the following chapters, MacLehose displayed political acumen, he understood the obligations to the colony and the sovereign, and most importantly, he had the ability to withstand pressure from his superiors. He significantly affected the course of Hong Kong's journey in the long 1970s.

---

37. Margaret MacMillan, *History's People: Personalities and the Past* (Croydon: Profile Books, 2015).

2
The Restive 1960s

Introduction

'Anyway, they didn't say to me: "look here, for goodness sake, when you go out do remember that Hong Kong isn't an independent republic". This wasn't the sort of line taken by anybody in fact. In so far as they had a line, it was: "for goodness sake get this marvellous place going. It's got such potential for everybody there and it seems to be a bit flat"',[1] Murray MacLehose recalled the FCO's message to him before he assumed the role of Governor in 1971. Further elaborating on his understanding of London's expectation, he continued: 'ministers wanted to feel that things were being done right here, not a subject of criticism either in the U.K. or the world, or with China; they wanted, like Ministers always do, peace and quiet and a feeling of pride.'[2] The Governor, in other words, believed he could expect considerable leeway for his own discretion, provided that he created no trouble for London and got the job done. Yet his governorship attests to the fact that this would be easier said than done.

He was certainly well qualified for the job. Born in Glasgow in 1917, Maclehose, like many of his contemporaries, was educated in prestigious institutions—Rugby School and Balliol College Oxford in his case—before joining the Colonial Office in 1939. He was soon transferred to Malaya as a cadet, but his service was interrupted by the war as he volunteered to join the Naval Service. He rejoined the civil service in 1947, but this time he decided to join the Foreign Office instead. This turned out to be a crucial move which marked the beginning of a long and distinguished career. His early postings included assignments in Czechoslovakia, New Zealand, and

---

1. Transcript of Steve Tsang's interview with Lord MacLehose, Bodleian Library, University of Oxford, 441.
2. Transcript of Steve Tsang's interview with Lord MacLehose, 507.

France, and by 1963 he was in charge of the Far Eastern Department of the Foreign Office. This upward trajectory continued as he landed the job of British Ambassador to Vietnam in 1967, and two years later he was appointed as British Ambassador to Denmark. His appointment to the Governorship of Hong Kong was further justified by his knowledge with the colony. He was sent to Hong Kong as a Political Adviser to the colonial administration between 1959 and 1962, an experience which helped lay the foundations for his governorship a decade later. Central to the job was to advise the Governor of the time, Robert Black, on matters related to the colony's relationship with China. He was thus fully aware of the intricacy and complexity of the challenge of engaging with the Communist regime. In fact, MacLehose had some close encounters himself with China in the post-war years. He served in the British Consulate in Hankou in 1949 and thus had the opportunity to witness the historic moment of the Communist takeover and its monumental impact up close.[3]

It is an understatement to say Hong Kong was 'a bit flat' by 1971. The colony was still licking its wounds after the trauma of the 1967 Riots when MacLehose arrived. While Hong Kong had managed to weather the storm, the confrontations exposed the gap between the government's performance and local expectations. After 1967, people had demanded a new social contract between the colonial government and local populace, including via a new approach to governance, with expansions in public expenditure and major investment in economic infrastructures. Yet an even more daunting task concerned the management of a 'new China'. Political radicalism in China had faded by the end of the 1960s, and the Communist regime finally decided to re-engage with the outside world by the early 1970s. China's admission into the United Nations in 1971 and the Shanghai Communiqué of 1972 heralded a new diplomatic approach by Beijing. The new pragmatism of the Chinese leadership entailed opportunities and room for compromise for Britain, which had never abandoned its commercial and diplomatic links with China since 1949. Yet a more outward-looking and confident China also denoted a change in Beijing's approach to Hong Kong. The city was valuable for its role in facilitating China's access to global economy and modernization programme, yet with the clock ticking, the issue of the future of Hong Kong was forecast to grow in salience during the 1970s. Britain's evaluation of its position in world politics and adaption to the reality of declining global influence also shaped the relationship with the colony. With the imperative of maintaining a 'special relationship' with the United States and the challenge of engaging with a rising China, the

---

3. 'Lord MacLehose', *The Guardian*, accessed 6 January 2023, https://www.theguardian.com/news/2000/jun/02/guardianobituaries1.

British government expected the colony to respond positively and cooperate in ways that accommodated these strategic calculations.

MacLehose also arrived at a time when the colony's relationship with London was far from harmonious. The tension inherent in the long disputes over Hong Kong's exports to Britain, the financial and economic cost of sustaining the sterling system, and grievances over the colony's expenditure on the British Garrison had prompted considerable local suspicion towards British commitments to Hong Kong. Yet this feeling was mutual. British officials calling the colony 'Hong Kong Republic' attested to their displeasure with what they perceived as Hong Kong's indifference to British concerns. MacLehose's predecessor, David Trench, who never shied away from robust arguments with London when Hong Kong's interests were at stake, was perhaps in the eyes of a few FCO officials, not a very pleasant Governor to work with.

The following discussion will expand on the various adversities which MacLehose inherited in 1971; challenges which set the parameters for his governorship as well as the contour of his relationship with London during his twelve-year period of in office.

Calling for a Blast of Social Reforms

The 1967 Riots represented the most serious challenge to the colonial authority since the end of Japanese Occupation in 1945. Triggered by an industrial dispute in a plastic flower factory in Kowloon, the colony was quickly swamped with incessant waves of demonstrations, strikes, vandalism, and bomb attacks, which resulted in the arrest of thousands and the deaths of fifty-one people. It was, in short, a full mobilization of pro-Beijing forces in the territory with local Communist leaders, desperate to prove their loyalty to the radical leadership of the Communist Party during the most violent phase of Cultural Revolution. What worried the colonial government most was the mainland authority's endorsement of the anti-imperialist efforts of compatriots in Hong Kong. Articles in the Party's mouthpiece, the *People's Daily*, and official statements from the Chinese Foreign Ministry helped sustain the morale of the protestors, displaying unequivocal support for the campaign in Hong Kong and criticisms of the misdeeds and atrocities of the colonial government. Furthermore, Beijing's assistance could be concrete as well as rhetorical. A few direct donations were made to local trade unions in order to encourage them to call for general strikes and even to attack British diplomats in Beijing. The clash at the border in July 1967 that resulted in the deaths of five police officers was most disconcerting for the colonial government as the possibility of further military action from the People's Liberation Army (PLA) looked genuine. The colonial government managed somehow to survive this storm with effective policing and repressive measures. The local community also took the side of the government, since the majority preferred stability to political fanaticism, even if the former entailed colonial rule. As the Cultural Revolution entered into a new phase in late 1967, with Mao resorting to de facto military rule across the country, the protests in Hong Kong gradually lost momentum.[4]

Despite the external instigation of these protests, the colonial government did not lose sight of the general frustrations felt by the local population, especially regarding social conditions. Grievances and bitterness against colonial rule in the post-war years had provided fertile ground for anti-government sentiments to ferment in the 1960s, and the local Communists had skilfully exploited these discontents in 1967. There was, undisputedly, ineffective communication between the government and the local communities. Even more importantly, a yawning chasm between the actual provision of social services and local expectations of them was discernible, with an influx of illegal immigrants from the mainland since the early 1960s undermining the colonial government's commitment to a more proactive approach in social policy. The local population continued to grow, and by 1970 had reached more than 3.96 million, almost double the level recorded in 1950.[5] This rapid expansion further exposed the vulnerability of underprivileged people in the territory. A study on living conditions in Hong Kong conducted in 1965 provides a vivid portrait of the abysmal life of the locals:

> When there is a principal tenant renting a premise, he usually divides the living space into cubicles by a maze of wooden partitions six feet high. This leaves a wide passage on the side of the entrance along which two to three-tier bunks are usually erected. As the houses are built side by side, there are windows at the front opening into a veranda about two feet high, if facing side streets and about seven feet wide if facing a main road and also a window in the rear onto a backyard. The cubicles in the middle are therefore without windows and are in permanent semi-darkness so that artificial lighting (usually by 25 watt electric lights or kerosene lamps) is necessary whenever the cubicles are in uses. Through draught between the front and the rear windows is prevented by the intervening partitions. The air within the cubicles is stagnant and stuffy . . . The only possible means of

---

4. Ray Yep, '"Cultural Revolution in Hong Kong": Emergency Powers, Administration of Justice and the Turbulent Year of 1967', *Modern Asian Studies* 46, no. 4 (2012): 1007–1032.
5. Kit Chun Lam and Pak Wai Liu, *Immigration and the Economy of Hong Kong* (Hong Kong: City University of Hong Kong Press, 1998), 10.

natural lighting and ventilation is through the space left between the top of the partitions and the ceiling, and there is no insulation in the roof.[6]

Together with lack of government support in other areas like healthcare, education, labour rights, and social security, there was an atmosphere of general frustration among the local population. This anxiety was expressed in various forms of anti-social behaviour. Crime had increased steadily during the first half of the 1960s (Table 2.1). Particularly noteworthy was the jump in drug abuse and gambling. Seizures of raw opium by the police had doubled between 1960 and 1965, whereas the figures for gambling offences in 1964 were three times higher than in 1962.[7] This vice, corruption, and the involvement of the triads in these crimes were genuine threats to law and order, but the fact that more and more people were inclined to engage in these pursuits to escape from reality was even more alarming.

Table 2.1: Crime statistics 1961–1966

Fiscal year	Total number of offences (Excluding minor narcotics offences)
1961/2	6,934
1962/3	7,474
1963/4	6,925
1964/5	8,672
1965/6	9,656

Source: *Hong Kong Police Annual Reports 1961–66*.

In fairness, the colonial government was not unaware of this situation. By late 1950s, the Hong Kong government had accepted the reality that the overseas emigration of the 'refugees' from China was not a viable solution and concluded that full local integration was the only way out of this 'problem of people'. A new philosophy of social policy thus gradually emerged. In 1961, the first territory-wide population census was conducted with the objective of collecting the data necessary for effective policy making.

---

6. *Journal of the Hong Kong Institute of Social Research* 1 (1965): 1–8, 25–28, 33–38, and 90–93. Quoted from David Faure, ed., *A Documentary History of Hong Kong: Society* (Hong Kong: Hong Kong University Press, 1997): 256–257.
7. Carol Jones and Jon Vagg, *Criminal Justice in Hong Kong* (London and New York: Routledge-Cavendish, 2007), 367–368.

Planning and Reviews

Since the early 1960s, there had been an increase in strategic reviews and long-term planning of welfare provisions in the colony. For example, the document *Development of Medical Services in Hong Kong* was released in the 1964, heralding a rising commitment to invest in medical services in the decade to come. More clinics would be built and new hospitals in Lai Chi Kok and Shau Kei Wan were proposed. A target of 5.72 beds per 1,000 people was recommended, and the total recurrent expenditure was projected to be HKD 156 million Hong Kong in the years 1967–1968. A more important document concerning the general welfare policy of the Hong Kong government was also published in the same year. The document, *Aims and Policy for Social Welfare in Hong Kong*, confirmed the government's responsibility 'to make provision for minimum public assistance consisting of shelter, clothing and food'[8] for those who were unable to fend for themselves, and reiterated the government's obligation 'to help individuals, families, groups or communities to overcome difficulties and handicaps which prevent them from attaining their full potential'.[9] Meanwhile, a comprehensive review of housing policy was also completed. Targets of providing 130,000 units of resettlement accommodation and 30,000 units of low-cost housing per year within the next six years were recommended.[10]

These initiatives were, unfortunately, too little too late to diffuse the social tensions before the confrontations in 1967. Yet this momentum did not wane after the riots. Instead, Governor David Trench perceived that colonial rule was fragile and there was a urgent need to shore up local support for the government in the aftermath of the confrontation. He argued that 'a loss of confidence could only too easily be generated by the successful exploitation of social and administrative problems by the Communists, or an erosion of our export markets by overseas interests'.[11] The traumatic experience of 1967, to a certain extent, helped pave the way for a more rigorous approach to social policy. The beleaguered situation of the riots had alerted the business community, who had persistently resisted increase in welfare expenditure, and were arguably indifferent to the needs of the vulnerable in local society.

Social reform was further fuelled by the general economic situation of Hong Kong by the late 1960s. The export-led industrialization of the colony

---

8. *Aims and Policy for Social Welfare in Hong Kong* (Hong Kong: Government Printer, 1964), 8.
9. *Aims and Policy for Social Welfare in Hong Kong*, 8.
10. *Review of Policies for Squatter Control, Resettlement and Government Low-cost Housing, 1964* (Hong Kong: Government Printer, 1964), paragraph 4.
11. Governor to the Right Honourable Michael Stewart, Secretary of State for Foreign and Commonwealth Affairs, 23 April 1970, FCO40/292, TNA.

continued, which increased tax revenues, creating a favourable position for considering a more expansive role for government. Asian economies had benefited tremendously from the recovery of the post-war economy in developed countries and the consequent demand for consumer goods and raw materials. The general increase in living standards reinforced a trend by which labour-intensive production in the core contracted, as it expanded in the periphery, and Hong Kong thrived during this structural adjustment of global capitalism. Compared with other developing economies in Asia, the colony enjoyed the extra advantage. The rise of socialist China had unintentionally facilitated Hong Kong's industrialization. While the arrival of Shanghai capitalists brought capital and expertise for industrial development after 1945, the inflow of masses from South China from 1949 also provided an abundant supply of cheap labour. The embargos on trade imposed on China by the United States and the United Nations during the Korean War also facilitated the colony's industrialization process. The colony's prosperity was no longer solely dependent on trade with China, as Hong Kong's share in China's total trade declined from 32 per cent in 1951 to 5 per cent in 1959.[12] Local entrepreneurs reoriented their efforts towards promoting industrial development.

The externally imposed isolation of the Communist regime also strengthened the colony's role as a conduit for China's access to the outside world, and, even more importantly, as a vital source of foreign exchange earnings. The Chinese government was prepared to support the colony with a steady supply of food, water, and other raw materials, which helped reduce the cost of labour for Hong Kong manufacturers. The colony's export economy was challenged by a new wave of protectionism in overseas markets—including the UK—and the rise of other industrial economies in the region like Taiwan and Korea. Nevertheless, Hong Kong exports of products such as textiles, toys, and electronics continued to spearhead the expansion of the local economy and maintain the momentum of growth, which led to rising wages, profits, and taxes.[13]

During the same period, the colony also developed gradually into a major regional financial centre. Several factors contributed to the rise of Hong Kong as a capital hub. The political instability and financial chaos on Mainland China in the 1940s had made Hong Kong a haven for flight capital and businesses fleeing from the Civil War and Communist takeover.

---

12. Catherine Schenk, *Hong Kong as an International Financial Centre: Emergence and Development 1945–65* (New York and London: Routledge, 2001), 11.
13. Alvin So, 'The Economic Success of Hong Kong: Insights from a World-System Perspective', *Sociological Perspectives* 29, no. 2 (April 1986): 241–258, and Catherine Schenk, 'Economic History of Hong Kong', in EH. Net Encyclopedia, ed. Robert Whaples, accessed 26 September 2022, http://eh.net/encyclopedia/econimc-history-of-hong-kong.

The colony was a particularly important destination for Shanghai capital. A member of the UK Trade Mission to China in 1947 observed that 'there is hardly a British firm in Shanghai which has not since the war transferred its principal office in that (part) of the world from Shanghai to Hong Kong'.[14] The consolidation of Hong Kong as an entrepôt and trading hub further attracted financial services and banks into the territory. The colonial government's reluctance to intervene in the financial sector probably attracted inward investment, including from elsewhere in South-East Asia. Hong Kong was notoriously famous for its lack of regulation of the banking sector in the post-war period. Any individual or company willing to pay in HKD 5,000 licence fee could accept deposits and operate as a 'bank'. In 1947, it was estimated that there were about 250 institutions offering banking services in the territory.

Foreign banks were particularly active in the Hong Kong market. While the overseas Chinese banks with headquarters in South-East Asian countries like Singapore, Malaysia, the Philippines, and Thailand were key players in the colony's rapidly growing banking sector, almost all of the foreign banks operating in China in the 1940s had also established offices in the colony. The growing presence of American banks attested to the rising prominence of Hong Kong in the Asian financial markets. Major players like Citibank and Chase Manhattan had been aggressively expanding their presence in the colony since the 1950s. Demands for banking services rose unabated with the growing domestic prosperity and the steady expansion of the trade volume of the colony. Between 1957 and 1965, there were 364 foreign banking companies registered in Hong Kong, bringing the total number to 1,957.

The capital inflow into the colony was further reinforced by the so-called 'Hong Kong gap' under the sterling system. The operation and significance of the system will be further discussed later, but the fundamental principle of the Sterling Area scheme was to have the currency of all members of the system pegged to the pound sterling, while the convertibility of sterling was restricted for non-members. However, given Hong Kong's status as an entrepôt, London allowed the colony to continue to operate as a free market for US dollars. This free market facilitated the flow of capital as well as trade in goods through Hong Kong.[15]

It is, however, incorrect to say that the colony had become an international financial centre of global significance before the arrival of MacLehose in 1971. Share trading began in the territory in 1865 and the Hong Kong Stock Exchange was founded in 1947. Yet by the end of 1960s, there were

---

14. Schenk, *Hong Kong as an International Financial Centre*, chapter 2.
15. Schenk, *Hong Kong as an International Financial Centre*, chapter 4.

fewer than seventy companies listed on the Exchange, and its development lagged far behind other Asian stock markets like Indonesia, the Philippines, Malaysia, and Singapore. The predominance of small family firms and easy access to bank credits rendered the option of share-issuing for raising capital less popular.[16] Nevertheless, the steady development of Hong Kong's economy led to the consolidation of the fiscal strength of the colonial administration. Between 1961 and 1971, the fiscal reserve had nearly quadrupled from HKD 493 million to HKD 2,886 million. The latter figure represented about one year's total government spending. The rapidly growing surplus justified a parallel increase in public expenditure. Between the fiscal years of 1968/1969 and 1971/1972, government spending rose by 12 per cent annually.[17] In short, the MacLehose administration was in a very good position to respond to the general call for the expansion of the government's role.

A Moderate Turn of Chinese Politics by the Late 1960s

The first two decades of the People's Republic of China were characterized by isolation and radicalism, and Hong Kong was haplessly confronted with the repercussions of various spillovers of the domestic fanaticism of its northern neighbour. Beijing was stricken with an obsessive siege mentality after its involvement in the Korean War in 1950. China's decision to side with the Soviet Union and the Communists in the Korean Peninsula had pushed the United States towards an antagonistic position. Washington instigated the United Nations embargo against China in 1951, which cut off China's trading ties with the rest of the world. Military alliances like the Southeast Asia Treaty Organization (SEATO) were also set up under American and British initiative in 1954, with countries like Thailand, the Philippines, Pakistan, Australia, New Zealand, Cambodia, Laos, and South Vietnam committing to collective defence against the possible aggression of Communist China. The eventual split from the alliance with Soviet Union had further pushed China into isolation and consolidated its sense of vulnerability. Despite the rigorous efforts to reach out to developing countries in South Asia, Africa, and Latin America, and its leading role in consolidate ties among the 'non-aligned' states, Beijing was essentially detached from the developed world by the 1960s. Yet this Cold War attitude towards diplomacy was also an extension of China's domestic politics. Ideological rigidity and dogmatism, together with Mao's desperation to regain leadership

---

16. Schenk, *Hong Kong as an International Financial Centre*, chapter 5.
17. Neil Monnery, *Architect of Prosperity: Sir John Cowperthwaite and the Making of Hong Kong* (London: London Publishing Partnership, 2017), 256.

after the failure of the Great Leap Forward ultimately led to the launch of the Great Proletarian Cultural Revolution in 1966. The country was soon drowning in incessant violence and relentless factional fights, and the unprecedented scale of the disruption and the unspeakable proportion of human loss pushed the party-state machinery into paralysis.

The spiral of escalating violence sustained by the survival instincts and political ambition of the Red Guards eventually drove the country towards the brink of civil war by late 1967. In the summer of 1967, cases of armed confrontation between Red Guards and the army, and even raids on arsenals, were reported. In August, serious armed conflicts broke out in major cities such as Nanjing, Changsha, Shenyang, and Chongqing.[18] Even Mao Zedong admitted that the mass movement had got out of hand and that the restoration of order was imperative. There were calls for the creation of Revolutionary Committees across the country as a basic governing structure, and the military was mobilized to restore control since PLA personnel were frequently core members of these new ruling bodies. This was followed by parallel changes at the top level of the power hierarchy. Radicals like Jiang Qing were sidelined and moderates such as Zhou Enlai gradually returned to the scene. While the Cultural Revolution did continue after this reconfiguration of power dynamics, the phase of extreme radicalism was essentially over by late 1968.

This moderate turn in China's politics had implications for the colony. The leftist protests which had been raging since May 1967 gradually lost momentum towards the end of the year. The fatigue of protestors and the firm response of the colonial authority accounted for this shift, but the waning of support from across the border in China was also important. The left-wing media attacks on the colonial government subsided, and the intensity of violence also dropped off. In the autumn of 1967, Governor Trench remitted his confidence in handling the situation in a communication with London:

> We knew earlier that the local Communists' campaign had been haphazard and misdirected; and there was a good deal of evidence that they had been dissatisfied with the amount of assistance they received from across the border. It was clear that they steadily lost support. Now, their 'struggle' has little effect on the daily life of the Colony.[19]

Trench's claims of victory over the local leftists was premature, as sporadic violence and bomb attacks persisted until the end of 1967.

---

18. Wenqian Gao, *Wannian Zhou Enlai* [Zhou Enlai in twilight years] (Hong Kong: Mirror Books, 2003), 232.
19. Hong Kong to CO, 21 September 1967, FCO21/202, TNA.

London found the dissipation of the conflict in Hong Kong an opportunity to improve the relationship with Beijing. The Anglo-China relationship had suffered as collateral damage of the protests in the colony during the 1967 Riots. In response to the colonial government's arrests of Communist journalists and banning of leftist newspapers in Hong Kong, the Hong Kong and Macao Office of the Chinese Foreign Ministry issued an 'ultimatum' to the British government on 19 August 1967, demanding the lifting of the suspension of the three newspapers and the release of all 'patriotic journalists' within forty-eight hours. On the day when the 'ultimatum' expired, the British Office was surrounded by thousands of angry Red Guards. Despite the efforts of local security officers to keep order, demonstrators eventually broke into the building and attacked the British personnel inside, including Percy Cradock, the political counsellor. The British government retaliated by imposing restrictions on the movement of Chinese diplomats in London. They were put under the close surveillance of the London Police and the Special Branch. On 29 August, a few dozen Chinese diplomats stormed out of their office with axes and baseball bats and confronted with the police outside.[20] Despite these serious altercations, London was determined to stay on good terms with Beijing. The British government was convinced that given China's command of thermonuclear technology and critical role in the Indochina region, engagement with the Communist regime was imperative for Britain's pursuit of regional balance and global peace. Economic considerations were another concern. Anglo-Chinese trade was relatively unaffected by the turbulence unleashed by the Cultural Revolution. During the first seven months of 1967, British exports to China increased from £16.5 million to £27.3 million. London also made serious efforts to sell British aircraft to China.[21]

Protestors jailed during the Riots in Hong Kong were a stumbling block inhibiting the development of a new Anglo-China relationship. London therefore put heavy pressure on Governor Trench to make early releases. Beijing was also eager to extend the olive branch to Britain. A clear signal of this came in early 1970. On 24 January that year, Zhou Enlai publicly criticized the Red Guards' burning of the office of the British mission and claimed that this had violated the diplomatic line of Chairman Mao. On another occasion soon after in February, Zhou subsequently apologized to the British diplomats for the incident and offered to repair the office at China's expense. China's eagerness to resume a 'normal relationship' with the world was reinforced by rising tensions with the Soviet Union. There had been sporadic incidents along the Sino-Soviet border since 1968. On

---

20. De La Mare to Brown, 29 August 1967, FCO21/86, TNA.
21. Morgan to Wilford, 11 September 1970, FCO21/668, TNA.

2 March 1969, forces on both sides fell into direct engagement on Zhenbao Island and the fighting continued for weeks. The growing threat of the Soviet Union provoked a major rethinking of China's diplomatic strategy and pushed Beijing towards Western Europe as a possible buffer against Soviet aggression. Although Britain was not yet admitted into the EEC at the time, its role and leverage in European politics were still valuable to Beijing.[22]

UK Prime Minister Edward Heath was particularly keen to develop a full diplomatic relationship with China. In addition to political and economic considerations, Heath was personally attracted to Chinese culture and was an admirer of Mao, whom he found to have the 'same qualities that he had seen in Churchill'.[23] Nevertheless, he had concerns about potential objections from the US. Beijing was prepared to entertain the prospect of a full diplomatic relationship on the grounds that London agreed to close her consulate in Taiwan and support Beijing's admission into the United Nations. Preservation of the 'special relationship' with the Americans had always been the priority for British diplomacy in the post-war years, and any move that might undermine this friendship needed to be handled with great caution. Yet Heath's concerns seemed unfounded. The Americans had in fact been making serious strides in establishing their own formal relationship with Beijing during the same period, and Heath was kept in the dark about Nixon's secret approaches to China. The growing schism in the Sino-Soviet relationship and China's command of nuclear weapons had prompted Nixon to reconsider the importance of engaging the Communist regime since 1969. The breakthrough came in 1971, when Kissinger secretly visited China on 9 July. His meeting with Zhou Enlai heralded a historic change in the contour of global politics and a new normalization of the Sino-American relationship. London, and indeed the whole world, was shocked when Nixon made a televised announcement of Kissinger's visit and his own upcoming visit to Beijing on 15 July. The British Ambassador to Washington was informed only thirty minutes in advance. This monumental episode quickly sparked a chain of events which placed the People's Republic of China back in the theatre of global diplomacy. By the time MacLehose assumed the office of colonial governor in November 1971, the People's Republic of China had been admitted to the United Nations and the Republic of China expelled on 25 October 1971. By March 1972, the full diplomatic relationship between the United Kingdom and the People's Republic of China had been confirmed, shortly after the pronouncement

---

22. Chi-Kwan Mark, *The Everyday Cold War: Britain and China, 1950–1972* (London: Bloomsbury Academic, 2017), chapter 5.
23. Mark, *The Everyday Cold War*, 161.

of the Shanghai Communiqué signed between Beijing and Washington. A more outward-looking and pragmatic China had emerged.

Unease with the Sovereign

Hong Kong's relationship with the sovereign had not always been easy and was particularly so in the 1960s. In fact, at the time MacLehose arrived at Hong Kong, it would be an understatement to describe the colony's relationship with London as jittery. As Priscilla Roberts argued, 'what might be termed an informal level of decolonization was already in place, with the interests and outlooks of Britain and Hong Kong effectively largely decoupled'.[24] On the economic front, there had been the devaluation of sterling in 1967 and the lingering trade disputes between Hong Kong and Britain had accounted for decades of heated exchange between the two. The dispute over the colony's contribution to cost of the British Garrison in Hong Kong further exacerbated the tension. The sovereign's commitment to the interests of the colony was questioned by both local elites and Governor Trench. London's insistence on the early release of prisoners from the riots, further soured disharmony between the governments of Britain and Hong Kong.

Devaluation of Pound Sterling

The altercation over the value of sterling and Hong Kong's exports to Britain arose from its status as a member of the Sterling Area. The evolution of the Sterling Area attested to the changing role of Britain in the global economy. During the heyday of Britain's power, sterling was naturally accepted as the primary currency for conducting transactions and for holding national reserves. Yet when Britain's pre-eminence started to decline after the First World War, efforts were made to encourage countries with close connections with Britain to peg their exchange rates to the floating pound to preserve the value of the British currency. The so-called Sterling Bloc was largely comprised of British dominions, colonies, and protectorates in the Middle East. Hong Kong was part of this informal group. With the further decline of Britain's status as a global economic power after the Second World War, London felt it necessary to strengthen the measures which protected the value of pound sterling, and the group was formalized as the scheduled territories of the Sterling Area in 1947.

---

24. Priscilla Roberts, 'Introduction: China and the Long 1970s: The Great Transformation', in *China, Hong Kong and the Long 1970s: Global Perspective*, ed. Priscilla Roberts and O. A. Westad (London: Palgrave Macmillan, 2017), 1–30.

In brief, there were three major components of this complex system of exchange controls. Firstly, members had to peg their exchange rates to sterling and maintain a common exchange control against the rest of the world. Secondly, they could enjoy freedom in currency and capital transactions within the Sterling Area. Thirdly, members were also required to maintain their national reserves in assets denominated in pounds sterling. In a word, the arrangement aimed to sustain the demand for sterling for international transactions and to minimize the convertibility of sterling into dollars. It made economic sense for Hong Kong to stay in the Sterling Area, since Britain and the Commonwealth were her major trading partners in the early post-war years and most of their transactions were concluded in sterling. However, although Hong Kong was obliged to impose exchange controls against the rest of the world, the colony was vitally given a special status that would allow her to operate as a free market for US dollars, without which it was impossible to function as an entrepôt. However, this still entailed that the fiscal health of the colony was entwined with the value of sterling.

At one point, Hong Kong held nearly a quarter of all externally held sterling balances within the Sterling Area,[25] but such a contribution did not mean much to London when it was decided to devalue the pound in 1967. Harold Wilson inherited a very large trade deficit when he came to power in 1964. By November 1967, Wilson concluded that a devaluation was inevitable. The pound was devalued by 14 per cent against the US dollar. Trench was informed of the decision a few hours before it was officially announced and made no effort to hide his anger in a response to London:

> I find it difficult to find words to express my feelings, and those of my Advisers, official and unofficial, on the manner in which Britain has now defaulted on its very large net financial obligations to Hong Kong . . . I find it very hard to excuse the manner in which responsibility for solving the exceedingly complex problems devaluation presented was thrust upon us without the least prior consultation as to where our interest lay (indeed after several refusals to enter into serious consultations), without advice of any kind, and without the same amount of warning was given to other independent countries.[26]

John Cowperthwaite, Hong Kong's Financial Secretary, succinctly summarized the impact of the decision on the colony:

---

25. Monnery, *Architect of Prosperity*, 24.
26. David Trench to the Commonwealth Office, 28 November 1967, OV 44/258, Bank of England Archives, quoted in Monnery, *Architect of Prosperity*, 229.

The act of devaluation imposed a very large immediate loss on Hong Kong (between 50–70 million pounds probably) and the problem was basically to distribute this loss while causing the minimum of dislocation, hardship and further loss. To follow the pound, while protecting the banks and the majority of merchants against exchange losses, would have lowered the living standards of the people and caused a loss of foreign exchange earnings due to the worsening of terms of trade. If on the other hand, the Hong Kong dollar's previous gold parity were maintained, there were prospects of serious consequences on industry and trade by reason of their sterling commitments, leading possibly to bankruptcies, factory closure and unemployment.[27]

Trench demanded urgent discussion of compensations and arrangements for the potential future devaluation. Hong Kong's fiscal reserve was a key issue here. At first, London did not provide any assurance, arguing that Hong Kong had suffered no worse than other sterling holders. Yet London was fully aware of the prevailing sentiment in Hong Kong. Anthony Galsworthy of the Commonwealth Office believed that if no solution could be found, several unofficial members of the Executive Council would resign, making the colony challenging to govern. The tension between London and the colony continued to run high, but Trench and Cowperthwaite were not prepared to back off. London eventually agreed to offer members of the Sterling Area some protection against the devaluation of the pound in the future. The Sterling Guarantee Arrangement was created under the Basel Agreement of September 1968, which guaranteed the US dollar value of official sterling reserves by members in excess of 10 per cent of their official reserves. Despite this 'victory', the Trench administration continued to fight for independence in exchange rate policy and diversification of reserve holdings, striving to minimize the possible impact of another British decision on the value of the pound on Hong Kong. Trench was convinced that the interest of the colony did not seem to feature significantly in the thinking of his colleagues in London.

Exports to Britain

Trade disputes between Hong Kong and Britain were also a major source of tension. A key aspect of the hostilities concerned the rising protectionism against Hong Kong exports and the anti–Hong Kong sentiment of British manufacturers and workers, which stemmed from the bestowment of the privilege of 'Imperial Preference' to Hong Kong in 1932. The British government decided to end its free-trade regime in response to the global

---

27. Cowperthwaite to Galsworthy, 21 December 1967, FCO48/78, TNA.

depression in 1930, and reimposed general tariffs for imports. Meanwhile, in order to strengthen ties between the colonies, Britain and members of Commonwealth agreed to reduce trade barriers within the Empire at the Ottawa Conference in 1932. For Hong Kong, this effectively created tariff-free access to the British market, a privilege that was particularly important after 1949. Communist China's growing trade ties with the Soviet Bloc and the US and United Nations trade embargos in 1950 rendered it imperative for the colony to find opportunities elsewhere. Her declining importance as China's entrepôt also encouraged the industrial development in Hong Kong. As a result of all these developments, Hong Kong's exports to the British market increased rapidly during the 1950s. For example, according to James Fellows, Hong Kong exports of grey cloth to Britain tripled between 1954 and 1956.[28]

In the face of mounting demand for protection for domestic industries, the British government 'encouraged' the largest suppliers of textile goods—India, Pakistan and Hong Kong—to limit their exports to the British market 'voluntarily'. Unsurprisingly, the Hong Kong government did not take this suggestion very positively. The colonial administration's adherence to the principle of laissez-faire made local bureaucrats very resistant to the idea of brokering a deal among the local industrialists, especially as the ethnic and linguistic divides of the domestic textile business (Shanghainese vs Cantonese, British Hongs vs local firms) rendered securing a general agreement a daunting task. With the textile and clothing industries employing 42 per cent of the colony's labour force, the limitation on Hong Kong exports would also harm the local economy and public livelihoods. Governor Alexander Grantham and his successor Robert Black resisted pressure from the British government for controls over Hong Kong exports, but protectionism prevailed in the end. In 1959, Hong Kong's cotton spinners and weavers 'volunteered' to limit their exports until 1962, which would buy the British manufacturers time to restructure and upgrade their production. Condemnation on the colony's exports continued unabated, but the focus was soon extended to the 'unfair competition' which Hong Kong's negligence regarding labour conditions produced. These sustained and organized attacks on the image of Hong Kong prompted the colonial government to organize a publicly funded public relations campaign in Britain, in which the Hong Kong General Chamber of Commerce and Government Information Service played a leading role.

The trade disputes turn further south in the 1960s. Britain's attempts to join the European Economic Community (EEC)—first in 1961, again

---

28. James Fellows, 'The Rhetoric of Trade and Decolonization in Hong Kong, 1945–1984' (PhD diss., Lingnan University, 2016), 36.

in 1967 and finally successfully in 1970—had major implications for the colony's trade prospects. The entire negotiation process was too complex and protracted to be elaborated here in full, but a key stumbling block in the negotiation of British admission which had direct relevance to the colony was over how to accommodate the interests of the constituents of the Commonwealth. Understandably, EEC members were reluctant to grant tariff-free status for these states, but for Britain this posed the challenge of how to reconcile this demand with the privilege of Imperial Preference granted to members of the British Empire. There was, however, a provision under the EEC which granted 'Associated Overseas Territory' (AOT) status to 'developing nations' which were former colonies of the member states, allowing them to enjoy certain tariff privileges. Yet Hong Kong was a victim of its own success. The EEC members saw her as a major threat to the European textile and garment industries due to its dominant role in global textile trade. Sensing the misgivings of the EEC members and their designation of Hong Kong as 'a special case', London eventually abandoned the pursuit of AOT status for Hong Kong. The protracted and secretive negotiations bred suspicion and resentment against the metropole in the colony. A member of the Hong Kong General Chamber of Commerce confronted various pro-Europeans MPs with this comment:

> In the light of the Prime Minister's expressed view that Britain must get into the Common Market, there was a feeling that Hong Kong's interest would be completely overlooked. This might well lead to a lack of confidence in Hong Kong towards the U.K. and in turn might curb British exports to Hong Kong.[29]

James Fellows summarized the uneasy relationship between Britain and Hong Kong during the negotiations with the following insight:

> Despite attempts by Hong Kong's business associations to influence the outcome of the negotiations, the colony was ultimately dependent on Britain's commitment to the interests of Hong Kong, and the lengths the British government would go in protecting them. Towards the end of the first (EEC) membership bid, this faith was wavering. By the time of the second bid in 1967, there were serious doubts that Hong Kong would be a priority. The British bid was in part born from domestic crises, and Britain seemed to be withdrawing from its imperial commitments during this period. In the end, the metropole's resolve was not tested as negotiations failed to materialize. Nevertheless, it was a crisis period in relations between Britain and Hong Kong and brought to the forefront the problematic nature of colonial status in a period of imperial retreat.[30]

---

29. Fellows, 'The Rhetoric of Trade and Decolonization', 119.
30. Fellows, 'The Rhetoric of Trade and Decolonization', 139.

Cost of British Garrison in Hong Kong

A concurrent controversy over Britain's financial commitment to cover the expenditure defending Hong Kong hardly improved the mood. The humiliation of the Suez Canal crisis in the mid-1950s had prompted a strategic rethinking of Britain's global military commitments. In 1961, Harold Macmillan set the ceiling for Britain's military expenditure and global commitment and decided on a withdrawal from military bases east of Suez. This decision had major implications for Hong Kong. With the reduction of the British military presence in Malaysia and Singapore, the colony would become even more vulnerable. This was compounded by a request from London to reduce the strength of the garrison from eight to five or six major units. The colonial government disagreed, and argued that the British Force was required not only for internal security but also for external defence against potential aggression from China, for which the sovereign should be responsible. Above all, these reductions 'would undermine the confidence of the civilian population in the resolve of the United Kingdom to defend Hong Kong'.[31] Eventually, a compromise was reached, and the colony was allowed to maintain a force of six and two-thirds units.

London however remained determined to cut military costs, and the colony was expected to make a substantial rise in financial contribution. From 1958, Hong Kong's contribution to the cost of the garrison stood at £1.5 million annually. In 1964, it was agreed that, starting in the financial year 1965/1966, the colony was required to pay an additional lump sum of £11.5 million over the next six years for local military infrastructures. Shortly after the publication of the Defence White Paper in February 1966, the colonial government was told that if Hong Kong wanted to maintain the current size of British garrison, an annual contribution of £11 million was required. Understandably, Hong Kong was not convinced. 'All shades of public opinion . . . are unanimously opposed to an increase in Hong Kong's defence contribution', was the conclusion of the Colonial Secretary, Frederick Lee, after his visit to the colony in July 1966.[32] London eventually managed to secure an agreement from Hong Kong to raise the colony's contribution to £5 million a year. Trench tried in vain to wrangle a better deal for Hong Kong with a proposed handover of land in the city occupied by the British Army. This was not the end of the story, however, since shortly after the agreement, London tried to back down from her promise by deciding to reduce the British garrison's strength by one major unit in

---

31. Chi-Kwan Mark, 'Lack of Means or Loss of Will? The United Kingdom and the Decolonization of Hong Kong, 1957–1967', *The International History Review* XXXI (March 2009): 45–71.
32. Glasworthy to Cass, 8 September 1966, DEFE13/534, TNA.

1967/1968. Nevertheless, the plan was delayed by the outbreak of the confrontations in 1967.

Release of Confrontation Prisoners

The arguments over trade and the garrison were not, however, the last altercations Trench had to endure before his departure in 1971. Towards the latter months of his term, he found himself engulfed in another round of heated debate with London, and this time, with the integrity of the local judicial system at stake, he was not inclined to back down.

During the 1967 Riots, more than 2,000 protestors were jailed and, for Trench, these arrests attested to his firmness in tackling the confrontations. While officials in London by and large trusted the Governor's approach to the crisis, voices calling for the early release of these prisoners gradually gathered momentum in the FCO towards the latter part of 1967. The debate over the case of Anthony Grey was the beginning of protracted altercations between Hong Kong and London on this matter. Grey was a Reuters reporter who was under house arrest in Beijing in retaliation against the Hong Kong government's arrest of some New China News Agency (NCNA) journalists in the colony. As early as August 1967, Donald Hopson, the head of British Mission in Beijing, had tabled a proposal for the early release of the NCNA reporters as a way to secure freedom for Grey. As a face-saving tactic for Hong Kong, Hopson recommended that these prisoners should be deported to the mainland.[33]

The suggestion of early releases as a tactic to defuse the tensions gradually gained momentum among officials in London. Sympathetic ears were also found among officials in the Commonwealth Office, suggesting support for the idea that 'an amnesty for those serving sentences for curfew breaking or minor breaches of the peace could be made at an opportune time'.[34] The Foreign Office was also under growing public and parliamentary pressure to demonstrate that efforts had been made to ameliorate Grey's conditions in Beijing,[35] and to entertain Hopson's proposal as a possible way to de-escalate tensions with China.[36] Trench, however, disagreed. Trench argued that a decision in favour of the early release of the confrontation prisoners 'would be widely interpreted as a sign of weakness' in Hong Kong, and if such a compromise were made, Beijing 'would merely pocket

---

33. Peking to Foreign Office, 14 August 1967, FCO40/113, TNA.
34. Commonwealth Office to Hong Kong, 5 October 1967, FCO21/193, TNA.
35. James Murray to Wilkinson, 2 May 1968, FCO21/227, TNA.
36. James Murray to Wilkinson, 23 January 1968, FCO21/193, TNA.

the concession and ask for more'.³⁷ For Trench, the unconditional or early release of these prisoners, who had committed criminal offences and been convicted through the correct legal processes in the colonial courts, was simply unacceptable.

Trench's resistance was, however, greatly undermined when Britain eventually decided to upgrade her diplomatic relationship with China. A decision to re-deploy ambassadors overseas made at the 9th Congress of the Chinese Communist Party held in April 1969 heralded a dramatic shift in China's foreign policy. Trench certainly felt the heat, and eventually made a major concession over the early release of a number of confrontation prisoners in the summer of 1969. Among the beneficiaries was Wong Chak, a journalist whose situation the Chinese authorities had equated to that of Grey. Originally, he was given a five-year term and was not due for release until 1971. Trench's compromise made Wong eligible for review and, more importantly, allowed him to walk free two years ahead of schedule.³⁸ The release of Grey followed shortly afterwards. Unfortunately, this was just the beginning of the Governor's journey down a slippery slope.

By early 1970, the call for early releases had gathered momentum, and London had become increasingly enthusiastic about exploring possible options for an early conclusion to this thorny issue. The gender, health, and age of various prisoners had been raised by officials in London as possible grounds for the remission of sentences. Officials in the FCO argued in late 1970 that 'the situation is now calm, three years have passed, and pressures are muted' and in 1971 it was specifically suggested that the Governor should release all remaining prisoners.³⁹

The issue had become a major irritant between London and Trench. According to Arthur Maddocks, Political Adviser to the Hong Kong government:

> The Governor took it pretty badly and he became a little neurotic, in my view, about London's desires: 'To improve relations with China'. These became almost fighting words with Trench . . . So, the more people wrote to him from London about improving relations with China, or the more Ministers, like Anthony Royle or Lord Shepherd, came to Hong Kong and spoke in these rather general terms, the more inclined he was to think that this was a pretty undesirable effort to get some benefits for London in China at the expense of Hong Kong.⁴⁰

---

37. Trench to Commonwealth Office, 19 January 1968, FCO21/193, TNA.
38. Document attached to Note No. 28, prepared by Gaminara, 11 March 1970, FCO40/252, TNA.
39. Morgan to Tomlinson, Monson & Deas, 31 December 1970, FCO40/253, TNA.
40. Transcript of Steve Tsang's interview with Arthur Frederick Maddock, n.d., Mss. Ind. Ocn. S340 Rhodes House Library, Oxford University, 64–65.

Although the floodgates were now open, Trench remained adamant over the handling of the 'hardcore' confrontation prisoners. Four prisoners jailed during the riots had either killed or seriously injured police officers or members of the public and had been given long sentences.[41] Trench refused to apply leniency in these cases and maintained his defiance against London's pressure till the end of his term. They were, however, granted early release shortly after his departure. MacLehose had declared his intention to 'work for a solution in the course of 1972' before his arrival in the colony.[42] All of the confrontation prisoners were released on 3 May 1973.[43]

Trench found all of these squabbles and fights with London to be a very frustrating experience. He certainly did not endear himself to his colleagues in Whitehall and he was fully aware that the feeling of uneasiness was mutual. In a message in January 1967, the Governor stated, 'the impression' had been given that Hong Kong is 'regarded at home not as the loyal supporter she on the whole is, but as a tiresome nuisance, to be slighted and made use of since she cannot quietly made away with'.[44]

Conclusion

MacLehose was seemingly an ideal candidate to succeed Trench. He had first-hand experience with the Scandinavian model of welfarism during his time as Ambassador to Denmark, which equipped him well for the colossal task of introducing social reforms in the colony in the aftermath of the 1967 Riots. MacLehose also had the right credentials for managing relations with China. His previous appointment as Political Adviser in Hong Kong, his wartime service in China, and his experience of engaging with another Communist regime in Czechoslovakia stood him in good stead for the challenge of handling a Communist regime across the border. Most importantly, London presumably wanted a more pleasant relationship with Hong Kong after years of beleaguered confrontations with Trench, whom FCO officials found very difficult to work with. There is evidence to support the truth of Leslie Monson's (the Deputy Under Secretary of the FCO) complaint about 'Sir David Trench's inclination when over-ruled

---

41. Hong Kong to FCO, 6 July 1972, FCO21/1025, SCR7/3371/68 II, TNA.
42. Guidelines for the Governor Designate, Hong Kong: Paper C, 18 October 1971, FCO40/329, TNA.
43. The Hong Kong Government did achieve a token victory by successfully removing Ho Cheung, a prisoner with a twenty-five-year sentence for murder, from the list of confrontation prisoners on technical grounds. The crime was committed in 1967, but Ho fled to the mainland afterwards. Ho returned to Hong Kong in 1971 and was subsequently arrested. Davies to Clark, 3 May 1973 and FCO Hong Kong to Peking, 28 April 1973, FCO21/1141, TNA.
44. Trench to Galsworthy, 5 January 1967, v, 3, 186–9, BDEE quoted in Mark, 'Lack of Means or Loss of Will?', 62.

to continue to harbour "ancient grudges"'. He went on to criticize the Governor's aberrance, stating that 'with other governors elsewhere in the past this would have called for a friendly personal letter from here, but this technique does not seem to work with Sir David Trench'.[45] As a former FCO colleague who had a better understanding of the thinking of his friends back home, MacLehose's appointment would hopefully pave the way for more cordial communications.

While MacLehose was probably aware of these expectations, there were still multiple unanticipated developments during his tenure in the 1970s. MacLehose was cognizant of the necessity of social reform and the imperative of developing the colony into a modern city. As part of his preparation for the role, he was particularly keen to learn from leading British experts about four specific aspects of city management: traffic control, town planning, police organization, and technical education. He was enthusiastic to hear their insights as to how these problems were approached in contexts comparable to Hong Kong—such as in Singapore and Japan. The size of the task was, however, much bigger than he imagined. Interestingly, he seldom mentioned the issue of corruption in the colony. Nor did he foresee that the most powerful advocates for an expansive approach in social policy were in fact from London rather than within local community. Engagement with China was certainly at the top of his agenda. The FCO was so keen to remind the Governor-designate of the importance of this matter that they gave him a copy of Richard Hughes's *Hong Kong: Borrowed Place, Borrowed Time* in his briefing package. MacLehose was certainly alert to the importance of preparing the colony for the ultimate negotiation over the future of Hong Kong in some distant future. Yet the 1997 issue was very much in the background when MacLehose arrived in the colony. Britain's position was that it was not possible to enter into any conversation with China on this matter before a post-Mao leadership emerged. Yet China's modernization drive and growing presence in global diplomacy had pushed the issue of Hong Kong's future to the forefront earlier than planned. Unlike Mao, Deng Xiaoping was not content with restoration of order in China. His vision was to transform China into a modern economy, even if this necessitated the abandonment of ideological orthodoxy and the embrace of capitalist practices. Engaging with a strong and confident China was a new experience both for the British government and for the Governor.

Last but not least, MacLehose had probably underestimated the disagreement between London and Hong Kong prior to his arrival. Yet he had been warned. His predecessor, Trench, had reiterated his fear that London was gradually eroding his capacity to govern, which the Hong Kong

---

45. Monson to Royle, 17 February 1971, FCO40/323, TNA.

authorities saw as detrimental to the interests of the colony.[46] FCO officials would certainly be inclined to attribute these 'biased accounts' to the difficult character of Trench and his failure to consider the situation in a wider context. Yet, this was hardly a matter of personal difference. Instead, it was a result of the process of 'decolonization in substance', as John Darwin called it, in post-war Hong Kong.[47] With the seismic change in Britain's position in the world and the parallel decline in resources and change in priorities after the war, the sovereign's will and capability to maintain its presence in the colony was questioned. The controversies over trade and military deployment in the 1960s were all extensions of this repositioning. MacLehose soon realized that America's relationship with China, the logic of Cold War politics, the roles and values of Hong Kong in the eyes of Beijing, London, and the British public, had all changed fundamentally. Locals were also becoming increasingly outspoken about their suspicions of Britain's commitments to the colony. MacLehose may have had the best credentials for the job on paper, yet the scale of the challenge was far larger than he conceived.

---

46. Bottomley to Monson, 17 February 1971, FCO40/323, TNA.
47. John Darwin, 'Hong Kong and British Decolonization', in *Hong Kong's Transition, 1842–1997*, ed. Judith M. Brown and Rosemary Foot (Basingstoke: Macmillan, 1997), 16–32.

3
Pre-empting the Sovereign
The Creation of ICAC and the Police Mutiny

Introduction

The introduction of Prevention of Bribery Ordinance and the creation of the ICAC were the most important institutional legacies of British colonialism in Hong Kong. Their success in eradicating the cancer of corruption from both the face of public administration and the social fabric of the colony within less than a decade was phenomenal. Working with Jack Cater, John Prendergast, and Charles Sutcliffe, Governor MacLehose's crusade saved Hong Kong from the purgatory of unrestrained corruption. MacLehose's initiative was met with strong opposition from the local police force. The colonial administration was confronted with the prospect of a police strike in 1977, and the Governor's resolve was put to the most severe of tests. Eventually, MacLehose conceded to an unprecedented amnesty, which was followed by the restructuring of the police leadership and the ICAC's priorities. Nevertheless, the ICAC persevered through all these challenges and continued to maintain its credibility as a fierce watchdog against corruption.

Since the beginning of colonial rule, the pervasiveness and magnitude of sleaze and fraudulence within the colonial bureaucracy had not gone unnoticed. The situation eventually deteriorated into a 'collective action problem'—citizens and political leaders alike did not have the will and incentive to contain corruption. That is, while everybody understood that they would stand to gain from erasing corruption, they had no reason to refrain from or work to confront corrupt practices because of a complete lack of trust that anyone else would join them in improving the situation.[1]

---
1. Robert H. Bates, *Toward a Political Economy of Development: A Rational Choice Perspective* (Berkeley: University of California Press, 1988); Donatella Della Porta and Alberto Vannucci, *Corrupt Exchanges: Actors, Resources, and Mechanisms of Political Corruption* (New York: Aldine de Gruyter, 1999); A. Persson, Bo Rothstein, and Jan Teorell, 'Why Anti-Corruption Reforms Fail—Systemic

The 'bus-riding' analogy for corruption in the colonial police force in post-war Hong Kong attests to this mentality. The practice of bribe-taking was said to be like taking a bus—even if you didn't want to get on it, don't stand in front of it. This was a common understanding among law enforcement personnel in the 1960s and 1970s.

Nevertheless, this chapter intends to shed new light on several key aspects of the dynamics of the reform process, rather than merely focusing on the heroic contributions of key colonial officials.[2] Firstly, decision makers usually 'inherit rather than make' policy[3] and changes in institutions are generally the result of cumulative developments over a protracted period with piecemeal modifications made at the margins. Complete ruptures with the past or variations of revolutionary proportions are few and far between. The trajectory of change is, in most cases, mundane, disjointed, or unspectacular, even though the narrative may appear theatrical and heroic in retrospect. The colony's campaign against corruption was no exception. MacLehose's achievements must be contextualized within the cumulative changes that preceded his tenure. More importantly, the 'London dimension' lurking behind the trajectory of his reforms must be acknowledged. MacLehose's ultimate decision to bring the protracted debate on the importance of creating an independent anti-corruption body to a conclusion was, in fact, very much driven by the prospect of London's enquiry into the corruption of the colony. The creation of the ICAC in 1974 was by and large a move to pre-empt London's intervention into this matter. Investigating the dynamics of the reform process and the handling of the crisis of police mutiny can thus help us uncover the intricate challenges faced by the governor in navigating the quagmire of domestic and external political pressure.

Assumption of the Ethnic Divide

The colony had been infected with the disease of corruption ever since the commencement of British rule in the territory. Governor Richard MacDonnell's communication with the Earl of Carnarvon of the Colonial Office in 1869 is probably one of the earliest official acknowledgements of

---

Corruption as a Collective Action Problem', *Governance: An International Journal of Policy, Administration, and Institution* 26, no. 3 (2013): 449–471.
2. Ray Yep, 'Beyond the "Great Man" Narrative: Scandals, Cumulative Reforms and the Trajectory of Anti-corruption Efforts in Colonial Hong Kong before MacLehose Years', *Social Transformation in Chinese Societies* 18, no. 2 (2021): 154–170.
3. Richard Rose and Phillip L. Davies, *Inheritance in Public Policy: Change without Choice in Britain* (New Haven, CT: Yale University Press, 1994).

the prevalence of sleaze and bribery. The Governor made no secret of his revulsion with the police force in the letter to his superior in London:

> I have no doubt that on my arrival more (than) half of the inspectors were in receipt of monthly allowances, higher than their salaries, from the keepers of Brothels and gaming establishments. In fact, every new police law was a new source of profit to them, and the Chinese had been early so habituated to similar practice on the part of the petty Mandarins and other officials in their own country, that such proceedings seemed to them quite natural.[4]

Another governor, William Robinson, shared MacDonnell's frustrations. He made his sentiments on the limited progress in repressing corruption in the colony clear in one of his very last dispatches to the Secretary of State for the Colonies, Joseph Chamberlain, in 1897:

> Thirty years ago it was well-known and was reported to your department that the efficiency of the Police was greatly impaired by the corruption of the force caused by its members receiving pay from the gambling hongs in Victoria, in consideration of which, the Police either sheltered the gamblers by not reporting their misdoings to the Captain Superintendent of Police, or gave notice to the gamblers of every intended raid on their gambling hong . . . [T]here has been a grave suspicion as to the inefficiency of the treatment of this evil and a further suspicion which I regret to say has been recently confirmed, that at all events part of the Police Force, which has been raised and maintained at such a great cost to the city, has for some years past been in league with the owners of gambling houses in this city.[5]

Robinson tried to address the situation with the introduction of the Misdemeanors Punishment Ordinance 1898. It was a landmark legal development in the history of anti-corruption campaigns in the colony: the offering of a bribe by a public servant as well as receiving one was made a criminal offence. However, it left the investigation of corruption cases to the police force, a government agency that was most vulnerable to pecuniary temptation, and no special unit was created within the police to handle bribery complaints. Despite its limitations, the Ordinance remained the colony's major anti-graft statute until after the Second World War.

Although the colonial government had admitted that corruption was prevalent in the territory, its assessment of the severity of the problem and formulation of a response was affected by its misguided assumption of the

---

4. MacDonnell to Lord Carnarvon, 7 January 1869, CO129/120, TNA.
5. Governor William Rob to Joseph Chamberlain, 13 August 1897, CO129/276, TNA.

existence of an ethnic divide in this matter. In short, colonial officials saw corruption primarily as a 'Chinese problem', and corruption was seen because of Chinese customs and culture. Like many other social ills ravaging the colony at the time, it was common for colonial officials to attribute these problems to the 'bad habits' of the Chinese, who were seen as creatures with truncated moral bearings. Their filthy habits were held accountable for the spread of diseases and the general miserable state of public health,[6] and this justified the residential segregation between the European and Chinese population.[7] Along the same lines, perceived Chinese low resistance to temptation and desire explained the prevalence of gambling, opium-taking, and concubinage in the local community. Corruption was just another natural extension of this Chinese moral aberration. It was assumed that their experience with the political chaos and public incivilities on the mainland convinced those who migrated into Hong Kong that bribery was essential for survival or access to public services.[8] As an official study on corruption in 1907 concluded:

> We must remind Your Excellency that in China the system of black-mailing is unfortunately a matter of everyday occurrence amongst Government officials (Yamen runners and others) and the civil population. Any Chinamen consequently settling here not only accepts but this is quite prepared to find similar conditions prevailing in this Colony as that which obtains in his own country.[9]

In some instances, corrupt European officers were even portrayed as 'passive' victims to these Chinese temptations:

> It is humiliating to read of Englishmen in the position of these men so utterly devoid of self-respect and lost to all sense of honour as to allow themselves to sink in such a life. Their conduct is evidenced in the report. Their conduct, gentlemen, drags the name of Englishmen of which every Englishmen ought to be proud, into the mire, tarnishes the national honour. On the other hand, the conduct a certain section of the Chinese

---

6. Ka-che Yip, *Disease, Colonialism, and the State: Malaria in Modern East Asian History* (Hong Kong: Hong Kong University Press, 2009).
7. Peak District (Residence) Ordinance, 1918.
8. H. J. Lethbridge, 'The Emergence of Bureaucratic Corruption as a Social Problem in Hong Kong', in *Hong Kong: Stability and Change*, ed. H. J. Lethbridge (Hong Kong: Oxford University Press, 1978), 214–237.
9. 'Report of the Commission appointed by His Excellency the Governor to Enquire into and Report on the Administration of the Sanitary and Building Regulations enacted by the Public Health and Building Ordinance. 1903, and the Existence of Corruption among the Officials charged with the administration of the Aforesaid Regulations', The Inquiry Commission, 1907, paragraph 388.

population in offering and even *pressing filthy bribes on men who in many instances never even asked for them* is most reprehensible. [my italics][10]

The general mentality of 'blaming the Chinese' for the epidemic of corruption derived not just from the racist bias of the alien rulers, but also stemmed from the colonial administration's lack of confidence and resources for getting involved in the management of the local community. During the early years of their administration in 'worthless' Hong Kong, the British exhibited a form of 'caretaker imperialism' commonly found in the less valuable possessions of the British Empire: 'hold on, hang on, do nothing'.[11] There was simply a paucity of administrative and human resources available for governors to do their jobs. Steve Tsang has summarized the situation eloquently:

> It is important to recognize that both the colonial society and the government were very small. The expatriate community numbered in the hundreds and the administration consisted of about 50 officials in its first decade. Thus, despite the grand title of certain offices and references to colony-wide interests, governance and administration of justice among the expatriates closely resembled that [of] a very small township. Thinking of Hong Kong as a crown colony being run by His Excellency the Governor, supported by his Executive and Legislative Councils and a civil service in the capital city of Victoria, gave a distorted picture of what colonial life and politics were like in the mid-nineteenth century.[12]

The small expatriate community was vastly outnumbered by the Chinese majority and the language barrier and cultural gap between the two communities entailed an acute sense of insecurity among the non-Chinese residents. As a result, the minority group's response was to keep the local population at a distance. Chinese and non-Chinese mostly lived among their own people, and the ethnic divide was present in most aspects of life. To a large extent, the colonial administration was indifferent to social ills such as gambling, public filth, and corruption.[13] Colonial officials

---

10. 'Report of the Commission appointed by His Excellency the Governor to Enquire into and Report on the Administration of the Sanitary and Building Regulations enacted by the Public Health and Building Ordinance. 1903, and the Existence of Corruption among the Officials charged with the administration of the Aforesaid Regulations', paragraph 388.
11. John Darwin, *Unfinished Empire: The Global Expansion of Britain* (London: Penguin, 2012), 391.
12. Steve Tsang, *Governing Hong Kong: Administrative Officers from the Nineteenth Century to the Handover to China, 1862–1997* (Hong Kong: Hong Kong University Press, 2007).
13. Ray Yep, 'The Crusade against Corruption in Hong Kong in the 1970s: Governor MacLehose as a Zealous Reformer or Reluctant Hero?', *China Information* 27 (July 2013): 197–221; Ray Yep, *Jingmo Geming* [Quiet revolution: The long campaign against corruption in Hong Kong] (Hong Kong: Chunghwa Bookstore, 2015); Yip, *Disease, Colonialism and the State*.

comforted themselves, however, with the belief that European officers at the core of the machinery of colonial rule were immune to these corrosions of public morality. All these factors helped account for the colonial government's evasive, ambiguous, and indecisive approach towards the issue of corruption and fraud, despite mounting evidence of its ascendance.

The Myth Debunked

The corruption scandals which occurred immediately before the Japanese invasion of Hong Kong in 1941, however, provide a powerful reminder that the supposed ethnic divide in corruption was a myth. With Japanese aggression against China in its heyday, the Air Raid Precaution Department (ARPD) was formed in 1937 owing to the expected bombing raids on Hong Kong.

It was the ARPD's plan to construct air raid shelters on both sides of Victoria Harbour. The Kowloon project was assigned to the Kin Lee Construction Company. The financial arrangement of the contract was that the government would reimburse Kin Lee the cost, plus 10 per cent as profit. In other words, the bigger the cost, the bigger the profit for the company. Kin Lee tried to exploit this loophole to its advantage through serial subcontracting arrangements. Bogus companies were set up which provided no service to the job, but instead inflated the total cost. It was also revealed that Kin Lee had exaggerated the size of the air raid shelter project and charged the government based on these bloated figures.[14] It was soon uncovered that Joseph Campbell, an engineer in the Public Works Department who was assigned with this duty, had received a bribe of HKD 2,000 and several gifts from Kin Lee during the construction period. It appeared that this was not just an isolated case of the corruption of an individual official, but that some form of syndicate was at work here. Campbell tried to kill himself during the investigation,[15] and Kin Lee's accountant, who was summoned to the inquiry committee, went missing along with all the related ledgers and receipts. Worse still, Steele Perkins, the ARPD commandant who oversaw the colony's entire air defence preparation, was also implicated. A concurrent investigation into the Island side project assigned to the Marsmans Company yielded no fewer accounts of irregularities and briberies.[16]

Governor Geoffrey Northcote was seriously disturbed by the scandal. Sensing the gravity of the issue of corruption, he warned the Colonial Office

---
14. *Ta Kung Pao*, 21 October 1941.
15. *Ta Kung Pao*, 9 September 1941.
16. *Ta Kung Pao*, 31 October 1941.

that 'how far into the Civil Service it will be proved that graft extends or has extended no one can say at the moment'.[17] The solemn words of Northcote did not go unheard. His successor, Mark Young, made the anti-graft one of his priorities. He decided to set up a new commission on corruption. Unlike the many other committees of inquiry that were founded to look into specific scandals, this was a new body with a much broader responsibilities, including advising the government about general anti-corruption strategy.[18] Unfortunately, the new corruption tsar did not have the chance to implement his proposals for how to clean up the colonial administration. On Christmas Day 1941, the Japanese captured the colony.

Institutional Breakthroughs before the Arrival of MacLehose

The traumatic experience of the Japanese Occupation significantly changed the attitude of both the Chinese and British communities in the colony. The locals felt betrayed by the British during their darkest hour, and any perception of the superiority and invincibility of the Europeans were obliterated by the feeble resistance put up by the British military against the might of the Japanese attack. There was a keen sense of shame among the British community. They were fully aware that something drastic needed to be done to win back the trust and support of the locals. It was amid this atmosphere of openness that the discussion on corruption was rekindled in the administration. In the meeting of the Executive Council held on 2 August 1946, the first post-war Police Commissioner, Duncan MacIntosh, expressed his dismay over the prevalence of corruption in the colony and stated that 'he had never seen such widespread corruption anywhere else before'.[19] Again, the myth of the ethnic divide was under question. MacIntosh disallowed a considerable number of undesirable European officers to return to the colonial force after the war. In his efforts to rebuild the force, the old, inefficient, and corrupt expatriate officers were either transferred to other dependencies or offered the chance to retire with a full pension.[20]

The momentum for change finally culminated in the passage of the Prevention of Corruption Ordinance in 1948. This was the first comprehensive legislation on corruption passed in the colony, since the issue had previously primarily been regulated by three sections of the Misdemeanors Punishment Ordinance, which only concerned public servants. The

---

17. Northcote to Gent (Colonial Office), 8 September 1941, CO129/590/18, TNA.
18. The Hong Kong Government Gazette, 31 October 1941, Hong Kong Government.
19. Minutes of the Meeting of the Executive Council, 2 August 1946, CO31/116, TNA.
20. Carol Jones and Jon Vagg, *Criminal Justice in Hong Kong* (London and New York: Routledge/Cavendish, 2007), 201–202.

provision of the new legislation concerning unaccountable wealth and possessions contained far-reaching implications. These were now legitimate evidence which a jury could use in a final judgement about whether the accused was guilty of corruption or not. This was very unusual in that it shifted the onus of proof to the suspect, a practice which was not entirely consistent with the English legal principle of 'innocent until proven guilty'. However, it opened up new ways by which law enforcement could indict a suspect. In 1959, the government introduced a further disciplinary measure for civil servants—Establishment Regulation 444. Any civil servant who failed to give a satisfactory explanation of their maintenance of a standard of living above that which was commensurate with his official income, or possession of wealth disproportionate to his official emoluments, could be dismissed or compelled to retire.

The colonial government was, however, hesitant to establish an independent task force against corruption. It is likely that Mark Young simply had too much on his plate, and remained cautious about this highly sensitive issue which would arouse strong resistance from the police force. The status quo still prevailed when Young retired. Instead, the government decided on a new specialized agency called the Anti-Corruption Branch. It was, however, still part of the police. An advisory committee on corruption was also subsequently established.

It was the perseverance of David Trench, who was appointed as Governor in 1964, which provided the final push for the legal breakthrough in the anti-corruption campaign. According to Hampton, among the populace there was a resentment of police corruption by the late 1960s that threatened to undermine the government's ability to govern:

> At the centre of public outcry against corruption were the often petty bribes demanded by police of small business owners. Although victims included a wide range of entrepreneurs, illegal hawkers perhaps the most vulnerable. Too poor to afford the rents paid by proper shopkeepers, and forced to keep their prices low both by fierce competition and the poverty of most of their customers, hawkers sold their products from unlicensed stalls that were neither recognised or genuinely forbidden, but were tolerated in exchange for 'tea money' paid to the police . . . Police demanded bribes from more sordid characters as well, for example from Triads who controlled prostitution and drug smuggling, but the continual extortion of honest (if unlicensed) entrepreneurs meant that the police were the most important public face of Government corruption.[21]

---

21. Mark Hampton, 'British Legal Culture and Colonial Governance: The Attack on Corruption in Hong Kong, 1968–1974', *Britain and the World* 5, no. 2 (2012): 228–229.

Trench was determined to intensify the effort against corruption and intended to equip the public prosecutors with more powers and leverages. Delegations were sent to Singapore and Ceylon to study their anti-corruption laws, and three reports were produced in 1968. Trench lost little time, and a proposal for legal changes incorporating many of the suggestions made by the Advisory Committee on Corruption was drafted. However, the legal advisers to the FCO and the Home Office were ill at ease with several of Hong Kong's suggested changes. In particular, the shifting of the onus of proof onto the suspect was still deemed too extreme and incompatible with the principle of presumed innocence. As Trench recalled:

> These (suggestions proposed by Advisory Committee on Corruption) were objected to by the legal advisers to the Foreign and Commonwealth Office who said that they were too extreme, that they were against the principles of natural justice . . . When I came, this was the position, that they had not exactly refused, but they had made it clear that they didn't like these changes and it stayed on [a] fairly official level in the Foreign and Commonwealth Office . . . Then I think it must have been in 1970 with this position still pretty deadlocked.[22]

Trench, a Governor with the reputation for never shying away from an altercation with his colleagues in the FCO if he thought such confrontation was warranted, eventually took a bold step to push his case forward. He explained:

> In the end, I said: 'right. It doesn't look as if you're going to give me these changes. When I get back to Hong Kong, I shall now write a formal dispatch to the Secretary of State and say that I didn't consider that I can accept the responsibility for corruption in HK any longer, and that I considered that failure to give us these changes in the law means that, in effect, the Foreign and Commonwealth Office must take the responsibility for corruption in Hong Kong.' Now that was a very serious step to take because a draft dispatch is something that can't be ignored and it's more or less a public document and it would mean that the Minister would have to admit in Parliament, if necessary, that he hadn't given us these facilities.[23]

This audacious move helped to sway opinion in the FCO, and the Prevention of Bribery Bill (1970), which appeared to be a turning point in the colony's campaign against corruption, was eventually given the green light from London. It was passed in the Legislative Council on 16 December 1970 after a decade of deliberation and hesitation. One of the

---

22. Transcript of Steve Tsang's interview with Sir David Trench, n.d., Mss. Ind. Ocn.s348, Rhodes House Library, Oxford University, 250–253.
23. Transcript of Steve Tsang's interview with Sir David Trench, 250–253.

most important facets of this legislation was that, from 14 May 1971 onward, 'anyone who, being or having been a Crown Servant, maintains a standard of living above that which is commensurate with his present or past official emoluments or is in control of pecuniary resources or property disproportionate to his present or past official emoluments shall, unless he gives a satisfactory explanation to the court as to how he was able to maintain such a standard of living or how such pecuniary resources or property came under his control, be guilty of an offence'.[24] This was 'a tough measure reflecting a tough attitude' towards the evil of corruption, as Trench put it.[25] It proved to be a very powerful weapon in the hands of the prosecution, and has been instrumental in the tremendous progress of the campaign against corruption since then.

The new initiative also rekindled the old debate on the separation of anti-corruption work from the police force. Denys Roberts, the Attorney-General who studied the anti-corruption model of Ceylon in 1968, was particularly enthusiastic about the idea of establishing a new and independent Anti-Corruption Office. In his view, such a move would help convey the government's determination to tackle the issue of corruption to the general public.[26] The Police Commissioner, Charles Sutcliff, who was conscious of the growing pressure for change, counter-proposed that the police now armed with the new powers, should at least be given some time to prove its mettle, before a final decision to establish up a new anti-corruption agency was made. There appeared to be a general consensus among decision makers on a three- or four-year observation period after the new Ordinance came into effect.[27] However, the escape of Peter Godber in 1973 provided the final push for the establishment of the ICAC.

The Precipitating Crisis of the Godber Case

Notwithstanding his vision for reforms and passion for social justice, MacLehose may never have envisaged himself as a crusader against corruption. At least, the documentary evidence available does not confirm this. In his maiden policy address delivered to the Legislative Council on 18 October 1972—which was regarded by many as a landmark document which depicted chains of social reforms on a seismic scale—MacLehose did not have a single word to say on the prevalence of corruption in the

---

24. Minutes of the Legislative Council, 16 December 1970, Hong Kong Legislative Council, 282.
25. Minutes of the Legislative Council, 1 October 1971, Hong Kong Legislative Council, 4.
26. *Second Report of the Commission of Inquiry under Sir Alastair Blair-Kerr* (Hong Kong: Government Printer, 1973), 43.
27. *Second Report of the Commission of Inquiry under Sir Alastair Blair-Kerr*, 44.

colony. Nor can we find any passing comment on the topic in the document entitled *Guidelines for the Governor Designate, Hong Kong* that was, in effect, an understanding between MacLehose and the FCO on the list of priorities that the former would focus on during his tenure.[28] As he admitted publicly in 1973, his suspicions of the true extent of corruption were more grounded than he had personally realized.[29] Rather than a saviour imbued with a self-assigned mission to eradicate fraud and sleaze from the bureaucracy, MacLehose was more of an accidental hero.

The case of the discovery of Peter Godber's corruption was the ultimate wake-up call for the colonial administration. Not only was the myth of the ethnic divide in corruption further debunked, but the prevalence of endemic corruption in the colony was confirmed. Godber was a legend in the police force for his heroic role during the confrontations in 1967 and appeared to live a modest life despite his rank as a chief superintendent. However, the Police Commissioner Charles Sutcliff was alerted to various suspicious transactions in Godber's bank accounts in April 1973. Further investigation by the Anti-Corruption Office determined that Godber had in fact accumulated an amount of wealth that far exceeded his total earnings for his service in the police force since 1952. His total net salary for the whole period of his service was less than HKD 800,000, but it appeared that the amount which had passed through his hands was in excess of HKD 1 million.[30] Under the Prevention of Bribery Ordinance, Godber could be prosecuted if he could not provide an explanation for his possession of assets disproportionate to his official emoluments. Although he was on the watchlist at immigration control, he somehow managed to gain direct access to the restricted area in Kai Tak Airport with his valid police warrant card and boarded a departing flight on 8 June. He arrived at London's Heathrow Airport the next day. This triggered a political bombshell in the colony. The credibility of the government's commitment to fighting corruption was seriously questioned. The integrity of the police force was particularly damaged. A conspiracy theory that the police had colluded in arranging Godber's escape to avoid embarrassment lingered on, despite the futile attempts of the subsequent government investigation to clear the police of any responsibility or wrongdoing.[31] Inevitably, the pro-communist

---

28. MacLehose to Leslie Monson, Wilford, Morgan and Lairn: Guidelines for the Governor Designate, Hong Kong, 18 October 1971, FCO40/329, TNA.
29. Minutes of Legislative Council, 17 October 1973, Hong Kong Legislative Council, 16.
30. Upon further investigation, Godber's financial resources totalled more than HKD 4.3 million. *First Report of the Commission of Inquiry under Sir Alastair Blair-Kerr* (Hong Kong: Hong Kong Government Printer, 1973).
31. *First Report of the Commission of Inquiry under Sir Alastair Blair-Kerr* (Hong Kong: Hong Kong Government Printer, 1973).

media seized this opportunity and pulled no punches in their attack on the colonial authority. The *Hong Kong Evening News* argued:

> [o]ne thing proved by the [investigation] report is that many laws in Hong Kong affect only the general public and not the privileged class.[32]

Even the non-communist papers were not fully convinced of the innocence of the administration. The *Keung Sheung Yat Po*, for example, opined:

> [T]he negligence involved in this incident should not be brushed aside as mere technical errors. People can interpret it as part of a plan to let off Godber.[33]

The repercussions of the saga went beyond the confines of the colony. The dramatic escape and the return of Godber to Britain inevitably drew the interest of politicians and the British media to the state of corruption in the colony. Parliamentary discussion of corruption in Hong Kong and the possibility of setting up a Royal Commission to investigate the colony's predicament were raised by MPs such as Patrick Jenkin and James Johnson. The pressure was sustained by the efforts of other campaigners like Alan Ellis, who alleged that his discharge from the Hong Kong Police Force in the early 1960s was a result of his refusal to collaborate with other police officers, and Elsie Elliot, who had tirelessly voiced her concerns over the rampant corruption in the colony to politicians in Britain and Hong Kong. These stories were finally picked up by the national media, including the *Sunday Times*.[34] Serious deliberation about the propriety of an external inquiry into Hong Kong's corruption was made among British officials. Fortunately for the Governor, officials at the FCO were wary of the potential damage to the authority of the Hong Kong government and to the morale of the local police that might be done by the prospective external inquiry. In addition, the fact that the practice of setting up a royal commission on the internal affairs of a dependent territory by the United Kingdom had not been deployed for many years also worked against the idea. FCO officials retorted to James Johnson's call for a judicial commission of enquiry into the organized corruption in Hong Kong that such move 'might be seen as calling in the question the authority of the Governor' and could have international repercussions.[35]

Michael Macoun, the Overseas Police Adviser of the FCO, however, saw the merit of an outside inquiry. Macoun had made a number of visits to

---

32. Press Review on Godber Case, 26 July 1973 to 1 August 1973, FCO40/453, TNA.
33. Press Review on Godber Case, 26 July 1973 to 1 August 1973, FCO40/453, TNA.
34. Paul Eddy and Richard Hughes, 'Drugs, Brothels, Bribery—and a British Colony's Police Force', *Sunday Times*, 29 July 1973.
35. Call on Mr. Amery by James Johnson, MP, 10 August 1973, FCO40/453, TNA.

the colony in the early 1970s and was not particularly impressed with the general quality of the Hong Kong Police. He believed that the colonial forces suffered from arrogance, believing that they had 'little to learn from the UK Police Service' and concluded that 'as an organization they are not as good as they think they are'. He strongly supported the idea of external inquiry and commented:

> [T]he appointment of an external UK Commission of Enquiry would indicate HMG's [Her Majesty's Government] concern in widespread allegations of corruption in Hong Kong and its determination to endeavour not only to substantiate or disprove these allegations but also to accept its responsibility was the administering authority of what is a Crown colony.[36]

Macoun was not alone. Richard Crowson of FCO, for example, also pointed out that:

> [I]f in the end we are going to appoint a Commission, it would I think be better to do so soon, rather than be seen to do so only when the pressure for one had become irresistible and after we had gone on refusing one.[37]

Unsurprisingly, MacLehose was unequivocally against the idea of external inquiry. He raised his unambiguous objection to the idea during his meeting with Anthony Royle, the Minister for Foreign and Commonwealth Affairs, in early August 1973.[38] He saw this prospective inquiry as an intrusion into the colony's autonomy which would seriously undermine his authority. MacLehose's speech to the Legislative Council on 17 October 1973 was a testament to his growing frustration:

> When we criticize faults here, we do so to an audience well aware of the strengths and achievements that make up the full picture of Hong Kong. But this is not so overseas.[39]

Sze-yuen Chung, an unofficial member of the Legislative Council, echoed the Governor's irritation with London's lack of understanding of the challenges faced by the colony. He argued:

> Occasionally, there are cases in which there are conflicting interests between Her Majesty's Government and the Hong Kong Government. Since Hong Kong is a colony and officials in the Hong Kong Government, with greatest respect, are basically members of the UK civil service and, strictly speaking, are under directives of Whitehall. Despite all their good efforts, the voices of Hong Kong people are seldom heard within the UK

---

36. Macoun to Crowson, 8 August 1973, FCO40/453, TNA.
37. Crowson to Guest, 8 August 1973, FCO40/453, TNA.
38. Mr. Royle Talk with Sir Murray MacLehose, 10 August 1973, FCO40/453, TNA.
39. Minutes of Legislative Council, 17 October 1973, Hong Kong Legislative Council, 19.

Government . . . In the recent past, there were some debates on matters concerning Hong Kong in both Houses without any direct participation from Hong Kong, and there were problems and issues about Hong Kong raised in both Houses without someone from Hong Kong to put them into proper perspectives.[40]

Meanwhile, MacLehose understood that he needed to respond swiftly in face of mounting domestic and external pressure. In his meeting with the Foreign Minister in August, the Governor disclosed his intention to set up a new body to investigate allegations of corruption in the police. In fact, by the time of the meeting, the Governor had already finalized the line-up of the new unit, with Jack Cater as the commissioner and John Prendergast, the former head of the Special Branch of the Hong Kong Police, as the chief of operations.[41] The creation of the ICAC was an astute move, since an independent agency in charge of anti-corruption activities was important not only as proof of the government's determination to uproot the evils of sleaze and dishonesty, but also a pre-emptive move against any prospective external investigation.

The independence of the new anti-corruption agency was underlined in all official pronouncements about the ICAC's creation. The new entity was formed as a statutory body outside of the ordinary structure of government, with its estimates and its commissioner and some other senior officers directly appointed by the Governor. The selection of staff was carried out by the commissioner and was not subject to the advice of the Public Service Commission. The primary and most significant institutional arrangement was, however, the organization's civilian headship. That is, it was not part of the Hong Kong Police Force. This separation was crucial in addressing the growing issue of the 'widespread loss of confidence in the ability of the Police to investigate corruption cases with impartiality and zeal'.[42] The protracted debate on the necessity of an independent anti-corruption body finally came to an end. The government also backed the ICAC with additional weaponry. A long list of recommendations for amendments to Colonial Regulations and local laws was made. These included an extension of the burden of providing a satisfactory explanation for possession of disproportionate pecuniary resources to close relations of the accused, the institution of disciplinary proceedings against a public servant irrespective of prospective or previous related criminal proceedings, and deployment of the 'Queen's pleasure' provision as a way to remove a public servant

---

40. Minutes of the Legislative Council, 31 October 1973, Hong Kong Legislative Council, 63.
41. Mr. Royle Talk with Sir Murray MacLehose, 10 August 1973, FCO40/453, TNA.
42. *Second Report of the Commission of Inquiry under Sir Alastair Blair-Kerr*, 51.

suspected of corruption. Despite the reservations of legal experts, the FCO eventually acceded to most of the colony's demands.[43]

Behind this celebratory fanfare of independence and allocation of legal powers was a more subtle but no less important message regarding the ability of the colonial government to clear up its own mess. This was clearly reflected in the Governor's speech on the staffing issue of the new Commission against corruption:

> We have taken very careful advice from the Overseas Police Adviser to the Secretary of State and others on what outside help we should enlist to get the operations unit of the Commission off to a good start, and build it up into the highly expert, effective and dedicated organization that it must be if it is to make headway. In the light of this advice we are appointing immediately Mr John PRENDERGAST to be Director of Operations. His record as a policeman is one of unbroken success in many different situations, and he has the advantage of experience of Hong Kong between 1960 and 1966 as Director of Special Branch. In due course we will be appointing one or two more from United Kingdom police forces, at different levels, with special experience of anti-corruption work. But these are all the importations we have in mind. Basically it is for us in Hong Kong to put our own house in order, and I know very well we have the men and women both inside and outside the police force to do it.[44]

The government's determination to maintain the indigenous character of this effort was illustrated by its willingness to take the risk of undermining public confidence in the new anti-corruption agency. The consequence of the deliberate staffing strategy in restricting the number of recruits from Britain was a reliance on the alternative source of expertise and experience in corruption investigation: the Hong Kong Police Force. As a result, 53 out of 255 staff serving in the Operations Department of the ICAC in its first year of existence were former police officers.[45] Despite Commissioner Jack Cater's promise that only former police officers of proven integrity and the right calibre would be recruited, and the commitment to turn the ICAC into a civilian organization as soon as possible, FCO officials were not entirely convinced of the wisdom of this recruitment strategy.[46] They questioned whether this was 'the ideal mix to provide enough local expertise without being accused of being too much part of the Hong Kong establishment',[47] and warned that this could invite 'accusations that the Hong Kong police

---

43. Stuart to Watson and Royle: Corruption in Hong Kong: Blair-Kerr Report, 15 October 1973, FCO40/454, TNA.
44. Minutes of the Legislative Council, 17 October 1973, Hong Kong Legislative Council, 18.
45. Annual Report of ICAC, 1974, Hong Kong ICAC, Appendix VI.
46. Stuart to Cater, 8 February 1974, FCO40/558, TNA.
47. Cater to Stuart, 26 February 1974, FCO40/558, TNA.

had merely moved across to take over the anti-corruption investigation and to keep out outsiders'.[48]

A Credibility Crisis: The Failure to Extradite Godber

The urgency of an institutional breakthrough which would placate the angry local community was further necessitated by the deadlock in arranging the extradition of Godber. This complication arose from the difference in criminal codes between Britain and the colony. While it was an offence for a civil servant to fail to account for possession of amounts of money disproportional to his total official emoluments under the colony's Prevention of Bribery Ordinance, ownership of unexplained wealth was not a ground for prosecution in Britain. And for this reason, the case against Godber did not constitute an extraditable charge under the British Fugitive Offenders Act.

The Hong Kong public was not impressed. The general sentiment was well captured in a comment by *Wah Kiu Yat Po* on 28 July 1973:

> The so-called 'restrictions of the law' and 'customs', etc. will not convince the people. We ask the Hong Kong Government to show sincerity and determination to get Godber back. If this cannot be done, the public will lose faith in senior European Government servants.[49]

Joyce Simmons, an unofficial member of Legislative Council echoed such sentiments:

> This summer our crisis was not caused by the heaviest rain in our history but by strange weakness in our link with Britain. Who can blame the many who firmly refuse to attempt to understand the legal aspects of Godber's flight and our inability to bring him back?[50]

MacLehose was obviously irritated by the lack of progress of the extradition and believed that the Act should be amended with retrospective effect to make Godber's extradition possible. The second report of the investigation commission led by Sir Alastair Kerr-Blair, which articulated a direct plea for the amendment of the British Fugitive Act in the form of an immediate waiver of the double criminality requirement with retrospective effect, was approved for release in September 1973. The logic of such a request was, as the author of the report claimed:

---

48. Cater to Stuart, 26 February 1974, FCO40/558, TNA.
49. *Wah Kiu Yat Po*, 28 July 1973.
50. Minutes of the Legislative Council, 31 October 1973, Hong Kong Legislative Council, 73.

Pre-empting the Sovereign 61

[I]n this dependent territory we live under the rule of law; and Her Majesty the Queen has the power to disallow any new legislation which she may consider not to be for the 'peace order and good government' of the Colony. She did not exercise Her power of disallowance in the case of the Prevention of Bribery Ordinance.[51]

In fairness, the FCO did try hard to find possible way to bring Godber back to Hong Kong. At one point, they even considered that Godber's taking of his police warrant and airport card out of Hong Kong could be seen as an act of theft, and could therefore form the basis of an extraditable charge. The Home Office, however, was not particularly sympathetic to the predicament of the colonial government. The officials were reluctant to put Godber under police surveillance as they were not comfortable with the idea of harassing a British citizen against whom there was no charge under British law.[52] In response to the FCO's concerns over on the potential results of the failure of Godber's extradition to Hong Kong, Brennan of the Home Office argued,

> The fact remains in that this is because the Hong Kong authorities were not able to prevent his leaving the Colony and have not been able, since he left, to produce a prima facie case against him of an extraditable offence under existing law. No doubt there are good reasons for both failures: but the resulting situation can hardly be laid at the door of the UK.[53]

Instead, Brennan reminded the FCO of the Home Office's reservations about the Prevention of Bribery Ordinance. Brennan reiterated the Office's discomfort with the legislation's entailment of the onus of proof shifting the suspect, an objection that had been strongly raised with David Trench in the 1960s. Politically, it was also unwise for the Home Office to amend the Act as proposed by MacLehose, Brennan argued:

> The rule (of reciprocity) is not only a safeguard to the individual: it protects the final authority in the requested country (in the UK my Secretary of State (for Home Affairs)) from the domestic and international embarrassment which might arise if there was an issue about the fairness of a law in the requesting country (in the present case, I suspect that there would be many in this country who would quick to point to the reversal of the usual burden of proof and the substantial interferences with individual privacy implied by Section 10 of the Prevention of Bribery Ordinance) . . . Even if an amendment of the law enabled the Hong Kong authorities to start extradition proceedings for Mr. Godber's return, it would still rest with a UK magistrate to decide whether the evidence was sufficient to

---
51. *Second Report of the Commission of Inquiry under Sir Alastair Blair-Kerr*, 42.
52. Corruption in Hong Kong: The Godber Case, 13 June 1973, FCO40/452, TNA.
53. Brennan to Stewart, 4 October 1973, FCO40/454, TNA.

justifying ordering his surrender. So, even if Mr. Godber was compliant enough to remain here, legislation which would probably cause a great deal of fuss might not, at the end of the day, achieve anything.[54]

The Governor was, however, not deterred easily. MacLehose understood that there would be strong resentment from the local public if London decided to reject the amendment request. His concern was not only for the damage to his authority, but he was also worried about the further deterioration of the London–Hong Kong relationship. To address this, he counter-proposed a future amendment of the Fugitive Act. This would not help to extradite Godber, but it would at least gain some mileage in convincing the Hong Kong community that the colonial administration had tried everything to address the loophole and avoid a repetition of the corrupt official's flight. More importantly, it would demonstrate London's responsiveness to the colony's concerns. With this amendment, the Governor believed he would be in a better position to defend London's decision of to reject the amendment of retrospective effect.[55]

As the deadlock dragged on, MacLehose intended to ramp up the pressure on London with a public criticism of the principle of double criminality for extradition in his address to the Legislative Council on 17 October 1973. Aware of the Governor's intentions, Alec Douglas-Home, the Foreign Secretary, wrote to dissuade MacLehose from raising these issues in his public speech, lest it may lead to embarrassing questions for him in Parliament.[56] Though he eventually agreed to soften his punch, the Governor retained the following paragraph, which vividly portrays his defiance:

> [T]he requirement of double criminality is hard to understand in the case of a dependent territory, such as Hong Kong, where HMG has a power to veto all laws passed, and the Secretary of State is obliged to answer for the laws of Hong Kong in the House of Commons.[57]

Colleagues in FCO were not impressed. Edward Youde, for example, blamed MacLehose for 'laying up trouble for the future in emphasizing so pointedly HMG's power of veto and the Secretary of State's responsibility for the laws of Hong Kong'.[58] Nevertheless, they were not indifferent to the predicament of Hong Kong government. In fact, there were intense exchanges on this matter between officials of the FCO and the Home Office in the following weeks. The scheduled visit of the Prime Minister to Hong Kong

---

54. Brennan to Stewart, 4 October 1973, FCO40/454, TNA.
55. MacLehose to FCO, 15 October 1973, FCO40/454, TNA.
56. Douglas-Home: Personal to MacLehose, 15 October 1973, FCO40/455, TNA.
57. Minutes of the Legislative Council, 17 of October 1973, Hong Kong Legislative Council, 18.
58. Youde to Stuart, 16 October 1973, FCO40/455, TNA.

Pre-empting the Sovereign 63

in January 1974 probably added a sense of urgency to the FCO's drive to resolve the contention.[59] Several options had been forwarded to the Home Office for consideration: (a) abandoning the application of the double criminality rule to all dependent territories; (b) including a list of dependent territory legislation which was to be exempted from the application of the double criminality rule; or (c) consideration of whether any special conditions should attach to service under the Crown by which public servants would be made answerable for their acts in all British territories.[60] In addition, a political argument about the possible repercussions of the issue on the relationship between the sovereign and the colony was also raised:

> It is a political problem of public confidence. The Hong Kong Government have set up a new and independent Anti-Corruption Commission. But as long as senior European officers are able to escape its operations and to live unmolested in the UK, public confidence in Hong Kong in the Commission, the Hong Kong Government and HMG will be diminished. If they believe that, in effect, the European administration are shielding their own people, the Chinese population will not come forward to give the evidence of corruption which should eventually make the special legislation unnecessary. Moreover, the fact that the law which impedes Godber's return is a UK one, increases, however unreasonably, the general political tension between Hong Kong and the UK which was the subject of Sir Alec's minute. If, as it very possible, another Hong Kong Government officer evades prosecution and settles in Britain, the effect on our relations will be serious. If no steps are taken to remedy the situation before the Prime Minister's visit to Hong Kong in January he will face questioning on this point.[61]

Home Office officials were not swayed. For them, the double criminality rule was a cornerstone of extradition arrangements, and its removal would diminish the degree of reciprocity. They saw no other law of any dependent territory which might warrant a similar exemption, nor did they find any call for change in the double criminality rule from other administrations under British rule. In short, they saw no compelling reason to concede to the demand of the FCO. This was backed by the Law Officers of the British government.[62]

---

59. Home Office, 'Note of a meeting held at the Home Office on 27 November 1973 to discuss the implications of the double criminality rule in the Fugitive Offenders Act 1967, in relations to Offences committed in Hong Kong', 30 November 1973, Stuart to Watson, 6 December 1973 and 'Watson to Youde,' 6 December 1973, FCO40/457, TNA.
60. Stuart to Watson and Royle, 2 November 1973 (note 313), FCO40/456, TNA.
61. Royle to Mark Carlisle, Home Office, November 1973 (date unspecified), FCO40/456, TNA.
62. Note of Meeting held at the Home Office on 27 November 1973 to discuss the Implications of the Double Criminality Offences committed in Hong Kong, 27 November 1973, FCO40/457, TNA.

By the end of January 1974, the FCO eventually accepted defeat in this fight and informed MacLehose accordingly. The Governor, however, preferred to drag the matter out. With the recent conclusion of the British general election in February 1974 and the possibility of major changes in personnel in the British government, the Governor insisted that the FCO should not give up the fight, in the hope that the new law officers might be more inclined to take a different view. He also reiterated his hope of tabling the amendment proposal formally in Parliament, although the chance of its passing was evidently rather slim. The optics of this would be better in the colony, he candidly confessed:

> It would be better, from our point of view, for the Bill to be defeated there, than for it not to have been presented at all. Nobody could then accuse us of not having tried.[63]

Just as the legislative approach seemed to be reaching a dead end, there came a dramatic twist in the saga of Godber's extradition. Shortly after the FCO informed the Governor of the Home Office's firm rejection of the amendment request, the colonial government informed them of a breakthrough in the Godber case. MacLehose was constantly reminded in the rebuttal against his plea for assistance by colleagues in London that 'it needs only one man to come forward and give conclusion of a corrupt transaction'[64] to get Godber extradited to Hong Kong. On 13 April 1974, the Governor's prayer was answered, although it came from the most unlikely source.

On that day, a woman contacted John Prendergast of ICAC that her husband, Ernest Hunt, a former police superintendent who was at that time imprisoned for corruption offences, had information that would help bring Godber back to Hong Kong. Hunt claimed that he had witnessed Godber taking a bribe of HKD 25,000 from another officer, Cheng Hon-Kuen, for his help in getting Cheng promoted to the post of divisional superintendent of the police division of Wanchai in 1971.[65] Apparently, Godber had written a very positive report on Cheng during the assessment exercise for the latter's promotion in 1970, which contradicted the appraisals on Cheng's ability provided by all other senior officers in the panel.[66] Hunt agreed to testify against Godber if he were granted immunity from prosecution for any further offence. This 'stroke of luck' did raise a few eyebrows and queries about the credibility of the deal with Hunt, a convicted corrupt

---

63. MacLehose to Duncan Watson, 26 March 1974, FCO40/457, TNA.
64. Douglas-Home: Personal to MacLehose, 15 October 1973, FCO40/455, TNA.
65. MacLehose to FCO, 26 April 1974, FCO40/554, TNA. and MacLehose to FCO, 24 October 1974, FCO40/557, TNA.
66. Penlington to solicitors of Lincoln Inn, 13 September 1974, FCO40/556, TNA.

officer, but MacLehose defended his decision by stating that it was Hunt who had initiated the contact, not the government. He went on to argue that, technically, there was no immunity that could be offered to Hunt as there was no pending charge against him when the approach by Mrs. Hunt was made. The government did attempt to prosecute Hunt further (over his German accounts) in 1973, but the case was a non-starter, since the Attorney General decided that the possibility of bringing further charges was a very slim one by November 1973, months before the dialogue between Prendergast and Mrs. Hunt.[67]

There was, however, a deal struck between the government and another party, Cheng, the officer who actually bribed Godber. It was agreed that no evidence concerning the alleged bribery of Godber provided during the trial would be used against Cheng and that no charge would be brought against him. Cheng was allowed to retire from the police force with his pension entitlement and would be offered assistance in gaining entry into another country once the case was concluded.[68] With the cooperation of the two Crown witnesses, Hunt and Cheng, Godber was finally extradited back to the colony on 7 January 1975 and the twenty-month long saga finally came to an end. Eventually, Godber was handed a four-year sentence, though most of the HKD 4 million in his possession remained untraceable.[69]

'The Honeymoon Was Over': The Police Mutiny of 1977

The masterstroke of MacLehose in diffusing both local and external political pressure through the creation of the ICAC and the eventual success in jailing Godber provided breathing space for the colonial administration. Jack Cater and his team were nevertheless fully aware of the challenge ahead and understood that the Commission had to fight hard to earn respect. Even the 'honeymoon period' of the ICAC was not entirely a smooth ride. Its credibility was damaged by the discovery of instances of its officers taking bribes and accepting private loans without permission. Some cynics seized the opportunity and ridiculed the ICAC as 'I Can Accept Cash'.[70] The business sector was uneasy with the powers of the ICAC and had been vocal in demanding that the Commission should confine its investigations to the public sector only,[71] while others questioned the accountability of

---

67. Stuart's letter to Scott, 12 November 1973, FCO40/554, TNA, and Scott's reply, 27 November 1973, FCO40/554, TNA.
68. A note by Rushford, 11 September 1974, FCO40/556, TNA.
69. *Ming Pao*, 15 September 1977.
70. Geoff Carter, former Head of Special Branch, interview by the author, 10 August 2007.
71. Annual Report of ICAC, 1975, Hong Kong ICAC, 2.

the Commission. Despite all these teething problems, the Commission did succeed in establishing its credibility as honest and effective against corruption within a reasonably short time. The public's trust was well reflected in the number of complaints received by the Commission. Even in its first year, the number of complaints received by the Commission represented a dramatic increase over the number of reports handled by the Anti-Corruption Office of the Police Force. A total of 1,167 complaints reached the ACO in 1972 but, as shown in Table 3.1, the average number of complaints made to the ICAC during the first three years was more than double this figure. These represented not just a rise in quantity, but also an improvement in the quality of these reports which reflected the growing trust of the general public. More and more reports were made which included the complainant's identity and substantiated information. As a result, there was a significant increase in investigations and convictions. Since the former ACO investigation of complaints never exceeded more than 200 cases a year and the number of successful convictions was kept to a few dozen, the ICAC was seen as more effective and credible: between 1974 and 1976 it investigated more than 1,000 cases every year and successfully put hundreds of corrupt officials in jail. These achievements certainly helped to convince the general public that the ICAC meant business. By the end of 1976, the Commission had developed into a substantial anti-corruption taskforce of 763 officers, more than quadruple of the strength of the ACO of the police force.[72] Lord Goronwy-Roberts was impressed and confirmed to MacLehose that 'ICAC was doing a good job and there was no need for an externally appointed Royal Commission (looking into the colony's corruption)'.[73] MacLehose's 'pre-emptive' move had worked.

Table 3.1: Complaints of corruption and investigation proceeded by ICAC 1974–1976

Year	Anonymous	Non-anonymous	Total	Investigated	Convicted	Referral for disciplinary action
1974	2,080	1,109	3,189	1,063	108	53
1975	1,944	1,235	3,179	1,403	218	76
1976	1,294	1,139	2,433	1,208	259	70

Source: *Annual Report of ICAC*, various years.

---

72. Annual Report of ICAC, various years, Hong Kong ICAC.
73. Record of a Meeting between Lord Goronwy-Roberts and the Governor of Hong Kong held at the Foreign and Commonwealth Office on Wednesday 9 April at 10:00 am, 24 April 1975, FCO40/646, TNA.

However, this success came at a price. Tensions between the ICAC and the police force had been rising since the founding of the former in 1974. As shown in Table 3.2, the police force had remained the leading target of public complaints against corruption in government, constituting almost half of the reports received by the ICAC. Concern was expressed that the Commission appeared to be carrying out a vendetta against the police. Jack Cater tried to diffuse the tension by attributing this perception to sensationalism from the local media:

> There can be no denying that investigations and prosecutions of members of the Police Force attract far more publicity and attention than any other group. This is a matter which I have discussed on a number of occasions with representatives of the media; many are agreed that the prominence given to Police corruption may seem unfair, but make the point that the media are in the business to 'sell newspapers', and that the headline 'Corrupt Cop' is more eye-catching and news worthy than a headline which reads 'Corrupt XYZ Department Employee'.[74]

Cater's conciliatory tone did little to allay fears among members of the police force. Since there was little sign of abatement in the Commission's enthusiasm for investigation and prosecution, there were also growing concerns about its impact on police morale. There were voices demanding a general amnesty, by which the ICAC should restrict its investigations to offences of corruption committed since the formation of Commission in February 1974. The pressure was substantial enough that it finally required the Colonial Secretary, Denys Roberts, to issue an official rebuttal in the Legislative Council in April 1975. Like Cater, Roberts also made a deliberate effort to placate the police force:

> From time to time, allegations are made that the Police Force is corrupt throughout. I have no doubt that honourable Members will agree with me that this is a gross exaggeration and unfair in the extreme to the thousands of members of the Force who are devoted, loyal and honest men, discharging a difficult, uncomfortable and frequently dangerous task with skill and determination. They are as anxious as we and the public to see a force which is free from corruption and is therefore a better instrument for dealing with crime, which unhappily remains a major social problem, because the force needs not only public support but public respect if it is to be fully effective.[75]

London was aware of the growing restiveness of the Hong Kong Police force. Macoun's report upon his return from a routine inspection of the

---

74. Annual Report of ICAC, 1974, Hong Kong ICAC, 24.
75. Minutes of the Legislative Council, 3 April 1975, Hong Kong Legislative Council, 680.

Table 3.2: Complaints, prosecution, and disciplinary action against police officers 1974–1976

Year	Number of complaints	Number of investigations	Number of convictions	Number of referrals for disciplinary action
1974	1,443 (3,189)	419 (1,063)	30 (108)	22 (53)
1975	1,492 (3,179)	602 (1,403)	58 (218)	20 (76)
1976	1,119 (2,433)	396 (1,208)	19 (189)	20 (75)

Source: *Annual Report of ICAC*, various years.
Note: Figures in brackets—total number of cases handled by ICAC.

colony's force further reinforced the unease of FCO officials. He was rather critical of the propriety of the procedures and methods adopted by ICAC and their damaging impact on the morale and operations of the police:

> Members of the European Inspectorate and certain junior Chinese officers whom I met informally were outspoken in their condemnation of the methods and procedures adopted by ICAC and categorically stated that they not only affected police morale but inhibited police operational effectiveness . . . Junior police officers stated that Chinese detective staff were often reluctant to pursue a criminal enquiry for fear of being 'fixed' through ICAC informants;

The resentment, according to Macoun, was not confined to the police but also could be found amongst the general public:

> Members of the public were equally critical of the overriding powers and presence of ICAC which had undoubtedly acquired an inquisitorial and pervasive role in the community . . . One particular aspect of ICAC procedures which would be intolerable in any free society is the arbitrary manner in which enquiries are conducted. Suspects can be required to attend for interrogation without being charged and placed under arrest if deemed to be uncooperative . . . the methods and procedures are far too inquisitorial and appear to absolve, under the existing anti-corruption laws, the ICAC from the need to observe normal legal procedures and to investigate in depth and assemble sufficient evidence before placing any suspect at risk. The result has been considerable inroads into personal freedom and the creation of an almost neurotic sense of apprehension in the community.[76]

Macoun was not alone in this regard, and concerns about the exceptional powers given to the ICAC were also raised by legal professionals in the

---

76. Minutes of the Legislative Council, 3 April 1975, Hong Kong Legislative Council, 680.

colony. One leading legal authority warned against the danger that ICAC operations might bring 'inconvenience, distress, irreparable damage and ultimately serious injustice to the innocent'.[77] FCO officials were thus fully aware of the grievances against the ICAC in Hong Kong. John Stewart of the Hong Kong Department of the FCO admitted that ICAC operations had had a considerable effect on the morale of police force and large swathes of the business and commercial community. He also conceded that some of the Commission's activities were 'difficult to reconcile with the principles of democracy and English-style justice'.[78] While stopping short of initiating a formal appraisal of the work of the Commission, officials were open to the idea of some form of review and appeal mechanism against ICAC malpractice.[79]

Despite growing discontent with the ICAC, MacLehose and Cater remained undeterred in their anti-corruption campaign against the police force. The Governor was of the opinion that the Police would have to endure another two uncomfortable years of being singled out for inquiry before the ICAC could break the back of the problem.[80] In a later communication with Macoun, the Governor hinted at a possible reduction in the size of the ICAC by 1977.[81] This was consistent with Cater's proposed time frame. In his annual report in 1976, Cater announced that the Commission would from then on concentrate on destroying corruption syndicates—groups of public servants colluding and collect bribes. According to Cater, although these syndicates could exist in any government department, the police force was the major victim of this particular evil. Additionally, there appeared to be a substantial connection between these police syndicates and triad societies: 'they have fed off each other and grown fat together,' claimed the ICAC.[82] It was found that in virtually every police division there was at least one syndicate in operation, and in some divisions several. Cater claimed that the money taken by the syndicates amounted to HKD 1 billion a year.[83] The Commissioner envisaged that 1976 and 1977 would be the crunch years for the Commission and for the community of Hong Kong.

---

77. Bernard Downey, 'Combatting Corruption: The Hong Kong Solution', *Hong Kong Law Journal* 6, no. 1 (1976): 63.
78. Stewart to Murray, 31 January 1977, FCO40/827, TNA.
79. Stewart to Murray, 31 January 1977, FCO40/827, TNA; also Duffy to Stewart, 22 February 1977, FCO40/827, TNA.
80. Record of a Meeting between Lord Goronwy-Roberts and the Governor of Hong Kong held at the FCO Office on Wednesday 9 April at 10am, 24 April 1975, FCO40/646, TNA.
81. Zhang Junfeng, *Fantan Tingbuliu* [The unstoppable anti-corruption campaign] (Hong Kong: Joint Publishing Ltd., 2010), 70–72.
82. Annual Report of ICAC, 1976, Hong Kong ICAC, 2.
83. Leslie Palmier, *The Control of Bureaucratic Corruption* (New Delhi: Allied Publishers, 1985), 146.

And Cater was right: the year 1977 turned out to be the most trying time for the ICAC. The police officers' anger eventually erupted into the infamous police mutiny in October 1977, triggered by the mass arrest in September 1977. More than 50 teams of ICAC officers were sent out to various locations, including the Yaumatei police station, the Kowloon CID Headquarters, and police quarters, in the early morning of 19 September. Eighty-seven police officers were arrested on this and the following day. Some 228 officers overall were implicated and were placed under investigation. The police community was shocked, and some decided to fight back. The first sign of trouble was a petition to the Police Commissioner by about 100 police officers, many of whom were currently under interdiction for corruption offences. They complained about the procedural fairness of the ICAC investigation and demanded better representation in the form of the creation of a rank-and-file association. Senior Assistant Commissioner Schouten tried in vain to diffuse the tension, and a mass meeting of about 3,000 police officers was held on 27 October. At this meeting, the organizers announced a march to the Police Headquarters on the following day. About 2,000 off-duty police officers responded to the call. The Commissioner and Deputy Commissioner received representatives of the group who presented them with another petition that was claimed to be signed by 11,000 out of 17,400 members of the Force. The Commissioner expressed his sympathy, and the crowd dispersed in orderly fashion soon afterwards. A small group of about forty officers, however, decided to vent their anger with the ICAC directly, and marched to the Commission's headquarters in Central. When the group tried to force their way into the offices of the ICAC, things got ugly. Windows were smashed, and a scuffle broke out in which a few ICAC officers suffered minor injuries.

The Governor confessed that there had been a grave misjudgement on the part of the colonial administration at this juncture. It seems that he put too much trust in various police associations' subsequent condemnation of the violence and disassociation from the protestors. Police management also believed that the general disgust at the attack would help to keep the protest peaceful and constitutional. As the force continued to perform its normal duty, senior officials in the government were confident that the formation of a new association for rank and file and a review of procedural matters related to the ICAC would be enough to wither the storm.[84] Yet this confrontation was just the beginning of the crisis, and an escalation of the tension was on the horizon. Support for the dissidents' demands quickly spread. On 3 November, about 400 inspectors of the Local Inspectors' Association expressed their support for the demands of their rank-and-file

---

84. MacLehose to Stewart, 19 November 1977, FCO40/837, TNA.

colleagues. In addition to the original demand for the creation of a rank-and-file association, an amnesty was also requested. Another meeting of about 300 officers from different divisions was held on 4 November at which the mood became increasingly militant and at which the option of a police strike was discussed.[85]

Prompt and drastic action from the government was imperative. The necessity of a swift and powerful response was confirmed when the Governor summoned the most senior police officers to an emergency meeting of the Security Committee on 5 November. The Police Commissioner's assessment of the situation was gloomy and unsettling. Notwithstanding that the force might continue to operate smoothly, he doubted the senior officers' ability to control the rank and file. He admitted that the concessions of the management had made no impact on the mood of the force and that there was a real possibility of another massive protest. He concluded that the longer it took to address the protestors' concerns, the more the dissatisfaction would escalate.

The Governor recalled:

> Though the meeting was calm and matter-of-fact, you can imagine the distress and shock with which one after another the senior officers confessed that they could not rely on their men to carry out orders, if I gave them, to intervene against the ring-leaders. When I asked them whether they would be able to carry out such orders given military support, again each one miserably answered he could not . . . On hearing this analysis, and realizing how rapidly the situation was evolving, and how consistently under-reported it has so far been, my appreciation was that we could be on the very edge of a breakdown in law and order. It would only need a rumour that the Police were off the streets for the night for looting to start. Indeed it would be all too easy for the Police ring-leaders to tip off triads to start something so that they could put pressure on the Government.[86]

When asked what could be done to bring the situation under control, the senior police officers unanimously proposed an amnesty and some procedures for investigating complaints against the ICAC. Jack Cater concurred with the former. In fact, only a day before the meeting, the Commissioner had suggested to the Governor that an amnesty was the only way out of this.[87]

The rest of the meeting focused on how to preserve the authority and dignity of the government and the ICAC given this monumental concession. The bottom line was that when announcing the amnesty, the government

---
85. MacLehose to London Telegram No. 1092, 5 November 1977, FCO40/836, TNA.
86. MacLehose to Stewart, 19 November 1977, FCO40/837, TNA.
87. MacLehose to Stewart, 19 November 1977, FCO40/837, TNA.

should not appear to have lost this round. Thus, it was decided that firstly, the amnesty would not be subject to further negotiation. Secondly, the ringleaders of the mutiny, many of whom were currently under investigation by the ICAC, should not be let off by the concession. The decision to make 1 January 1977 the cut-off date, with the exception of those who had already been interviewed by the ICAC, suggests that most of the organizers of the various petitions would not be exempted. Lastly, the government also proposed to amend the Police Ordinance to give the Police Commissioner the power of summary dismissal of disobedient officers.[88]

The rapid unfolding of the events deprived the Governor of the chance for a full consultation with all the concerned parties. Members of the Executive Council, except for Yuet-Keung Kan, were not consulted, and even the FCO was not given sufficient time to deliberate on the decision of partial amnesty. FCO officials were not entirely happy with the situation, as they were only informed on 5 November when the decision had already been made. Some went on to criticize the Governor and the Police Commissioner's poor judgement on the state of police morale and their persistent denial of the concern for the impact of ICAC work on the spirit of the police force raised by the FCO months before the mutiny. Yet the FCO officials reasoned that the Secretary of State should show his full support for the Governor's decision, since 'less than complete confidence in the Governor would make the situation between Police and the public in Hong Kong worse than it is'.[89]

Rebuilding after the Crisis

The partial amnesty succeeded in diffusing the crisis. Despite the resistance of a hardcore who persisted in demanding a full amnesty, the move achieved the objective of isolating the ringleaders from the majority of the police force. The general public also saw this as a way out of the predicament, caught as they were between the danger of a breakdown in law and order and the importance of the anti-corruption campaign, and showed their support for the government. The management of the police force also accelerated the work of forming the Junior Police Officers' Association and succeeded in containing the influence of the radicals in the process.[90] There was, however, more work to be done between the police and ICAC in the aftermath.

---

88. MacLehose to Stewart, 19 November 1977, FCO40/837, TNA.
89. Stewart to Murray, 7 November 1977, FCO40/836, TNA.
90. Background Note: Royal Hong Kong Police Force (RHKPF) and Junior Police Officers' Association (JPOA), 1 February 1978, FCO40/1022, TNA.

Holding the ringleaders of the mutiny accountable was one of the priorities of the government. A substantial number of these dissidents were related to the Yaumatei case, which concerned some 180 officers, of whom the majority had been interdicted from the terms of the amnesty announced in 1977.[91] The prosecution, however, proved to be difficult and complicated as the Attorney General could not identify clear connections between all of the suspects. Instead, there appeared to be groups and clusters of corrupt officers operating independently of each other. Proceedings against each group needed to be launched separately. Worse still, the success of the prospective prosecutions largely hinged upon the testimony of witnesses, of whom many were convicted drug traffickers. It was believed that it could take four to five years for all the trials to conclude, even if the credibility of the witnesses could stand the interrogation of the defence attorneys. In the end, the government decided to adopt a selective approach and pressed charges against twenty officers and recommended no further action against another thirty-seven. The remaining 118 were, however, informed that their service was to be terminated at the 'Crown's displeasure' in accordance with Colonial Regulation 55. This may not have been what the Governor had hoped for, but pragmatism prevailed. Most of the ringleaders of the 1977 mutiny were, at least, punished in one way or another as the Governor desired.[92]

The review of the operations of the ICAC was a more challenging task. The general feeling that they were being unjustly harassed by the ICAC lingered among the police officers in the aftermath of amnesty. The immediate damage to the morale and credibility of the ICAC inflicted by the 'rethinking' of its operations and priorities was obvious. The Operations Department had to abruptly terminate eighty-three investigations as a result of the amnesty.[93] Jimmy McGregor, who had served and witnessed the rampant corruption in the Department of Commerce and Industry until the mid-1970s, regarded such a 'retreat' as a missed opportunity to tackle corruption head on.[94] The Governor also backed off from his resistance to London's demand for the creation of an Ombudsman for the ICAC and conceded to the introduction of a mechanism to investigate

---

91. These policemen were arrested or interviewed by ICAC between February and October 1977. All these officers had allegedly received money for providing protection for drug dealers. The ICAC originally hoped to prove a conspiracy between all these officers. The evidence however did not confirm the existence of a single syndicate but a series of smaller one; many received money on individual basis.
92. Stewart to Murray, Hong Kong: Yaumatei Corruption Case, 1 February 1978, FCO40/1022, TNA, and MacLehose to FCO, 31 March 1978, FCO40/1022, TNA.
93. Annual Report of ICAC, 1977, Hong Kong ICAC, 9.
94. Jimmy McGregor, 'Fighting the "Vermin of Society"', in *Hong Kong Remembers*, ed. Sally Blyth and Ian Wotherspoon (Hong Kong: Oxford University Press, 1996), 156.

complaints against the Commission in the form of a Committee under the chairmanship of Yuet-Keung Kan. The ICAC was subject to further scrutiny by a team of Special Police Advisers headed by Jim Crane, which was sent from Britain in January 1978. Although the team's primary objective was to advise the police force on organization and communications, they were also 'invited' to review the ICAC's procedures for investigations and its relationship with the police. It is hard to deny the cumulative negative impact of all these developments on the public perception of the credibility of the Commission. The drop in the number of complaints received in 1978 was a testament to the damage. The ICAC received 1,234 complaints that year, the lowest since its founding in 1974, and a significant drop of 28 per cent compared to the previous year.[95]

It is perhaps unfair to say that MacLehose had withdrawn his support for the anti-corruption campaign spearheaded by the Commission since the crisis. The Commission persevered, and succeeded in attacking syndicated corruption, as evidenced by the prosecution against the Yaumatei syndicates in 1978. The Governor also continued to show his unyielding support for the anti-corruption body in terms of budget. By 1980, the Commission had developed into a force of 1,099,[96] a rapid expansion from the 369 personnel in 1974. Yet their approach to handling the police was now more moderate. From 1977 onwards, improving police morale and the relationship between the Commission and the police force appeared to be the government's primary concern. Joint seminars, co-training, exchange of intelligence, and joint operations with the police were developed on the recommendation of Jim Crane's team. The appointment of John Luddington, the former chair of the Public Service Commission, as the successor to Jack Cater was also illustrative of the Governor's priorities. Jack Cater had embodied MacLehose's commitment of the campaign against corruption. His promotion to the post of Chief Secretary in July 1978 was indicative to some degree of the fact that 'there was a good deal of public concern about the possibility that the Commission was likely to be wound up'.[97] Yet the Governor saw this as an opportunity for moderation and reconciliation with the police:

> Now that the Commission had been built to the full strength and has considerable success in reducing corruption to acceptable levels, the new Commissioner needs to be someone who is not so much a crusader or

---

95. Annual Report of ICAC, 1978, Hong Kong ICAC, 75.
96. Annual Report of ICAC, 1980, Hong Kong ICAC, 11.
97. Annual Report of ICAC, 1978, Hong Kong ICAC, 9.

Pre-empting the Sovereign

innovator as someone whose appointment will indicate the importance the government attaches to the Commission's work and who will have the personality and experience to lead the Commission and keep it on the rails. And hopefully, without conceding anything, he should be able to create a better working relationship with the police.[98]

This preoccupation with improving relations with the police force coincided with a shift in the focus of the ICAC's investigation work. Although police-related complaints still contributed the largest share of investigations in the public sector, the Commission's preoccupation with the police force appeared to have eased by the late 1970s (see Table 3.3). This was probably a result of the success of previous efforts in eradicating syndicated corruption and the impact of the partial amnesty in 1977. It was evident that the Commission had also begun to pay increasing attention to corruption in the private sector during the same period and had achieved considerable success. Offenders involved in corruption related to the Hong Kong Telephone Company and the China Motor Bus Company were eventually brought to justice, heralding a new frontier in the anti-corruption campaign. As seen in Table 3.3, by 1980, the number of cases under ICAC investigation relating to the private sector exceeded those of the police force. Although there is no evidence to suggest that this was deliberately intended to let the police off the hook, the diversification in investigations certainly helped improve the relationship between the ICAC and the police force.

Table 3.3: Investigation of corruption cases by ICAC

Year	Percentage related to private sector	Percentage related to Police Force
1974	15.3%	39.4%
1975	15.5%	42.9%
1976	25.5%	30.9%
1977	25.5%	38.6%
1978	25.6%	41.2%
1979	24.6%	37.2%
1980	33.3%	28.7%

Source: *Annual Report of ICAC*, various years.

---

98. MacLehose to FCO Telegram no. 392, 30 March 1978, FCO40/935, TNA.

Conclusion

MacLehose's contribution to the creation of the ICAC and the colony's anti-corruption campaign was critical part of his legacy. Lethbridge was of the opinion that MacLehose's efforts against corruption were a part of the Governor's grand moralizing project that was designed to instil a new sense of civic responsibility and community amongst the locals.[99] However, like most public administrators, colonial governors did not simply make but also inherited policy. The institutional foundations for the anti-corruption campaign were already in place before MacLehose reported for duty in 1972. The statutory powers that shifted the onus of proof onto the suspect—a means that proved to be instrumental in bringing many culprits of corruption to justice—was secured by David Trench, and the removal from the police of the responsibility to investigate cases of corruption was the result of decades of debate.

Nevertheless, MacLehose should be credited for maintaining this momentum and seizing the opportunity to set up the ICAC. He demonstrated his extraordinary political acumen in diffusing the crisis triggered by Godber's escape. By creating a long-awaited independent anti-corruption body, MacLehose managed to pre-empt a possible external inquiry by London and put a halt to the downward spiral in public confidence in the colonial government's commitment to fighting corruption. In this stroke of political genius, the Governor managed to keep the damage done by the crisis to the authority of his administration to a minimum. Yet the impact of the police mutiny seems to have shaken his resolve. Regardless of any façade of dignity and firmness in the announcement of a partial amnesty, and this was the darkest hour in the history of the ICAC. The Governor had little choice but to sanction a moderation in the Commission's operations. Fortunately, the ICAC persevered and weathered the storm, and its eventual success in institutionalizing the principles of integrity and honesty into the conduct of public service and the social fabric of the colony added a crucial chapter to the story of the Hong Kong miracle.

The history of the ICAC and the anti-corruption campaign also reveals a love–hate relationship between the Governors and the bureaucracy of Whitehall. The legal and constitutional frameworks defined by the Crown restrained the scope of policy making in Hong Kong, the saga of Godber's extradition and the debate over the double criminality requirement attest to this. Nevertheless, there was flexibility inherent in the Queen's royal prerogative allowing leeway to pursue the colony's agenda. The notion of the

---

99. H. J. Lethbridge, 'Corruption, White Collar Crime and the ICAC', *Hong Kong Law Journal* 6, no. 2 (1976): 169.

Queen's displeasure towards Colonial Regulations, for example, proved to be a powerful instrument in cleansing up corruption in the aftermath of the police mutiny. In most cases, success in mobilizing these legal assets to the colony's advantage hinged upon the Governor's persuasive power. As shown in the altercation between the Home Office and David Trench over the shifting of the onus of proof to the suspect, the determination (and even threats) of a Governor could stretch legal limitations. Bureaucratic politics in the British government also played a key role here. Departments with different responsibilities and concerns responded to the plight of the colony differently. As shown by the anti-corruption campaign in the 1970s, FCO officials were relatively well-informed of the general situation of the colony, and were by and large receptive to the Governor's accounts. They believed in the importance of respecting the tradition of colonial autonomy in handling domestic crises, and minimizing the impact of their decisions on the authority of the Governor. In this case, the FCO acted to a large extent as a spokesperson for the colony, pursuing the case of Hong Kong by tireless appeals to the Home Office, a ministry which was more concerned with legal principles and the rights of British citizens like Peter Godber, than the political predicament of a governor administering a colony. The outcome of this bargaining and negotiation depended on the willingness of each department involved to give and as well as validity of their respective arguments. Nevertheless, the FCO's determination to make a case for the colony was also affected by the political atmosphere within Britain. The national embarrassment and media interest in the corruption in Hong Kong which Godber's escape to Britain stirred up had made the FCO more vulnerable to parliamentary pressure and attacks from the opposition. Although this could have reinforced their desire for a quick fix and thus made the FCO more motivated to lobby on behalf of Hong Kong, its officials could also have found it tempting to resort to a more intrusive and direct solution such as to address the crisis in the colony as well. It was up to the Governor to demonstrate his ability to clear up his own mess and relieve FCO of the pressure of direct intervention into the domestic business of the colony. During the corruption crisis in the 1970s, MacLehose did a great job of thwarting most of the threatened interventions from London, and his various pre-emptive actions and canny political moves offered more space for the FCO to handle the situation on the British side. Nevertheless, as we will see in the forthcoming discussion, when the tempo and drive for intervention came from more powerful and motivated interests in Britain, the scope for Hong Kong's resistance shrank rapidly. This was the case for social reforms of the 1970s, to which we will now turn.

4
Pushing Back
Social Reforms and the Hong Kong Planning Paper

Introduction

The so-called MacLehose era has been fondly remembered as a period of significant expansion of social services and extension of welfare rights.[1] MacLehose's ambitious Ten-Year Housing Programme, the launch of nine years of free universal education, the development of partnerships with the voluntary sector in providing welfare services, and expansion of public health facilities were perceived as the foundations of a new social order for Hong Kong society.[2] The Governor has very frequently been credited for the initiation of these social reforms:

> More than anything, however, it is one man's vision: a product of the 'wildcard', protracted presence in the Colony of Governor Sir Murray MacLehose. No doubt, the aftermath of 1966–1967 would have seen numerous officials, perhaps even senior policy spokesmen, making a conscious effort to 'correct for past mistakes' as they variously perceived them. But only a Governor could speak explicitly for Government as a whole and perhaps (this in an age of television) even personify the entire apparatus. And Sir Murray proves no ordinary Governor.[3]

Notwithstanding the role and contribution of the Governor, the prevailing narrative has missed several key issues concerning the dynamics of the reform process. Firstly, as in the case of anti-corruption campaign, the momentum for reform was already in place before MacLehose took over. His predecessor, David Trench, was fully aware of the inadequacy of the

---

1. Ian Scott, *Political Change and the Crisis of Legitimacy in Hong Kong* (Hong Kong: Oxford University Press, 1989), 127.
2. Scott, *Political Change and the Crisis of Legitimacy in Hong Kong*, chapter 4.
3. Catherine Jones, *Promoting Prosperity: The Hong Kong Way of Social Policy* (Hong Kong: Chinese University of Hong Kong Press, 1990), 210.

social services, and major reviews and consultations had commenced or been completed even before the 1967 Riots. Moreover, it is important to recognize the role of London in these reforms. Comparing MacLehose's initial views on reform, delivered in his earlier public addresses, with the actual programme implemented under his governorship, it is possible to reach a conclusion that there was a leap in the scope and pace of reform from 1976 onwards. Unbeknown to the Hong Kong public, the FCO had in fact bestowed upon the colonial administration a blueprint for social reforms that very year, *The Hong Kong Planning Paper*. The Labour administration under Harold Wilson and James Callaghan, driven by the party's ideological concerns and strategic calculation of the future of Hong Kong and relations with China, buoyed by the growing resentment of British businesses against the influx of Hong Kong products and rising unionism, was determined to accelerate social reforms in Hong Kong. Contrary to popular perception, MacLehose was actually a reluctant reformer with a strong faith in low taxation and fiscal discipline. He defended a vision of the colony's interests that brought him into altercations with his colleagues in the FCO. Snapshots of the negotiations, interactions, and confrontations between the colony and the sovereign during this process provide therefore a way of understanding Hong Kong autonomy.[4]

Momentum for Reform before MacLehose

Post-war Hong Kong saw the rapid growth of the local population. The return of locals from the mainland after the war, the baby-boom in post-war years, and the inflow of mainlanders triggered by the Communist takeover of China and the famine in the late 1950s accounted for these changes. Between 1945 and 1965, the population dramatically increased from 1.5 million to 3.5 million, which led to a massive demand for public services. The support of extended kinship networks or self-help, theorized as the cornerstones of the colonial social order according to Lau Siu Kai's notion of 'utilitarian familism', could no longer accommodate the needs of the rapidly growing community.[5] Equally important was the fact that by the early 1960s, the colonial government was convinced that overseas emigration was no longer a viable solution for the massive number of Chinese refugees who had arrived in Hong Kong during the post-war years. Full local integration of these immigrants was deemed the only solution to

---

4. Ray Yep and Tai-Lok Lui, 'Revisiting the Golden Era of MacLehose and the Dynamics of Social Reforms', *China Information* 24, no. 3 (2010): 249–272.
5. Siu Kai Lau, *Society and Politics in Hong Kong* (Hong Kong: Chinese University of Hong Kong Press, 1982).

the 'problem of people', and a new approach to public services was thus required.[6] Calls for change had become more vocal within policy-making bodies by the early 1960s. For instances, a white paper *The Development of Medical Services in Hong Kong* and the working party report entitled *Review of Policies for Squatter Control, Resettlement and Government Low Cost Housing* were published in 1964. This was followed by the white papers *Education Policy* and *Aims and Policy for Social Welfare in Hong Kong* in 1965.[7] At about the same time, the colonial government's first white paper on social welfare— authored by Lady Williams of the University of London—was published. She was invited to visit Hong Kong 'for the purpose of advising the Government whether a survey of social welfare services in Hong Kong would be feasible and valuable'.[8] A working party was set up in 1966 to investigate the idea of establishing some kind of social security system, and its report was published in 1967. These reviews of the changing needs of the Hong Kong people and the role of government in the provision of services were, at best, rudimentary and should not understood as locking the colonial administration into a commitment to make fundamental changes. However, they were indicative of the colonial administration's growing awareness of emerging social needs and the imperative of framing policies to meet these expectations.

The 1967 Riots further reinforced the government's motivation for formulating policies that responded more effectively to a rapidly changing social environment.[9] Colonial officials remained wary of Hong Kong's vulnerability to Communist threat which could exploit the failure of the administration to address concerns about the welfare of ordinary people. Hugh Norman-Walker, the Colonial Secretary, for example, warned that the Communists remained determined to win wider support by posing as champions of the people who were more considerate of their needs and interests than the colonial authority. 'Let there be no mistake about this. The Communists have in no sense abandoned their efforts to secure control over Hong Kong affairs,' Norman-Walker cautioned.[10] He called for more forward-looking public service programmes which should include the acceleration of major initiatives in education, housing, medical services, and amenities, plus urgent attention given to infrastructure investment, the

---

6. Chi-Kwan Mark, "The 'Problem of People': British Colonials, Cold War Powers, and the Chinese Refugees in Hong Kong, 1949–62," *Modern Asian Studies* 41, no. 6 (2007): 1145–1181.
7. Jones, *Promoting Prosperity*, chapter 6.
8. Gertrude Williams, *Report on the Feasibility of a Survey into Social Welfare Provision and Allied Topics in Hong Kong* (Hong Kong: Government Printer, 1966), 1.
9. For a critical review of the impacts of the 1967 riots on policy changes, see Alan Smart and Tai-Lok Lui, 'Learning from Civil Unrest: State/Society Relations Before and After the 1967 Disturbances', in *May Days in Hong Kong: Riot and Emergency in 1967*, ed. Robert Bickers and Ray Yep (Hong Kong: Hong Kong University Press, 2009), 145–160.
10. Countering Subversion—Government Policies, 11 May 1969, HKRS742-15-22, HKPRO.

amendment of labour legislation, and the development of public assistance scheme.

Norman-Walker's concern of the Communist threat was echoed by Alastair Todd, the Defence Secretary,

> We have to show clearly where we best can, that they (the local Communists) are not the champions of the people that they claim to be and that they are no more considerate of the people's needs and interests than the Government, as they would wish public to believe.[11]

The 1997 Factor

MacLehose certainly saw the merits of these arguments and agreed that Hong Kong's government must meet the people's expectations. In one of his earlier dispatches to London, he argued:

> People are more concerned with conditions of life for themselves and their children and with their prospects of betterment. This makes the social policy of the Hong Kong Government and what is done to improve living conditions of particular significance for the Colony's future. Moreover I find that in the last ten years the population has become much less fatalistic about conditions of life and more expectant of Government.... While this increased awareness and expectancy represent a potential danger to the government if it acts beneath public expectations, it also offers opportunity to the Government if it sets out to meet them and is believed to be doing so. The increased awareness and expectancy, if met, could generate a civic pride that could not have been stirred amongst the more fatalistic and apathetic and desperately preoccupied refugees of 20 or even 10 years ago.[12]

A sense of civic pride, MacLehose believed, would be imperative for the effective governance of the colony:

> A new generation is growing up—55% of our population is under 25— and is demanding more from Government, often rightly. Like any other government this one must govern by consent and must do so without the aid of the electoral system. If that consent is to be retained, not only must legitimate demands be satisfied, but the population must be conceived that such satisfaction is genuinely the objective of Government. The need is not only for administrative action producing physical results; there is

---

11. Aims and Policies of the Hong Kong Government: Text of an Address by the Defence Secretary at a Seminar, September 1970, HKRS742-15-22, HKPRO.
12. Governor to the Rt. Hon. Sir Alec Douglas-Home, KT, MP, 1 January 1973, FCO40/439, TNA.

also a need to secure the active confidence of the population. We cannot aim at national loyalty, but civic pride might be a useful substitute.[13]

MacLehose considered the China factor to be an important component of his overall governing strategy, though he was more concerned with Hong Kong's longer-term political future. By the 1970s, China was beginning to renew its interest in participating in international affairs and crucially in rebuilding diplomatic relations with the West. These changes created a new environment within which Hong Kong's social development needed to be planned and visualized. Indeed, as early as late 1971 when MacLehose was preparing the documents on 'The Guidelines for the Governor Designate, Hong Kong', he reckoned that the importance of the 1997 factor and argued,

> We must work out policies in Hong Kong consciously designed to prolong confidence and so gain all possible time for conditions to emerge in China in which a favourable negotiation would be possible. Conversely we must avoid actions and administrative procedures in Hong Kong which tend to highlight the diminishing term of the Lease . . . Hitherto the Hong Kong Government has believed that the security risks involved in forward planning were greater than any advantages derived from it. My own view is that the balance of advantage now lies in initiating a highly secret but thorough look at the future. While I do not think the critical period will commence before the second half of this decade, the planning process will have to start now.[14]

MacLehose was certainly not the only one who pondered over the 1997 issue and its impact on colonial governance. The 1967 Riots had provoked serious reflection on the British status of Hong Kong beyond 1997 at the very top level of the British government. In the report, 'Hong Kong: Long Term Study', a document prepared by the Cabinet Ministerial Committee on Hong Kong in 1969, the pessimism of the top British decision makers over the future of Hong Kong was vividly expressed. The study stated that 'it is inconceivable that any communist Chinese government would "negotiate" an extension of the Hong Kong lease' and 'the Chinese intention is to take

---

13. Governor to the Rt. Hon. Sir Alec Douglas-Home, KT, MP, 1 January 1973, FCO40/439, TNA.
14. Guidelines for the Governor Designate of Hong Kong: Paper B-Domestic Policies, 29 October 1971, FCO40/329, TNA. The document is a joint effort between Murray MacLehose and the Foreign and Commonwealth Office. And in a related exchange sent by MacLehose to Sir Leslie Monson of FCO, the former agreed that the document 'set out what subjects the Office and I consider to be of priority for my attention in Hong Kong and, where possible, how we think they might be tackled'. Also C. M. MacLehose to Sir Leslie Monson, Mr Wilford, Mr Morgan and Mr Laird, 16 October 1971, FCO40/329, TNA.

over Hong Kong by 1997 at the latest'.[15] However, the late 1960s were not considered to be an opportune moment to approach Beijing on this matter. It was not perceived to be possible to do business with the radical leadership in China during the height of the Cultural Revolution, and Beijing, as reflected by the 1967 Riots, appeared to be content with the status quo in Hong Kong and in no hurry to take over the colony. The cabinet report recommended British negotiators should wait 'for the successor Government to that of Mao to emerge, establish itself throughout China, and define a general foreign policy against which to judge the nature and timing of any approach on Hong Kong'. Nevertheless, the report did highlight the merit of more proactive preparations for the inevitability of negotiation. It argued that Britain's strongest bargaining position came from the economic value of Hong Kong to China and therefore from a maximum degree of economic progress and tranquillity in the colony. It was imperative that this be achieved during the run-up to the proposed negotiations with China about Hong Kong's future in the mid-1980s.[16] Social development and reform were therefore not only crucial for maintaining the confidence of the local community in the colonial authority, but they were also essential to meet the strategic concerns of the sovereign.

MacLehose, who was convinced of this logic argued that there must be major development efforts in the colony,

> I think we should do everything we can to make Hong Kong a model city, of international standing, with high standards of education, technology and culture, as well as industrial, commercial and financial facilities, from which China can gain great benefit, but which China might be reluctant to try to absorb while she still has some need of the material benefits it offers and while her own conditions remain so different. This might conceivably gain additional time for conditions in China to evolve, and might even influence the Chinese Government to consider an eventual continuing special status for Hong Kong, perhaps under Chinese sovereignty, which would to some extent safeguard the way of life of the populations and the British and other foreign interests in the Colony. Conversely if we made a mess of things in Hong Kong, so that it became so impoverished that China could draw no benefit from it, and its international standing was correspondingly low, I see no reason why China should not take it over immediately. So both for these political reason, and in any case because I

---

15. Cabinet Ministerial Committee on Hong Kong, 'Hong Kong: Long Term Study', K(69)i, 26 March 1969, CAB134/2945, TNA.
16. Cabinet Ministerial Committee on Hong Kong, 'Hong Kong: Long Term Study', K(69)i, 26 March 1969, CAB134/2945, TNA.

am sure it is what HMG would wish on its merits, we should go for Hong Kong as a model city.[17]

MacLehose came to the conclusion that,

> a major effort must now be made to put a term to the deficiencies that exist and have therefore drawn up major programmes, to be completed within the next decade in the fields of Housing, Education, Medical and Health Services and Social Welfare . . . Suffice it to say that when completed there should be little about Hong Kong for which any European observer need feel shame, and much for which Asians will feel admiration. The programmes have caught the imagination of the public, and generally improved its confidence in the Government and in the Government's concern for public welfare.[18]

In short, MacLehose saw his government as 'a Government in a hurry',[19] racing against time to build civic pride amongst the local Chinese population under colonial rule before the question of Hong Kong's future was put on the negotiating table. London concurred with the Governor's views. In his reply to the Governor's telegram in February 1973, Alec Douglas-Home, the Foreign Secretary, commented on the colonial administration's mission:

> I also agreed that the conjunction of continued prosperity in Hong Kong with the present period of better relations with the Chinese Government makes this the right moment to push forward the development of Hong Kong as a place where the mainly Chinese population will wish to live and work; and that the Hong Kong Government must be a Government in a hurry if the necessary development is to be completed within a reasonable time scale.[20]

The Changing Political Climate in London

MacLehose followed up his intention with action seeking progress on the 'four pillars' of public housing, education, medical and health services, and social welfare was evident from 1972 onwards.[21] For example, an Industrial Relations Bill that was intended to replace the more restrictive Illegal Strikes and Lock-out Ordinances was in an advanced stage of planning, and by 1974, a Severance Bill that would offer a better deal for the workers

---

17. MacLehose to James Callaghan, 27 May 1974, FCO40/547, TNA.
18. MacLehose to James Callaghan, 27 May 1974, FCO40/547, TNA.
19. Governor to the Rt. Hon. Sir Alec Douglas-Home, KT, MP, 1 January 1973, FCO40/439, TNA.
20. The Secretary of State for Foreign and Commonwealth Affairs to the Governor of Hong Kong, 17 April 1973, FCO40/439, TNA.
21. Jones, *Promoting Prosperity*, 210.

under the current arrangements was also under consideration. Meanwhile, policymakers were also deliberating over the regulation of working hours and wages for overtime. In terms of social security, public assistance by means of cash payments instead of relief in kind was introduced, and provision of disability allowances and non-means-tested infirmity allowances for persons aged over seventy-five were also launched.

However, due to a mood swing in British politics, the colony's developments in social policy were now gauged through a different lens. Swift and comprehensive social reforms were deemed imperative under the Labour Government who came to power in 1974. Yet concerns for the conditions of workers in Hong Kong was nothing new. George Foggon, the Overseas Labour Adviser to the FCO who visited Hong Kong during the height of the 1967 Riots, was disturbed by the general neglect of workers' welfare in the colony. He came to the conclusion that although the confrontation was primarily political in origin, it was wrong to ignore the significance of the material and social conditions of the working population to the long-term stability of Hong Kong. He warned that a conventional narrative of government-cum-business improving living conditions via market-led growth would not have much mileage among young people, 'unless there is some evidence of a conscious drive on the part of the leadership of the Hong Kong government and employers—to ensure that the lower echelons of society to which the bulk of the younger people belong have an opportunity of sharing the fruits of such growth'.[22] Seven years later, in another assessment of the colony's situation, Foggon conceded that while there were limited but welcome signs of change, his judgement on the dire state of labour welfare in the colony lingered:

> There is little doubt that intervention by the Hong Kong Government to improve the working conditions of the labour force could have been carried forward at a faster pace over the past the years without jeopardizing economic growth.[23]

The reputation of Hong Kong's welfare policy was not particularly high amongst members of the Labour Movement in Britain during the post-war years, and the return of Harold Wilson as Prime Minister in March 1974 encouraged more criticisms of the colony's labour affairs and fermented leftist ideas in policy-making. Left-wing politicians and unionists were particularly concerned with the compatibility of Hong Kong's labour legislation with the Conventions of the International Labour Organization, such as the status and development of trade unions and the general

---

22. Visit of Oversea Labour Adviser, FCO, 11–16 October 1967, FCO40/718, TNA.
23. Report by Overseas Labour Advisor, FCO, Visit: 9–21 February 1974, FCO40/616, TNA.

welfare entitlement of the workers. By the mid-1970s, of the sixty-eight International Labour Conventions ratified by the UK, only twenty had been fully applied to Hong Kong, and ten had been applied with some modification. This did not compare favourably with other Asian economies such as Japan, which fully ratified thirty-one Conventions.[24] The Trade Union Congress, for example, had requested an on-site inquiry into the state of labour affairs in the colony. However, it was the Fabian Pamphlet entitled *Hong Kong: Britain's Responsibility* by Joe England,[25] that really galvanized the British public to question the Hong Kong government's efforts to protect the local working population.

Joe England's verdict on the miserable conditions endured by the workers in Hong Kong damaged the colony's image, for he contended that,

> It is possible to view the 1950s as the period of "take off" when the provisions of jobs was more important than anything else. The 1960s, however, were the unequivocally a period of intense exploitation. Economic and political power united to ensure that capital grew at the expense of labour . . . The protection afforded to industrial workers was indeed minimal.
>
> The disgraceful record of the 1960s needs to be underlined because it illustrates a basic fact about the power elite in Hong Kong: their vast disregard for human consequences of their kind of 'success'. The booming 1960s was a time when much could have been done to improve conditions. It was not done because, in the eyes of the rulers, nothing needed to be done; the system was working beautifully without 'interference': the indices of growth all proved. The existence of economic growth eliminated the need for social development.
>
> Finally, the basic fact which should never be lost sight of is Hong Kong is not a 'developing economy'. It is a rich state half the size of Greater London yet exporting more than the whole of India. But it is a political economy which ensures that 'the worker gets not what he earns, or what the market forces in a so called *laissez faire* economy decide is a fair return for his labour; he gets what his masters deem surplus to their own requirement'.[26]

At least ten Parliamentary questions were triggered in the aftermath of the report.[27] MacLehose was furious with England's remarks and no punches in his response:

---

24. Speaking Notes for Lord Goronwy-Roberts, Minister for Foreign Affairs, meeting the Foreign Affairs Group of Parliamentary Labour Party: Applications of ILO Conventions (in Hong Kong), 9 May 1975, FCO40/614, TNA.
25. Joe England, *Hong Kong: Britain's Responsibility*, 1975, FCO40/721, TNA.
26. England, *Hong Kong: Britain's Responsibility*.
27. For example, Parliamentary Questions on Hong Kong Child Labour's Situation by Ronald Atkins, MP, 11 February 1976, Question by Lord Brockway, 19 July 1976, and Question by Robert

Mr. England has wrongly assumed that Hong Kong's problems are best solved by applying principles well suited to British conditions. He makes no attempt to analyse the differences in culture, aspirations, attitude towards government, and life style which exist between eastern and western people ... It is written by an expatriate who left Hong Kong five years ago and with whom local people will find it difficult to identify, particularly when we applies U.K. type solutions to Hong Kong problems, without sufficient regard to the underlying differences between the two countries.[28]

Officials in the FCO were not impressed by MacLehose's positioning on this matter. In one of their internal communications about the Governor's remarks, Foggon of the Hong Kong and Indian Ocean Department opined,

I am not very happy about the confidential assessment contained in Hong Kong Telegram 59. Mr. England is criticized for assuming that 'Hong Kong's problems are best solved by applying principles well suited to British conditions' (para 3)—a criticism repeated in para 7. So far as housing and education are concerned, these surely are universal and have nothing to do with differences in 'life style which exist between Eastern and Western people'. Indeed, Hong Kong takes credit in the same documents for improvement in social welfare. These improvements are based mostly entirely on British practice and were in fact devised by an officer seconded from the DHSS in this country. The glaring effect is that Hong Kong has failed to follow what her neighbours in Asia have done in the social service field and has chosen instead Elizabeth poor law.[29]

Fortunately for MacLehose, England's suggestion of a commission of enquiry to investigate the conditions in the colony was not supported by the British government. Nor was it seen appropriate to appoint a House of Commons Select Committee to handle the matter further.[30] The call for interventions in the colony's labour welfare provisions was, however, mounting. And a Granada TV production, *World in Action: Made in Hong Kong*, which aired on national television in the UK was highly critical of the colonial government's indifference to the issues of child labour, industrial safety, and inadequate compensation for industrial injuries.[31]

However, the demand for social reform did not only come from the left wing of British politics, it was also strongly echoed by the British industries. With British manufacturing in decline and the world economy troubled by the oil crisis in the early 1970s, businesses in the UK questioned whether

---

Perry, 7 December 1976, FCO 40/718, TNA. See also Meeting between Lord Goronwy-Roberts and Mr James Johnson MP at 11:00 a.m. on Wednesday 10 February 1976, FCO40/721, TNA.
28. MacLehose to FCO, 22 January 1976, FCO40/721, TNA.
29. Foggon to Janvrin, 22 January 1976, FCO40/721, TNA.
30. England, *Hong Kong: Britain's Responsibility*, 25.
31. Granada TV, *World in Action: Made in Hong Kong*, 13 December 1976.

Hong Kong was an 'industrial slum'. For British manufacturers, particularly those in the textile industry, Hong Kong's success in flooding the British market with their products was predicated on its negligence towards workers' welfare, which led to low production costs. Hong Kong's export boom, they argued, was largely due to its ability to 'undersell British manufacturers because of its low wage economy' and consequently its ability to sustain 'cut-throat competition' with British products.[32]

Such demand for protection against unfair competition dated back to early post-war years. From 1948 to 1959, there was intra-British Empire free trade, and so Hong Kong–made goods were not subject to import duties in the UK. As a result, the British cotton textile industry, which was based primarily in Lancashire, faced severe competition from industries in Hong Kong, India, and Pakistan, all of which enjoyed tariff-free entry into the UK. The enlargement of the EEC and the prospect of the termination of the preferential treatment enjoyed by Hong Kong prompted British manufacturers to embark on a campaign of sustained propaganda and lobbying efforts against the colony. In the late 1960s, the UK Cotton Board launched a 'Buy British' campaign, which disseminated black propaganda about low wages and long hours of work in Hong Kong, and which was linked to allegations that corruption was endemic in the colony. MPs like Ernest Thornton played a major role in this campaign. Thornton had a distinctive political agenda: to protect the interest of his constituents, who were heavily dependent on the cotton textile trade. He was the Secretary of the Rochdale and District Weavers', Winders', Reelers', Beamers' and Hosiery Workers' Association, and the Labour Party's chief spokesman on cotton textiles. He was an advocate for the imposition of import control from producers selling goods at a 'ridiculously low price'.[33] Seeing the Hong Kong economy as a 'crass and corrupt form of Chinese capitalism', he claimed that the colony was a 'sweat shop', that was 'guilty of the most scandalous exploitation of labours'.[34] Thornton tabled nineteen parliamentary questions about Hong Kong in the 1959–1960 session. These campaigns coincided with UK government-sponsored negotiations between industrialists in India, Pakistan, and Hong Kong about voluntary limits on the growth of certain types of export, which culminated in the signing in October 1959 of the Lancashire Agreement. This agreement was a three-year interim measure but was afterwards renegotiated. Into the 1960s and 1970s, Lancashire textile producers thus continued to lobby for the formal

---

32. Note of a Meeting held between Governor MacLehose and MPs at Congress House on Wednesday 3 December 1975, 3 December 1975, FCO40/617, TNA.
33. 'MP suggests import board for textile', *The Guardian*, 17 January 1964, 20.
34. 'Hong Kong deal "will not end cotton troubles"', *The Guardian*, 29 October 1958, 3.

protection of their interests in the form of state-imposed import quotas and the renewal of voluntary restraints. During these years, debates about the UK's commercial policy were complicated by discontinuous negotiations over Britain's entrance into the Common Market. This lobbying was accompanied by demands for 'social protection', including the extension of labour laws, demands which intensified after the 1967 Riots. Allegations that working conditions in Hong Kong were 'sweated' persisted into the 1970s, including reportage on child labour. When Labour governments were in power (1964–1970 and 1974–1979), demands for social protection, led by trade unionists and campaigning MPs, intensified.[35]

The embarrassment which MacLehose faced during a trade promotion event organized by the Hong Kong government in 1975 was illustrative of the predicament faced by the colony. The Governor was warned by the FCO not to host a media stand-in session at a scheduled trade promotion event in London organized by Hong Kong Trade Development Council, as there was 'a faint risk that those people who are determined to regard Hong Kong as a sweat-workshop 'may comment unfavourably on the presence of the Governor in London to sell Hong Kong goods'. Princess Alexandria, a member of the British royal family, was originally invited to be the guest of honour for the event, but she was also advised by officials not to accept the offer lest it draw the criticism of Lancashire MPs who were hostile to Hong Kong. Hong Kong was 'however unjustly, widely regarded as the greatest threat to British textile industry in its own market', the Governor was told.[36]

London: Hong Kong's Value Exaggerated

MacLehose's frustration with British policy and the business community was to a certain extent indissoluble from his belief that the colony must be seen as an asset for Britain. He found those British attitudes 'coloured by an unsubstantiated assumption that the UK loses money on the Colony' very irritating.[37] The Governor argued that 'the advantages Hong Kong offers the United Kingdom are great and could be even greater'. In his dispatch to Douglas-Home in 1973, MacLehose attached a document entitled, 'Who Benefits from Hong Kong?', which contained a detailed account of the value of Hong Kong to Britain:

---

35. David Clayton, 'Buy British: The Collective Marketing of Cotton Textiles, 1956–1962', *Textile History* 41 (2010): 217–235. See also Mark Hampton, *Hong Kong and British Culture, 1945–1997* (Manchester: Manchester University Press, 2016), 42–72.
36. Duncan Watson to MacLehose, 10 February 1975, FCO40/619, TNA.
37. Duncan Watson to MacLehose, 10 February 1975, FCO40/619, TNA.

> Hong Kong lies at the heart of the Pacific region, the fastest growth area in the world. I believe that as a base Hong Kong has assisted British exporters and investors to exploit this area. I also believe that if they wish to exploit it more vigorously Hong Kong offers an excellent starting point. It does this as a large and rapidly growing market in its own right, and as a major manufacturing centre, but also as a focal point in international banking and in communications by sea and air, and with well-established British houses of great size, strength and experience with connections throughout the Pacific region . . . I should make an additional point on this. Hong Kong has a great potential as a British shop window in the Pacific region . . . so the key to the use of Hong Kong as a British commercial shop window in the Far East must lie in a determined attempt to ensure the window is a full of British rather than competitors' goods.[38]

Unfortunately, colleagues in Whitehall were not entirely convinced. Central to their displeasure with Hong Kong was the colony's lack of preferential treatment for British firms. Goodfellow of the Hong Kong and Indian Ocean Department of the FCO, summed up the general sentiment succinctly:

> Almost all Sir Murray MacLehose's arguments to the advantage of Britain apply equally to any of the other free nations of the West. This I think is the crux of the difficulties inherent in the colonial position between ourselves and Hong Kong . . . it could be argued as a general point in respect of trade and commerce the United Kingdom benefits little or nothing in the colonial relationship as compared with our competitors.[39]

One of the controversies at the time was the Governor's refusal to grant special treatment to British firms who wanted construction contracts for the Mass Transit Railway in Hong Kong. FCO officials saw this as a litmus test of the benefits which the Governor believed London would accrue from its relationship with the colony. They argued that it would help if this 'fundamental unity' occasionally had 'practical results'.[40] Nevertheless, despite their persistent lobbying efforts and not so subtle hints, the contract was eventually offered to a Japanese consortium led by Mitsubishi in 1974. 'This would be seen as a severe defeat for British industry', the Governor was warned.[41]

---

38. 'Who Benefits from Hong Kong?', The Governor of Hong Kong to the Secretary of State for Foreign and Commonwealth Affairs, 11 October 1973, FCO40/439, TNA.
39. A note by M. A. Goodfellow, Hong Kong and Indian Ocean Department FCO, 29 October 1974, FCO40/439, TNA.
40. A. C. Stuart to Youde and Watson, 21 November 1973, FCO40/439, TNA.
41. A note by M. A. Goodfellow, Hong Kong and Indian Ocean Department FCO, 29 October 1974, FCO40/439, TNA.

This perceived deprivation only exacerbated negative feeling towards Hong Kong among British officials. Voices concerned about the cost of keeping the colony were becoming more audible. Some even argued that Hong Kong had in fact been a constant cause of embarrassment in the UK–China relationship.[42] A FCO official noted that the burning of the British diplomatic mission in Beijing as a result of the 1967 Riots in Hong Kong was the first since the Boxer Uprising in the late Qing years. Interestingly, Edward Youde, the eventual successor to MacLehose, was among those who were sceptical of the colony's value to the UK. He believed that the Governor's rose-tinted vision of the Hong Kong–Britain relationship was questionable.[43] Some FCO officials even concluded with a rather cynical comment,

> at the end of the day I believe it is in our interest to stay in Hong Kong because it is there and because we have a responsibility to the four million Chinese who choose to live and work there. We would not today have chosen to create Hong Kong if it did not exist.[44]

The change in government in Britain in 1974 and the subsequent reshuffle in personnel at the FCO did not lead to any major shift. London's prevailing attitude towards Hong Kong remained sceptical. A comment by Laurence O'Keeffe, the head of the Hong Kong and Indian Ocean Department of Foreign and Commonwealth Office in 1975, attested to the lingering of such a sentiment:

> the people who benefited most from the existence of Hong Kong were the Japanese and the Americans and to a lesser degree I think, even the Australians. But the big Hong's, the big so-called 'British' companies were based in Hong Kong and did not pay British tax. They were not acting on behalf of British interests but specifically their own. The problem was that we were holding the baby and there was absolutely no way that we could drop it at that time. This came as a bit of a surprise to me. I had hitherto always assumed that the colonies were run for the benefits of the colonisers from which the colonised actually got some benefits too in terms of peace and prosperity. It had never occurred to me that we would actually be holding on to something where we were the least favoured.[45]

---

42. Addis to Youde, 7 November 1973, FCO40/439, TNA.
43. A note by Edward Youde, 27 November 1973, FCO40/439, TNA.
44. A. C. Stuart to Youde and Watson, 21 November 1973, FCO40/439, TNA.
45. 'BDOHP interview: (Peter) Laurence O'Keeffe', accessed 6 January 2023, http://www.chu.cam.ac.uk/archives/collections/BDOHP/OKeefee.pdf.

Hong Kong Planning Paper

London's vision for social reforms in Hong Kong was crystallized in the document Hong Kong Planning Paper in 1976. MacLehose certainly had a plan for social reforms which sought to meet the rising local expectations of a better quality of life, and shrewdly recognized the need 'to satisfy this demand before it becomes too strident'.[46] MacLehose also reckoned that the legitimacy of the British alien rule in Hong Kong hinged primarily on the superiority of living standards in the colony when compared with the mainland. Nevertheless, his vision for change had a strong conservative and incrementalist flavour. No major upheaval in labour legislation was envisaged. While MacLehose was just as aware of local inertia towards improvements in labour welfare as of the fact that pre-1967 legislative initiatives had 'run into the sand',[47] his position appeared to be ambivalent. He claimed that he had 'not come to any conclusion about what is needed'. Even in his maiden speech to the Legislative Council in 1972, an occasion that was seen by many as the coronation of a reform-minded governor, MacLehose appeared vague and did not commit to any specific reform programme. On the topic of labour welfare, the Governor did not go beyond reiterating the progress in labour legislations made under David Trench and his rhetoric amounted to the conclusion that 'a good deal remains to be done'.[48]

Whatever the blueprint for change was that MacLehose had had in mind, his vision was clearly dwarfed by the grand scheme of the reforms outlined in the 'Planning Paper on Hong Kong'. The paper was a product of the British government's political calculations over the future of the colony, an acceptance that 'Hong Kong was a difficult political problem which is likely to become more acute as 1997 approaches'.[49] The new initiatives for social reform were thus part of the preparations for the prospective negotiations with China and a strategy for maintaining stability in the colony. The paper claimed that in order to discharge the responsibilities of the British to the people of Hong Kong, the colonial government should 'take account of their desires and feelings'. The principal concerns of the Hong Kong people, according to this document, included confidence in the government, assured employment, personal safety, adequate housing, decent educational and medical services, and, most importantly, a social welfare net which would prevent the poor, elderly, disabled, sick, and

---

46. MacLehose to Leslie Monson, 18 October 1971, FCO40/329, TNA.
47. MacLehose to Leslie Monson, 18 October 1971.
48. Address by the H.E. the Governor, *The Legislative Council Debates Official Report*, 18 October 1972, Hong Kong Legislative Council, 15.
49. 'Planning Paper on Hong Kong', n.d., FCO40/704, TNA, 1.

unfortunate from falling below the subsistence level.[50] Rapid reforms in two areas were seen as imperative to the social well-being and stability of the colony: labour rights and social security.

Specific objectives had been laid down for the reform of labour rights. Firstly, Hong Kong's labour conditions should be made equivalent to the highest nearby standard in the region. Secondly, the reforms must ensure faster progress in the application of the International Labour Organization Convention in the colony. Both targets were to be completed within a five-year period, with specific time-frames for the implementation of reforms already under considerations of the Hong Kong government. These included better provision for rest days and statutory holidays (both by 1 January 1977), the introduction of compulsory annual leave with pay (1 January 1978), and the prohibition of the employment of minors under fourteen years of age by 1979 and under fifteen by 1980. The paper also requested the broadening of industrial safety regulations and improvements in sickness benefits and redundancy wages. Nevertheless, the paper also urged that more controversial issues such as minimum wage and statutory hours of work be considered, changes which MacLehose had not been seriously contemplating.[51] The paper's verdict on the gaps and weakness in Hong Kong's system was critical, as is shown by its diagnosis of the limitations of the colony's social security system:

> There is no direct provision for unemployment benefits; pensions are small and available only to persons of 75 and over; sickness benefits, an employer's liability, does not extend beyond 24 days and there is no pension for widows.[52]

Despite such profound differences between metropolitan and colonial plans, MacLehose tried to demonstrate his compliance in his Policy Address in 1976. MacLehose set out in his speech a comprehensive review of 'what needs doing to complete the safety net of our society and make sure it has no holes'. He informed the Legislative Council that the coverage of the public assistance scheme would, as suggested by the paper, extend to able-bodied persons between fifteen and fifty-five in the coming financial year. He went on to pledge that the administration would make more of an effort in improving the employment conditions of Hong Kong workers with legislative initiatives for severance pay and sickness benefits. The study of further safety legislation and the compensation of workers in cases of bankruptcy or liquidation would also be high on the government's agenda. London's

---

50. 'Planning Paper on Hong Kong', 7.
51. 'Planning Paper on Hong Kong', 12–13.
52. 'Planning Paper on Hong Kong', 15.

scheme had extended the scope and accelerated the pace of reforms. Amendments to the Employment Ordinance were made to provide one week's holiday with pay and one rest day a week in 1978 and 1979 respectively, as suggested in the paper's timetable for implementation.[53]

London, however, remained sceptical. 'We must in particular try to carry the Governor with us,' Hugh Cortazzi reminded his colleagues in the FCO.[54] In fact, there were intensive exchanges, if not altercations, between the Governor and FCO officials before the speech was finalized. FCO officials found the early version of MacLehose's Legislative Council (LegCo) speech not entirely 'satisfactory for the UK audience'. They were particularly irritated with all the Governor's emphasis on his qualifications of the reforms and his reservations with respect to implementation. For example, MacLehose's caution on the necessity of requiring specific checks in order to prevent abuse in the newly extended Public Assistance Programme, and his call for the new measures to be implemented in different phases, were seen as evidence of his lack of any sense of urgency in making major reforms.[55] Lord Goronwy-Roberts even tried to dictate a revised paragraph of the address to the Governor, and opined a sentence such as 'I have decided that the time has come to launch a new programme of social development to provide a necessary improvement in the well-being of our less fortunate citizens' would better reflect the determination of the colonial administration. 'I should greatly welcome a forthright statement that the intention is to make progress as quickly as possible according to the timescale in the Planning Paper,' the minister added.[56]

Although the Governor decided to accept most of the suggestions to amend his speech, his displeasure was evident. 'Since action lies here I hope you will allow me my own presentation,' MacLehose protested. He confronted Goronwy-Roberts, saying that the suggested phrase 'to launch a new programme of social development' was factually incorrect, exaggerated, and pretentious, as these welfare projects had always been the priorities of the colonial administration. This was not the first time that the pair had clashed on the matter of Planning Paper implementation. When in a meeting shortly after the pronouncement of the document Lord Goronwy-Roberts informed the Governor that the social reforms listed in the paper

---

53. Address by the H.E. the Governor, *The Legislative Council Debates Official Report*, 6 October 1976, Hong Kong Legislative Council.
54. Cortazzi to Stewart, Hong Kong Planning Paper: Future Action, 13 September 1976, FCO40/705, TNA.
55. Milton to Stewart, Governor's Statement to the Legislative Council, 28 September 1976, FCO40/705, TNA.
56. Crosland to Hong Kong: Personal for Governor from Lord Goronwy-Roberts, 1 October 1976, FCO40/705, TNA.

represented 'the minimum' which British government could regard as acceptable, MacLehose retorted that it represented 'the maximum he thought possible to attain in Hong Kong'. He contended that 'it would be difficult for him if additional measures were added as it would be for HMG if Hong Kong were to fall behind in implementing the programme'.[57]

For MacLehose, London must reckoned the challenges he faced locally and the necessity for 'balance' in introducing social reforms into account:

> Opposition is not just 'conservative', it is also communist and from owners of small and medium factories. Owners of large factories are more likely to like a broad long-term view. The line-up could be commercially formidable if I give a wrong impression of the scope of what is proposed . . . It is your Government's aim to build into our society: a balance . . . The first side of the balance—comparative economic freedom—is perfectly compatible with social and commercial responsibility. We know this is so, and we must keep it so. The other side—social provision is equally compatible with Hong Kong's traditional virtues of realism, will to work, and self-reliance. These too are precious and essential to our society and must be preserve. I am convinced that in the construction of this balance lie Hong Kong's nest prospect for prosperity, social harmony and international respect.[58]

Metropolitan Intervention Intensified

MacLehose's 'defiance' attested to his displeasure with the FCO's new interventionist approach in overseeing the colony's social development, involving a policy blueprint onto the colony. While he conceded that the British government was obliged to monitor the progress and administration of the colonies and that the Secretary of State was constitutionally entitled to issue guidelines and directives, he contended that there was a tradition of giving 'the man on the spot' who had the last word on how his jurisdiction should be governed. To his knowledge, there was no precedent for the Colonial Office to impose a comprehensive programme of reforms in various aspects of government activity on a colony in the form of a Planning Paper. The primary obligation of a colonial governor, in his opinion, was to serve the interests of the population of the territory, as pre-war governors had succeeded in doing. He reminded a FCO official on a duty tour to Hong Kong that the Secretary of State could, as a last resort, sack a governor if he found his service failed to further the interests of Her Majesty's Government.[59]

---

57. Record of Meeting between MacLehose and Lord Goronwy-Roberts, 21 July 1976, FCO40/704, TNA.
58. MacLehose to FCO, 4 October 1976, FCO40/705, TNA.
59. Milton to Cortazzi/Hong Kong: Call on the Governor, 16 July 1976, FCO40/704, TNA.

Despite MacLehose's dissatisfaction with London's management of the policy making process, the momentum for reform appeared to show no sign of abatement, and more changes were proposed in the Policy Address of 1977. The maximum penalty for employing child labour was raised to HKD 10,000. Further extensions of the public assistance scheme were introduced, including a supplement for those who had been forced to rely on welfare benefits for over eighteen months, and the lowering of qualifying age for Old Age Allowance from sixty-five to sixty. And, for the first time, the idea of the self-contributory scheme for employees that had been advocated by the authors of the Paper was formally put on the agenda of the colonial policy makers.[60] The Governor proclaimed that the government 'might introduce a semi-voluntary contributory scheme providing insurance cover against sickness, injury and death, and perhaps also a small retirement benefit'.[61] This scheme would:

> Cater for an area of need, which cannot be met satisfactorily through the Public Assistance Scheme because the persons concerned or their families have means above the level of eligibility for public assistance, but are so far above it has to be insulated against the financial effects on the family of the prolonged sickness or death of a bread-winner.[62]

Yet the Governor's frustration with the FCO's request for rapid changes lingered, and MacLehose did not shy away from revealing his feelings in public statement, as shown in his Policy Address in 1977:

> [I]t has become apparent that the pace of legislation has outrun the administrative and enforcement capacity of the [Labour] department. The staff of the department are of high calibre, but there are too few of them. It is therefore that in the coming year the department should have time to consolidate and build up its resources.[63]

His attitude was creating a vicious cycle by which the Governor's defiance reinforced the FCO's distrust of his commitment, justifying further instructions and an even more interventionist approach, including elaborate mechanism for monitoring progress. Hugh Cortazzi, a senior official in the FCO justified this by saying that they 'must monitor carefully progress on the Planning Paper' because they had 'doubts about the willingness and determination of some officials and unofficials in Hong Kong to put

---

60. Address by the H.E. the Governor, *The Legislative Council Debates Official Report*, 5 October 1977, Hong Kong Legislative Council.
61. Address by the H.E. the Governor, *The Legislative Council Debates Official Report*, 5 October 1977, 34.
62. Address by the H.E. the Governor, *The Legislative Council Debates Official Report*, 5 October 1977, 34.
63. Address by the H.E. the Governor, *The Legislative Council Debates Official Report*, 5 October 1977.

the programme into effect in the time scale envisaged'.[64] Thus, in addition to progress reports from the colonial government and regular visits from the Governor and from officials from both administrations, a new standing committee was established to monitor the Hong Kong Planning Paper. The Committee was comprised of economists, overseas labour advisers, legal advisers of the Ministry, and representatives from relevant geographical units—for example, the Hong Kong Department and Far East Department—and was chaired by a Superintending Under-Secretary. It was to meet quarterly and bi-annually and discuss the progress of the implementation of the Planning Paper. FCO also considered appointing a second Political Adviser to the Governor with a responsibility for the 'UK dimension', which would have been 'seen by the present Governor as a vote of non-confidence in his capacity to exercise his function as HMG's representative in Hong Kong'. MacLehose retorted that 'he thought that his own UK conscience was fairly alert and that he probably knew as much as anybody', and this appointment never materialized.[65]

The Dispute over Fiscal Philosophy

London and MacLehose also differed on the fiscal approach behind all the social reforms. The line taken by the Governor was that Hong Kong must maintain its pro-business policies, and given that the colony had an open economy, the size of the public sector should be carefully managed.[66] His faith in the conventional wisdom of 'trickle-down economics', the idea that economic growth is key to the improvement of general living standards for all, is evident. For MacLehose, the low-tax regime of Hong Kong's economy was simply untouchable. So, despite his spirited call for social reforms, he argued that 'it will be a time to decrease rather than increase in taxes and charges. So problems should be faced and solved now, within the next decade, at whatever cost is necessary compatible with the continued expansion of the economy and its attractiveness to investors, in the hope of being able to ease up in the 80's'.[67]

For London, the proposed reforms should take priority over fiscal discipline. They believed that options such as raising the direct taxation rate, broadening the tax base, and even deficit budgeting should be considered. As one FCO official put it, 'conservatism in financial policy was not

---

64. Cortazzi to Stewart, 13 September 1976, FCO40/705, TNA.
65. Record of Meeting between Governor and the Minister of State for Foreign and Commonwealth Affairs, 9 December 1976, FCO40/712, TNA.
66. Hong Kong—Domestic Policies Up to the '80s, 6 March 1976, FCO40/701, TNA.
67. MacLehose to James Callaghan, 27 May 1974, FCO40/547, TNA.

as necessary as Hong Kong officials commonly stated it to be', and public expenditure could be increased to about 25 per cent of the colony's GDP.[68] FCO officials had long desired that the colonial government implement a more proactive fiscal approach, and they had repeatedly made their views known to the Governor. For example, Foggon, the Overseas Labour Advisor, challenged the fiscal conservatism of the colony in his report on Hong Kong situation in 1974:

> One might well ask, therefore, whether the current budgetary theology in Hong Kong is quite such an essential formula for success as is popularly supposed. Up to the early 1960s, the Spartan rigidities of the budget policy were no doubt right. Have they been so right since? The policy of meeting capital expenditure wholly from the recurrent budget, for example, has meant a tight squeeze on normal recurrent items. Expenditure on education suffered badly in the 1960s; social welfare and the relief of poverty were almost non-existent. The standard of subsidized housing—single rooms with no kitchen—is another legacy of that period. Would it not be possible in these more affluent days for Hong Kong to get away decisively from building one-room 'flats' for families? Are not Hong Kong people ready to pay for a degree of privacy and comfort in the housing to be built under the new 10 year plan? Could there not perhaps be a greater readiness to borrow for capital projects to release resources from the recurrent budget for accelerated improvements in education, medical services and social welfare, for example? These are questions that go far beyond this report but they are the crux of whether prosperity can be shared in the future in Hong Kong to a greater extent than it is now.[69]

Goronwy-Roberts was more specific in his diagnosis: an increase in taxation was necessary for social reform in Hong Kong. In his communication with James Callaghan, the Foreign Secretary at that time, he argued:

> All these [reforms] will require a great deal of money and extra tax will be needed. In my discussion with officials I made the point that taxation in Hong Kong is criticized here as being too low. No doubt Hong Kong having no natural resources of its own is dependent on attracting business into the colony; to do this its taxation structure must be competitive with that of its neighbours. Nevertheless I believe there is scope for increasing taxation, for redistributive and welfare purposes, as does the Governor.[70]

The fiscal conservatism enshrined in Philip Haddon-Cave's Budget Speech of 1976 was hardly comforting for the reform-minded FCO. The

---

68. Note by Galsworthy, 16 March 1976, FCO40/712, TNA.
69. Hong Kong: Report by Overseas Labour Adviser, FCO, Visit 9–21 February 1974, FCO40/616, TNA.
70. Goronwy-Roberts to Callaghan, 21 February 1975, FCO40/615, TNA.

colony's Financial Secretary was no stranger to the British administration, as he had been a staunch defender of Hong Kong's agendas in previous battles over the pound sterling rate and export quota. For many bureaucrats in the FCO, Haddon-Cave personified a form of fiscal conservatism that would thwart the full implementation of their reform blueprint. And the 1976 Budget Speech undoubtedly provided ammunition for those who wanted to get rid of the Financial Secretary. Contrary to views of officials in London, Haddon-Cave emphasized the importance of a balanced budget and laid down the guiding principles for public expenditure in his address to the Legislative Council. In his Budget Speech delivered in February 1976, Haddon-Cave set out the need for there to be a ceiling for public expenditure explicitly:

> Public expenditure tends to be determined by political and social, as well as economic considerations and so it is important that the size of the public sector does not exceed a certain limit. Otherwise, there is a risk that the public sector activities will damage the growth rate of the economy. It is a matter of opinion when this limit is reached, but it is clearly lower in an open economy such as ours, necessarily dependent on a relatively narrow range of industries manufacturing for export, than in a closed economy. But in my opinion, if one measures the size of the public sector in terms of the ratio of total expenditure to the GDP, the outside limit should be set at 20%; and when the economy is enjoying strong growth, the ratio should fall.[71]

He went on further to elaborate the specific parameters for public expenditures, such as that:

(a) the recurrent expenditure should absorb no more than 80% of the recurrent revenue;
(b) at least 60% of capital expenditure should be financed by the surplus on recurrent account; and
(c) at least 88% of total expenditure should be met from recurrent revenue.[72]

These articulations were evidently at odds with the reformist fiscal philosophy advocated by FCO officials. More importantly, they found that Haddon-Cave's views were also contrary to those of the Governor, who, in his early exchanges with London had conceded that public expenditure could safely rise to 22.5 per cent of GDP.[73] There were concerns that Haddon-Cave's fiscal caps might hinder the implementation of the reform programmes,

---

71. The Budget for 1976–1977, 25 February 1976, Official Report of Proceedings, Hong Kong Legislative Council.
72. The Budget for 1976–1977.
73. Hong Kong: Briefing for Mr. Cortazzi's Visit, 28 April 1976, FCO40/710, TNA.

and the idea of transferring the Financial Secretary away from Hong Kong was under consideration. As a paper prepared by the Hong Kong and Indian Ocean Department of the FCO concluded, some officials thought that this risk was worthy of serious consideration:

> Removal would, we judge, cause serious difficulties in our relations with Hong Kong; but in the last resort, Ministers may conclude that this is the only course.[74]

Galsworthy, Private Secretary to Lord Goronwy-Roberts, concurred:

> It was agreed that if excessively conservative policy in Hong Kong were to be avoided in future, it might well be necessary to change some of the senior appointments there.[75]

In a meeting with the Governor in July 1976, Lord Goronwy-Roberts expressed his concerns with the general tenor of the Budget Speech and pulled no punches in criticizing Haddon-Cave. He believed that the Financial Secretary's views were inconsistent with the aims of the Planning Paper. In short, the minister saw Haddon-Cave's budget a challenge to London's pursuit of social justice.[76]

The Governor's response to these attacks on the Financial Secretary was balanced. On the one hand, he understood that the Budget Speech created difficulties for colleagues in London and he assured them that if revenue was required to finance the reform programmes, Hong Kong would without hesitation find means to acquire it. On the other hand, he did feel that there was an ill-conceived 'hate' for the Financial Secretary, whose position was political and who had his Hong Kong constituency to consider. However, if the Governor's thoughts on his Financial Secretary's stance on fiscal management were remotely ambiguous, the next aggressive move by London undoubtedly cemented the 'bonding' between the Governor and his Financial Secretary.

In a meeting in July 1976, Lord Goronwy-Roberts reiterated that the implementation of the Planning Paper should not be derailed by financial difficulties, and that the proposed reforms must be introduced within the agreed timetable. And as an insurance policy, he argued that the Secretary of State would like to be informed in good time of the Hong Kong government's annual budget proposals so that he could, if necessary, offer comments. The Governor was horrified at the prospect of potentially having to negotiate a budget with London, and contended that this 'intrusion' was a

---

74. Hong Kong: Briefing for Mr. Cortazzi's Visit.
75. Galsworthy to Larmour, 16 March 1976, FCO40/702, TNA.
76. Record of Meeting between MacLehose and Lord Goronwy-Roberts, 21 July 1976, FCO40/704, TNA.

grave departure from the Colonial Office's fiscal tradition. Fiscal autonomy had always been cherished by the colonial administration, and the postwar Governor Mark Young had made it a top priority of his term. By 1948, Alexander Grantham, Young's successor, was able to proudly proclaim that while London's approval of the annual estimates, large investments, or new loans was still required, the metropole's command over Hong Kong was largely theoretical. In 1958, Governor Robert Black proudly informed the Legislative Council in his inaugural address that the Secretary of State had told him that in view of the good financial and administrative standing of Hong Kong, the colony was no longer required to submit the budget for approval.[77]

MacLehose further argued that the timescale for the final formulation of budget figures had always been tight, and decisions were usually made at the very last moment. The proposal could therefore only arrive in London at a time that left little room for change. However, Lord Goronwy-Roberts retorted that the difference between the Governor's early pledge and the 1976 Budget had demonstrated the need for London to know what exactly was envisaged in advance. As a compromise, the Governor agreed to explain the 1977 Budget in general terms during his scheduled visit to London in December 1976 and to supplement this with a written prognosis a fortnight before Budget Day.[78]

The heated exchanges of this meeting did not eradicate the difference in fiscal philosophy between the two sides, and the Financial Secretary remained defiant. For the FCO officials, the 1977 Budget was another disappointment. Though no longer stating the ceiling of public expenditure to GDP ratio explicitly, Haddon-Cave's general tone of fiscal prudence and by implication, a lack of enthusiasm for social reforms lingered.[79] James Stewart, the Head of FCO's Hong Kong Department complained that:

> there is one main criticism of the Budget which is of overriding importance and should be made to the Governor, i.e. that the Minister of State would wish to see the Budget expresses explicitly the strategic, fiscal and budgeting planning of the Hong Kong government during the foreseeable future to take account, among other things, of the need for the expansion planned in Government spending, particularly in the social and related fields . . . It is, I think, true to say that the Budget, as presented in March 1977, did not, as it should have done, correspond and expand on

---

77. Neil Monnery, *Architect of Prosperity: Sir John Cowperthwaite and the Making of Hong Kong* (London: London Publishing Partnership, 2017), chapters 5 and 8.
78. Monnery, *Architect of Prosperity*, chapters 5 and 8
79. The Budget for 1977–1978, 2 March 1977, Official Report of Proceedings, Hong Kong Legislative Council.

the expenditure proposals and the strategy propounded in the Governor's speech at the opening of Legislative Council in 1977.[80]

Haddon-Cave's unwillingness to increase taxes alienated him from the London establishment. Given the current state of fiscal health and the expected opposition from local community, he saw no ground for raising the rate of direct taxation. London, however, thought otherwise. In the eyes of FCO officials, the budgeting philosophy of Hong Kong was conservative, out-of-date, and failed to live up to the expectations of the Planning Paper's grand scheme of changes. 'The attitude of Hong Kong seems to be estimate revenue and then decide on expenditure rather than determine policies and then decide how to finance them through revenue,' Cortazzi, who now chaired the Standing Committee to Monitor the Planning Paper complained.[81] A FCO economic adviser went further to point out that 'there is no economic cause for budgeting for a balanced budget and that there is a good social case for budgeting for a deficit'.[82] For them, budgetary balance was nothing but proof of Hong Kong officials' inability to see the big picture which had been bestowed upon them. As pointed out by Lord Goronwy-Roberts, the 'fundamental point was that higher taxation would produce better services'.[83] The steady rise in revenue which a rise in taxation guaranteed would ensure that social reform programmes held no risk of being cut back due to fiscal difficulties.[84] Yet, despite all this pressure, there was no major change in Hong Kong's taxation system between 1976 and 1977 and the fiscal discipline advocated by Haddon-Cave prevailed.

Conflicts over a New Contributory Scheme of Benefits

MacLehose was, however, determined to resist the idea of comprehensive social security scheme. Unlike other reforms proposed in the Planning Paper, MacLehose appeared very reluctant to agree with London on this matter, and progress was sluggish. The Governor perhaps felt frustrated with London's persistent criticism of his lack of effort in improving welfare support in Hong Kong. In fact, there was a significant rise in public expenditure on social welfare between 1975 and 1978, with the total expenditure increased from HKD 352 million in the fiscal year of 1975/76 to a new

---

80. Stewart to Murray/Cortazzi-Hong Kong: Standing Committee to Monitor the Planning Paper: the 1977/78 Budget, 12 May 1977, FCO40/754, TNA.
81. Cortazzi's Summary for Lord Goronwy-Roberts, 14 November 1977, FCO40/755, TNA.
82. Stewart to Murray/Cortazzi-Hong Kong: Standing Committee to Monitor the Planning Paper: the 1977/78 Budget, 12 May 1977, FCO40/754, TNA.
83. Governor's meeting with Stewart/Cortazzi at FCO, 21 November 1977, FCO40/761, TNA.
84. Lord Goronwy-Roberts to the Secretary of State, 1 July 1977, FCO40/755, TNA.

height of HKD 433 million in 1977/78.[85] The increase in projected expenditure on social security between the fiscal year of 1978/79 and 1982/83 was no less spectacular; the allocation would increase from HKD 53 million to HKD 177 million over this five-year period (see Table 4.1).[86] London, however, remained unconvinced of the Governor's commitment. Central to the FCO's concerns was not merely the rise in resources allocated for social welfare, but also reforms in terms of extension of coverage and innovation in institutional settings. High on their wish list was the introduction of some form of contributory scheme which would provide protection for a wide range of contingencies. As pointed out above, the Governor did in fact commit himself to 'a semi-voluntary contributory scheme providing insurance cover against sickness, injury and death, and perhaps also a small retirement benefit' in his 1977 Policy Address.[87] Yet this public pledge

Table 4.1: Estimated public expenditure on social services 1978–1983

Fiscal year	Social security (cash payment)	Elderly (excluding medical cost)	Services for youth	Rehabilitation	Total
1978/79					
Recurrent	53.0	7.0	20.0	19.0	99.0
Capital	–	0.1	1.6	19.0	20.7
1979/80					
Recurrent	102.0	13.0	25.0	37.0	177.0
Capital	–	0.3	–	25.0	25.3
1980/81					
Recurrent	134.0	19.0	33.0	51.0	237.0
Capital	–	0.4	0.2	18.0	18.6
1981/82					
Recurrent	158.0	28.0	34.0	63.0	283.0
Capital	–	0.8	0.2	14.0	15.0
1982/83					
Recurrent	177.0	34.0	36.0	76.0	323.0
Capital	–	0.5	0.2	11.0	11.7
Total	624.0	103.1	150.2	333.0	1210.3

(unit: million HKD)

Source: TNA, FCO 40/756, MacLehose to FCO, Tel. 820, 12 August 1977.

---

85. The Budget for 1977–1978.
86. MacLehose to FCO, Telegram No. 820, 12 August 1977, FCO40/756, TNA.
87. Address by the H.E. the Governor, *The Legislative Council Debates Official Report*, 5 October 1977.

hardly satisfied his impatient colleagues back home. In order to speed up the process of change, Heppell, Assistant Secretary in the Department of Health and Social Services of the British government who had been seconded to the Hong Kong government between 1972 and 1974, was sent to the colony. Before his departure, Heppell was reminded of the Governor's pledge on social reforms and the implementation deadline set out in the Planning Paper. More importantly, he was urged to ensure that developments in the colony's social security system could be presented in a good light in the UK.[88]

Heppell's mission had mixed results. On the one hand, he managed to secure a proposal for a voluntary contributory scheme from the Hong Kong government. The scheme would operate on a self-financing basis with a contribution rate of 2 per cent from the employer and was planned to be implemented by 1982. However, the proposed scheme would only provide benefits for sickness, injury, and death; there was no extension of unemployment benefits under this scheme. Heppell was sympathetic to the Hong Kong government and believed that the colonial administration had 'gone as far as feasible'. He viewed the proposed scheme as 'a first step from which progress could be made'.[89] The Governor was not forthcoming on this matter. He argued that:

> [T]he sickness, injury and death benefit scheme, assuming it receives general support, will represent a very considerable innovation in Hong Kong, the significance of which you will of course appreciate. It makes no attempt to emulate social insurance schemes as they have developed in western countries. But we must start off our scheme in a way that is manageable administratively and acceptable socially . . . If we were to go for a fully compulsory scheme, or for a more expensive scheme with higher contributions, we should be unable to carry the Hong Kong people with us.[90]

In an almost self-congratulatory manner, MacLehose believed that he had already done enough to demonstrate his commitment to reforms, claiming that,

> When the parallel new schemes for services to the handicapped, elderly and youth are added, the scale of social security development proposed is pretty ambitious. When it is all put together in a White Paper we will have a clearly defined and comprehensive scheme of payments and services across the whole field.[91]

---

88. A note prepared by Milton, Hong Kong Department, 25 March 1977, FCO40/756, TNA.
89. Record of Meeting held in Mr. Stewart's Office 24 November 1977, FCO40/756, TNA.
90. MacLehose to John Stewart, 30 July 1977, FCO40/756, TNA.
91. MacLehose to John Stewart, 30 July 1977, FCO40/756, TNA.

The FCO officials did not share his confidence as their central complaint was the Governor had failed to meet the agreed timetable for reforms. In short, they found that the Governor's proposal was defective in many ways and was not exactly what London had been pressing for.[92]

The Governor's irritation with these discouraging remarks from London was apparent. MacLehose eventually exploded in a meeting with FCO officials in London in late 1977. When the Labour Adviser argued that the contribution rate of 2 per cent was too low and that the three and a half-year period of implementation was too long, the Governor retorted that under the present social security scheme in Hong Kong, nobody was in serious want and nobody was put in humiliating circumstances, and there had been a major improvement over the last five years. He went on to confront the FCO officials present in the meeting by asking them 'to examine their consciences' as to whether accelerated reform 'would be desirable as a means of improving the welfare for 4½ million people in Hong Kong or to make the scheme look better in the UK'.[93] MacLehose presented himself as representing Hong Kong rather than UK interest.

Conclusion

By the end of 1977, numerous changes in social services and labour legislation had been introduced, MacLehose however had not endeared himself to FCO officials overseeing the implementation of the Planning Paper. In London's eyes, the Governor's commitment to reforms was seen as tentative as MacLehose had not delivered a rapid and comprehensive overhaul of the colony's welfare and social security system that could meet London's strategic and political concerns. For them, what the colonial administration had offered was too little too slow. David Owen, the Foreign Secretary, lectured the Governor in a meeting in late 1977 on his views of the progress so far:

> The principal complaint was that many of the expatriate civil servants there (in Hong Kong) seemed completely out of touch with British ideas and that the public service perhaps needed an injection of new blood. As far as social development was concerned, Hong Kong was proceeding in the right directions. Our only concern was that perhaps the pace was too slow.[94]

---

92. Minutes of the 4th Meeting of the Planning Committee to Monitor the Hong Kong Planning Paper on 11 November 1977, FCO40/755, TNA.
93. Notes taken at the Governor's meeting with Mr. Stewart and Mr. Cortazzi at the FCO on 21 November 1977, FCO40/761, TNA.
94. Minutes of the Meeting between Governor and David Owen, Secretary of State for Foreign and Commonwealth Affairs on 30 November 1977, FCO40/755, TNA.

The Labour administration did not slacken off its efforts to push for further social reform in the colony. During his visit to Hong Kong in April 1978, John Stewart, the Head of the Hong Kong Department of the FCO, presented the Governor with a document which outlined possible developments in the colony beyond the time covered by the Planning Paper. This document was never made known to the general public. London demanded a comprehensive social security system with coverage of unemployment and retirement benefits. MacLehose argued that the people in Hong Kong would dislike the ideas, seeing it as a move towards a Western welfare state. Furthermore, the Governor resolutely refused to commit himself to an overhaul of the colonial system's budgetary system and fiscal procedures.[95]

It was the British voters who came to the 'rescue'. The Labour Party was voted out of power in the 1979 General Election and the momentum for reforms consequently subsided. The neoliberal Thatcher government downgraded the priority of social reforms within the new administration's agenda for Hong Kong. Meanwhile, the Hong Kong government was busily occupied with the arrival of refugees from Vietnam and the influx of illegal migrants from the mainland since 1975. While the impact of refugee inflow had subsided considerably after 1975, there was a dramatic upsurge in late 1978. With all these seismic changes in the broader social, economic, and political environment, attention to labour conditions in Hong Kong reduced significantly. The deceleration of reform was apparent in various fields and the contributory scheme proposed in 1977 was not implemented until the very end of colonial rule under Chris Patten.[96]

This chapter has not set out to tarnish the reformist legacy of MacLehose. Our primary concern has been on the issue of the colony's autonomy. The altercations and dynamics uncovered here reveal that Hong Kong's scope for action was largely determined by the position of the sovereign. Driven by domestic pressure from the left and the right, as well as strategic calculations over the future of Hong Kong, the FCO did not hesitate in imposing a grand scheme of social reforms onto the colonial administration. Officials back home were largely undeterred by or simply indifferent to the Governor's concerns throughout this process. They had little sympathy for MacLehose's reservations about the pace and scope of these changes and their possible repercussions for the local economy. Yet despite London's drive to deviate from its traditional approach and get muddled

---

95. Call by the Governor of Hong Kong on Lord Goronwy-Roberts, Steering Brief: Social Development in Hong Kong after 1980, 25 April 1978, FCO40/954, TNA.
96. For example, the reduction of target of production of public housing units was dropped from 45,000 a year to 35,000 a year was announced in the 1979 Policy Address. Address by the H.E. the Governor, *The Legislative Council Debates Official Report*, 10 October 1979, Hong Kong Legislative Council.

up in the colony's development, the trajectory of these reforms shows that the metropole simply could not unilaterally dictate the course of developments and preordain outcomes. MacLehose and Haddon-Cave stubbornly defended their vision of local interests and tried to implement the reforms at their own pace, even under a façade of subservience and accommodation they had. They were not pushovers, and seemed not to be in thrall to the constitutional asymmetry of power. Through persuasion (via carefully crafted communications with London), by referral to conventions ('the FCO has never done this before'), using threat ('London could ultimately sack the Governor'), by reference to local opinion ('anti-British feeling has been mounting in Hong Kong'), deploying occasional outbursts or even direct confrontation ('the FCO should examine their consciences'), the Governor steered the reform onto a direction he found more comfortable. As an agent with political acumen and skill, MacLehose articulated local concerns even in face of highly motivated intervention from the sovereign. Nevertheless, his room for bargaining was contingent upon a key variable: the strategic interests of the sovereign. When the sovereign found that major concerns were at stake, MacLehose's space for negotiation shrank. The Governor modified, delayed, or even scaled down many of London's initiatives, but most of the proposals listed in the Planning Paper were implemented one way or other. This outcome was also apparent in the case of the Vietnamese boat people crisis, as we will see in Chapter 5, a zero-sum game scenario between London and Hong Kong.

5
Humanitarianism Outsourced
The Vietnamese Refugee Crisis, 1975–1979

Introduction

Colonial Hong Kong was trapped by the politics of the Cold War. As Priscilla Roberts insightfully pointed out, 'economically, intellectually, socially, and culturally, the Cold War years were crucial in ensuring that Hong Kong became a unique and cosmopolitan metropolis'.[1] In the process, the colony had to adapt, respond, and transform its policies in accordance with the demands, challenges, and opportunities unleashed by the global tensions between ideological camps and superpowers. The challenge manifested in the colossal problem of forging a working relationship with the Communist regime across the border was complicated by Hong Kong's role as a platform for the Americans' anti-China propaganda and surveillance.[2] The Cold War's impact on Hong Kong stretched much further than the arduous task of living with China. This chapter concerns a neglected episode from this era: the Vietnamese refugee crisis of 1975–1979.

The exodus of refugees from Vietnam in the immediate aftermath of the conclusion of the Vietnam War was due to the dislocation of the communist takeover in Vietnam. However, it was subsequently accelerated by the realignment of the major powers in the latter part of 1970s. China backed the Vietnamese communists between 1970 and 1975, but this level of support was unsustainable. The deteriorating Sino-Vietnamese relationship prompted the Beijing-backed regime of Pol Pot in Cambodia to attack Vietnam in 1977, leading to Vietnamese counter-offensive that toppled Pol Pot's authority. Beijing retaliated with a brief war with Vietnam in 1979,

---

1. Priscilla Roberts, 'Prologue: Cold War Hong Kong: The Foundations', in *Hong Kong in the Cold War*, ed. Priscilla Roberts and John Carroll (Hong Kong: Hong Kong University Press, 2016).
2. Nancy Tucker, *China Confidential: American Diplomats and Sino-American Relations, 1945–1996* (New York: Columbia University Press, 2001); John Carroll, *Edge of Empire: Chinese Elites and British Colonials in Hong Kong* (Cambridge, MA: Harvard University Press, 2005).

and anti-Chinese policies in Vietnam triggered a massive exodus of local Chinese. The rising role of the Soviet Union in Indo-China also drove Beijing closer to the West.

Hong Kong was caught up in this crisis. As a gateway to the 'free world', Hong Kong became an ideal halfway point for the refugees. Even more importantly, the approach and response of the colony was primarily driven and dictated by the obligations and duties attendant on its role as a colony of Britain. Britain had been obsessed with its special relationship with the United States, with maintaining cordiality with Washington a priority of the British Government since 1945. While the United States was prepared to accommodate a substantial number of Vietnamese with American ties, Washington also expected a global response to the humanitarian crisis, and thus Britain was 'obligated' to entertain the concerns of its most valuable ally.

This is a tale of the colony's balancing act in accommodating both domestic pressure and the expectations of the sovereign power and international community. London's proclaimed commitment to humanitarianism did not manifest in deeds. Despite its prevailing rhetoric of good citizenship in the global community, British government's assistance to Hong Kong was limited. The UK arguably outsourced her humanitarian responsibility to Hong Kong. As a result, the colony shouldered the burden of supporting tens of thousands of refugees, in spite of her own acute housing crisis and influx of illegal immigrants from mainland China. The rise of Margaret Thatcher and her proactive approach in addressing the crisis was a false dawn. Hong Kong benefited from the United Nations Conference in Geneva in 1979, but the colony was still compelled to allow a substantial number of refugees to remain in Hong Kong. The Conference however confirmed Hong Kong's role in the US-designated global scheme for tackling the crisis. The colony was assigned as the role of port of first asylum, a holding space where applicants for refugee status and resettlement elsewhere would be pre-screened. This is a story of the futile attempt of the colony to negotiate with London. Instead, Hong Kong was deployed a leverage in London's attempt to evade responsibility in the theatre of international politics. When the sovereign's key concerns were at stake, the colony's room for bargaining promptly evaporated.

The Arrival of the *Clara Maersk* in 1975

Hong Kong watched the development of the Vietnam War in the early 1970s with great trepidation. The signs of an exodus were already on the horizon with the escalation of military action and the growing vulnerability of the

US-supported regime in the south of Vietnam. In 1974, a group of 119 Vietnamese was smuggled to Hong Kong with the assistance of criminal networks, but the colony handled this inflow with relative ease, and succeeded in repatriating the majority of these people to Vietnam. 'We will be keeping a close watch on events and deal with any situation when it arrives. All is quiet now,' said the Director of Immigration, attempting to put on a brave face in anticipation of what was in store.[3] This encounter was, however, a mere harbinger of the crisis to come. The eventual withdrawal of American forces from Vietnam and the fall of Saigon in April 1975 unleashed a global humanitarian crisis with inflows of refugees into Hong Kong lasting next two decades.

4 May of 1975 was a day of historic significance for the colony. The local community was in a jubilant mood as HRH Queen Elizabeth II and Prince Philip commenced their first royal visit to the colony. On the same day, however, a Danish-registered ship, *Clara Maersk*, with 3,750 Vietnamese on board, arrived in the proximity of Hong Kong waters. The mayhem began. The refugee crisis could not have hit the colony at a worse time, for Hong Kong had been struggling with an acute housing shortage in the post-war years and had just taken major initiatives to tackle the issue. The challenge was further compounded by the massive influx of migrants from China which had continued since the communist takeover in 1949, spiking during the famine in the late 1950s and the chaos of the Cultural Revolution. In the year of 1975 there were, on average, 3,000 mainland Chinese illegally entering the territory of Hong Kong every month. The Vietnamese refugee crisis thus could not be tackled in isolation. As MacLehose noted, 'the fact that illegal Chinese emigrants are being sent back to China makes it hard for the local population to accept that non-Chinese Vietnamese with no claim on Hong Kong should be allowed to remain here while their own people are returned.'[4]

How would Hong Kong respond? The Hong Kong government honoured its duty as the Danish ship's port of first call offering these refugees temporary shelter. Special camps were set up where they waited for decisions of foreign governments on whether they could be admitted. The stranded refugees were fed and given medical care. The colony was praised as a 'beacon of civility' during this trying time.[5] American officials, for instance, were full of appreciation for the efforts of the Hong Kong government. A report of an American Congressional study mission to Hong Kong stated:

---

3. *South China Morning Post*, 4 April 1975.
4. MacLehose to FCO, 8 May 1975, FCO40/651, TNA.
5. Diana Lary, 'Review of *Elusive Refuge: Chinese Migrants in the Cold War*, by Laura Madokoro', *Pacific Affairs* 90, no. 4 (2017): 793–795.

> The civilians and the officials of the Government of Hong Kong should be commended for their efforts on behalf of these refugees who suddenly descended on them . . . Even though the facilities were crude, under the conditions prevailing in the area, they were satisfactory and showed a human concern for the refugee plight.[6]

In short, Hong Kong was acclaimed for its 'generosity, magnanimity, humanitarian assistance commodities to help them start starting a new life in free countries'.[7]

Hong Kong's concern for refugees was to a certain extent attributable to its long history of relief work as provided by international organizations, local philanthropy, and religious groups. The charitable works of local groups such as Tung Wah were crucial to the survival of the underprivileged in the territory, and services supplied by the Roman Catholic Church had been critical in the provision of social support for the poor and unfortunate in the colony. The arrival of the London Missionary Society, the Lutheran World Federation, the Methodist Committee for Overseas Relief, and later the American Friends Service Committee, further consolidated the central role of international and religious groups in relief work.[8]

Yet underneath, the Hong Kong government's benevolent stance was not wholly driven by altruism. From day one, Hong Kong officials were fully aware of the gravity of the refugee issue. Hong Kong could provide transitory accommodation, but it assumed that the ultimate solution required a global response. The Hong Kong government expected its liberal approach might help garner positive feedback from the international community, especially in the United States, as Washington acknowledged publicly its obligation. As outlined by President Lyndon Johnson in his address to a joint session of Congress on the eve of the fall of Saigon,

> I must, of course, as I think each of you would, consider the safety of nearly 6,000 Americans who remain in South Vietnam, and tens of thousands of South Vietnamese employees of the United States government, of news agencies, of contractors and businesses for many years whose lives, with their dependents, are in very grave peril. There are tens of thousands of other South Vietnamese intellectuals, professors, teachers, editors and opinion-leaders who have supported the South Vietnamese cause and

---

6. Congress on Indochina Evacuation 1975, 'Study Mission Report of Minority Counsel Prepared for the Use of the Subcommittee to Investigate Problems Connected with Refugees and Escapees of the Committee on the Judiciary, United States Senate, July 8, 1975', 8 July 1975, RG0342, Entry P89, Box 7, National Archives and Records Administration (hereafter 'NARA'), 39.
7. *Wah Kiu Yat Po*, 10 June 1975.
8. Lary, Review of *Elusive Refuge*.

the alliance with the United States, to whom we have a profound moral obligation.[9]

The Congress swiftly passed the Indochina Migration and Refugee Assistance Act, authorizing the admission of 130,000 Vietnamese to the United States. These included 4,000 orphans under 'Operation Babylift'. Among the rest were relatives of American citizens and permanent resident aliens, employees of the American government, firms, or voluntary agencies, and individuals of high intelligence value to the US government. The military base in Guam was designated as a holding area for these refugees before they were relocated to other facilities for further processing and resettlement.[10]

'Maximum internationalization' was, nevertheless, the cornerstone of American response to the refugee crisis. Washington wanted a global response and used Hong Kong to secure one. The US Consul-General informed the colonial administration that it was highly unlikely that Washington would agree to admit the group which had come to Hong Kong to Guam, as the facility there was already overcrowded. Besides, such action would likely draw 'severe criticism' from Congress as, unlike those who were included in the evacuation operation, the group picked up by the Danish vessel had fled Vietnam on their own initiative.[11] State Department officials reiterated their irritation with the negative response or indifference of other countries and were determined to bring their concerns before the international community. Reciprocity was thus expected from anyone who wanted support from the United States in tackling the immediate refugee crisis, and that was where Britain made itself a nuisance to the colony.

Indifference of London

Hong Kong government consulted London about the handling of the *Clara Maersk* incident, given the diplomatic implication for UK–US relationships. The British government was, however, very reluctant to offer substantial assistance to the colony. Arrival of non-white immigrants and refugees had been a divisive issue in British politics since the 1950s. During the colonial era, the British government actively encouraged British passport holders of South Asian origin to move to the territories now known as Kenya, Uganda,

---

9. Congress on IndoChina Evacuation 1975, 'IndoChina Evacuation and Refugee Problems: A Study Mission Report Prepared for the Use of the Subcommittee to Investigate Problems connected with Refugees and Escapees of the Committee on the Judiciary, United States Senate', 9 June 1975, RG0342 Entry P89 Box 7, NARA, 5.
10. Congress on IndoChina Evacuation 1975, 7.
11. MacLehose to British Embassy in Washington, 5 May 1975, FCO40/651, TNA.

Humanitarianism Outsourced

and Tanzania to help develop their local economies. These Asian immigrants settled down as indentured labourers, traders, shopkeepers, and small business owners, successfully forming the middle layer of East Africa's political economy. After independence in these African countries, however, the fate of the small Asian communities took an unpleasant turn. They were regarded as economic exploiters and were scapegoated for the shortcomings of fellow Africans. The new governments in Nairobi, Kampala, and Dar es Salaam deprived them of immigration and trading rights, as well as property. Consequently, Asians started leaving East Africa. As British passport holders, most migrated unrestricted to the UK, but their arrival soon provoked hostile reactions from the public. The British government was under immense pressure to restrict this inflow and legislations were passed in 1962 and 1968 with stricter border control. The Commonwealth Immigrants Act of 1962 required all British nationals in the Commonwealth to apply for a limited number of employment vouchers. The law was amended in 1968 with the introduction of the concept of 'belonging'—'UK belongers' were confined to those who were born in, naturalized, or adopted to the UK or had at least one parent or grandparent in that category. The Heath government imposed further control with a new legislation in 1971 that virtually equalized the status of British passport holders outside Britain to that of aliens.[12]

These legislative efforts were however futile in reversing the tide with the development in Uganda in 1972. In January 1971, General Idi Amin Dada took power in Uganda in a military coup. On 4 August 1972, Amin announced the expulsion of all Asians within ninety days. By the deadline, about 27,000 Ugandan Asian citizens of the UK and colonies migrated to Britain.[13] Overall, by 1973 approximately 103,588 Asians had entered Britain from East Africa.[14] At a time when Britain was under the challenges of rising employment, a housing shortage, growing inflation and strikes, it was thus hardly surprising to see the rise of xenophobia and racism in British politics.[15] Protests with signs like 'Britain for the British' and calls for the end to all immigration had been common since the 1960s, and the toxic mood was further sustained by xenophobic speeches by politicians

---

12. Sara Cosemans, 'Undesirable British East African Asians. Nationalities, Statelessness and Refugeehood after Empire', *Immigrants & Minorities* 40, no. 1–2 (2022): 210–239.
13. Cosemans, 'Undesirable British East African Asians', 229.
14. John Mattausch, 'From Subjects to Citizens: British "East African Asians"', *Journal of Ethnic and Migration Studies* 24, no. 1 (1998): 135.
15. Saima Nasar, 'When Uganda Expelled Its Asian Population in 1972, Britain Tried to Exclude Them', *New Line Magazine*, 12 August 2022.

like Enoch Powell.[16] Under these circumstances, the Hong Kong government hardly endeared itself to Britain with the Vietnamese refugee issue.

Britain's assistance in alleviating Hong Kong's predicament was limited. Whitehall departments were mostly indifferent to the colony's plight, although there were a few voices in the FCO advocating for the colony to be supported. '[We] cannot expect the Hong Kong population to play its part if there is no evident concerns on ours', a FCO official proclaimed candidly.[17] Yet in a reply to the internal lobbying in the FCO on the behalf of Hong Kong, a Home Office official in charge of aid allocation showed little sympathy for the colony:

> As I do not have to tell you, Hong Kong is among the richest of the 'developing' territories and not normally regarded as a suitable recipient of aid funds. While I take the cost of a relief operation would put some strain on the colony's financial resources, the financial resources of the United Kingdom are at present under strain themselves and I think that it would be argued that this was a contribution to the refugee problem which the colony could reasonably be expected to undertake itself.[18]

Another official also tried to justify London's reluctance to help on the grounds that such generosity could offer other countries an escape route:

> We do not, however, want to run the risk of offering so much that potential recipient countries will feel relieved of the necessity to offer permanent homes; nor to take on an open-ended commitment which would imply that the remaining refugees will be staying on in Hong Kong indefinitely.[19]

Fortunately, the relentless lobbying effort of Hong Kong eventually persuaded London to raise its financial assistance from £20,000 to £70,000, though the colony had to shoulder two-thirds of the total cost of HKD 4.28 million in accommodating the *Clara Maersk* group,[20] and was asked to pay HKD 93,000 to the British Ministry of Defence for the services of the British armed forces in receiving and accommodating the refugees from the *Clara Maersk*.[21] Haddon-Cave, the Financial Secretary of Hong Kong, was also

---

16. Enoch Powell, Conservative MP, made his infamous 'Rivers of Blood' speech in Birmingham on 20 April 1968, criticizing mass immigration into Britain. This speech created a political storm and led to his dismissal from the Shadow Cabinet by Edward Heath.
17. Rae to O'Keeffe, 21 April 1975, FCO40/651, TNA.
18. Rae to O'Keeffe, 21 April 1975, FCO40/651, TNA.
19. O'Keeffe to Williams, 16 June 1975, FCO40/653, TNA.
20. Dinwiddy, Hong Kong and Indian Ocean Department to Drace-Francis, Assistant Political Adviser to Hong Kong Government, 29 August 1975, FCO40/654, TNA, and Vietnamese Refugees in Hong Kong between 1 August 1975 and 30 November 1975, 22 March 1976, FCO40/719, TNA.
21. Hong Kong Government to FCO, 26 June 1975, FCO40/653, TNA.

reminded by the British Treasury that he would 'have to produce detailed evidence that he has not embezzled the money'.[22]

UK financial assistance was not the primary concern of the Hong Kong government; what mattered most was Britain's acknowledgement that it must admit a substantial number of refugees from the *Clara Maersk* group, which would, in turn, make similar commitments by other powers more likely. Initially, Britain only agreed to consider seventy-one refugees from the group stranded in the colony, so long as these applicants had proven British ties.[23] While the number was lamentable since, by then, even the colony had agreed to accept at least fifty-eight refugees, the main concern of the Hong Kong administration was the influence of this paltry British commitment on other countries. Local officials warned that it would be difficult to elicit sympathy from America if Britain appeared to have done so little.[24] Officials of the United Nations High Commission for Refugees shared a similar observation. They believed that the lobbying efforts in other former British territories, such as those in the Caribbean, would be difficult if the UK herself had taken no refugees.[25] Even British diplomats found the situation embarrassing. 'One further reason for our not taking a stronger line (of lobbying) with the Americans is of course our own performance,' a FCO official admitted.[26] A more candid view can be found in another communication:

> There has been no suggestion, either from this Department or from the Hong Kong Government, that the UK might be a haven of last resort for the residue who have nowhere else to go. The crucial point, as I explained on the telephone, is that unless and until the refugees wanting to come here are allowed to do so, we are effectively unable to assist Hong Kong in any new initiative to seek homes (in the United States or elsewhere) for the rest. Moreover, the continuing delay is the subject of increasing embarrassing criticism in Hong Kong which, in the absence of a favourable decision, would almost certainly give rise to questions in Parliament after the recess.[27]

Understandably, the lukewarm response of the sovereign power drew the colony's ire. Members of the Executive Council were resentful. British officials were even warned by the Governor that they would receive a hostile reception during their prospective visit to Hong Kong:

---

22. Drace-Francis to O'Keeffe, 6 August 1975, FCO40/653, TNA.
23. From MacLehose, 26 May 1975, FCO40/653, TNA.
24. Note for the Record: Vietnamese Refugees by Drace-Francis, 14 July 1975, FCO40/653, TNA.
25. Note for the Record: Vietnamese Refugees by Drace-Francis, 14 July 1975, FCO40/653, TNA.
26. Wotton to O'Keeffe, 1 August 1975, FCO40/653, TNA.
27. O'Keeffe to Taylor, Home Office, 12 September 1975, FCO40/654, TNA.

One difficulty which further representations in Hague or elsewhere are likely to encounter is if the authorities approached ask what Britain has done to help Hong Kong in this matter. I apologise for harping on this point, but I have just come out of an Executive Council meeting where there was some overt sarcastic comment, particularly by senior Chinese Unofficials, on the fact that none of the Vietnamese refugees here have yet been accepted by Britain. I fear that you will meet considerable criticism on this score when you come out here next month unless you can bring with you some Indication of whether the UK would be prepared to accept some of the refugees who have applied to go there.[28]

The Home Office was eventually swayed to make a concession, with the maximum intake quota raised to 150, but it was reiterated that this was 'an exception to the general policy' of the British government on the issue of refugees. The colony was also made aware that this was the 'final contribution to this refugee resettlement problem related to the Danish vessel in Hong Kong' and with London 'not prepared to accept responsibility for any residue left in Hong Kong'.[29] Hong Kong was also told that this concession was also 'made on the understanding that (British) government funds will not be committed' to pay for the travel and relocation expense of these refugees.[30]

An American Plan for Hong Kong

The British approach to the refugee crisis was simple: pay lip service to international obligations, ensure that humanitarianism was not misread as commitment to financial contribution and refugee intake, keep a low profile, and let others take the lead in handling this crisis. There was, however, one issue with this approach: the imperative of placating the United States. The handling of another refugee ship, the *Ava*, in 1976, illustrates the British priority of addressing the American concern.

In early July 1976, a Burmese vessel with ninety-nine Vietnamese refugees on board arrived in Hong Kong waters. The vessel was originally scheduled to unload 1,700 tons of cargo in Hong Kong, and for another 7,000 tons to be discharged in Japan. Learning from the painful experience of the *Clara Maersk* crisis the previous year, the Hong Kong government was determined not to grant landing permission to the ship. The colonial administration was worried that a lenient response might set a precedent

---

28. Drace-Francis to O'Keeffe, 6 August 1975, FCO40/653, TNA.
29. Home Office to O'Keeffe, 3 October 1975, FCO40/652, TNA.
30. Telegram from Callaghan, 13 October 1975, FCO40/652, TNA.

that may encourage other ships to bring refugees to Hong Kong.[31] Hong Kong officials believed that since the vessel was registered in Burma, it was the responsibility of the Burmese government to accept these refugees.[32] The Hong Kong government even offered to airlift this group to Rangoon. Unsurprisingly, the Burmese rejected the proposition flatly.[33]

Hong Kong officials remained undeterred. Denys Roberts, the Colonial Secretary, launched an ardent defence of the colony's position in a communication to the FCO arguing that the colony had already done more than its fair share by offering temporary shelter for more than 4,000 refugees the previous year. The Secretary went on to criticize the United Nation Higher Commission for Refugees (UNHCR) for making 'little practical contribution' to the resettlement of refugees. He found the Commissioner's proposed solution to the *Ava* crisis unacceptable. The Commission pledged to offer financial support in return for Hong Kong granting permission for the *Ava* to land. Roberts argued that, if the UNHCR was prepared to be 'generous', it should extend the same offer to Burma in return for the latter's role as a temporary place of first asylum. For Hong Kong, this was the 'test case', with a danger, if mishandled, of becoming a dumping ground for any refugees rescued in the South China Sea. Unfortunately, this was exactly what Washington expected Hong Kong to do in the global response to the refugee crisis. On this matter, London initially stood behind Hong Kong, but its position changed quickly after an intervention by the United States.

The Americans had a three-pronged approach for tackling the Vietnamese refugee crisis. Firstly, the US admitted key responsibility in addressing the issue and was prepared to make major contributions in terms of financial support and refugee intake. Secondly, all other nations in the world should also contribute, with UNHCR playing a major role in coordination and logistical support. Lastly, nations in South-East Asia should perform a distinctive role as port of first asylum, a temporary refuge for those rescued at high sea, pending resettlement decisions across the world. For the US, the *Ava* issue was thus a test case to turn her grand global response scheme into reality. Understandably, Washington was extremely irritated by the Hong Kong government's firmness in refusing the *Ava* permission to land.

Washington appealed to the UNHCR to 'exert moral leadership' and reiterated its expectation that host governments allow ships with refugees

---

31. Hong Kong, 6 July 1976, FCO40/719, TNA.
32. O'Keeffe to Cortazzi, 13 July 1976, FCO40/719, TNA.
33. Hong Kong to FCO, 9 July 1976, FCO40/719, TNA.

on board to land and promise to provide them with 'reasonable assistance'.[34] The pressure was swiftly raised with a targeted comment on Hong Kong, that 'the correct policy, based on standard international practice and basic humanitarian considerations, should be to allow the refugees to land' in a US rebuttal to London's defence of the colony's position.[35] Meanwhile, a team of officials from the American Consulate-General in Hong Kong was airlifted to the *Ava*, where they conducted a series of preliminary interviews with the refugees on board. This led to an interim decision that thirty-nine members of this group would be considered for entry visas to the United States, providing that further rounds of interviews could be arranged. The US State Department insisted, however, that formal interviews and the final assessment of eligibility must take place on shore.[36] In other words, no landing permission, no chance of any American intake. The Hong Kong government, however, was not prepared to budge.[37] American officials became therefore 'extremely disturbed' and warned about of the 'disastrous consequence', that ships' captains could be incentivized to turn a blind eye to refugees in unworthy vessels in the future.[38] Washington could not stomach that her grand plan was derailed by this tiny British colony.

At this boiling point of diplomatic wrangling, a dramatic twist occurred. The UNHCR, which coming under intense pressure to resolve the dispute, gained permission of the Japanese government to unload *Ava* in Yokohama.[39] The Hong Kong government was elated and quickly commenced arrangements for the departure of the vessel. The Americans were furious. On the instruction of the State Department, the American Embassy in London demanded that the *Ava* should not be allowed to sail for Yokohama. London was swayed by the reaction of its most important ally and instructed Hong Kong to put plans on hold. After further deliberation in the FCO, with ministers heavily involved in discussions, a 'difficult decision' which 'much depends on the attitude of the Americans' was conveyed to the colony: the captain of the *Ava* should be told to land in Hong Kong.[40]

The Hong Kong government was frustrated by this 'difficult decision'. A further delay of the landing arrangements provided the trigger point for their ultimate confrontation. Colonial officials believed that it would look better to the local population if the whole matter was handled by UNHCR officials, and so they wanted to wait for its representative,

---

34. From Roberts, Hong Kong to FCO, 16 July 1976, FCO40/719, TNA.
35. From Washington to FCO, 16 July 1976, FCO40/719, TNA.
36. Ramsbotham to Hong Kong, 20 July 1976, FCO40/719, TNA.
37. Roberts to FCO, 23 July 1972, FCO40/719, TNA.
38. UK Mission in Washington to FCO, 23 July 1976, FCO40/719, TNA.
39. Tokyo to FCO, 23 July 1976, FCO40/719, TNA.
40. O'Keeffe to Larmour, 26 July 1976, FCO40/719, TNA.

Rajagopalan Sampatkumar, to arrive before the landing and relocation proceeded. Officials in London were unimpressed. The Foreign Minister, Lord Goronwy-Roberts, found it irritating and his suspicion of Hong Kong's defiance was further aroused by a public statement from the colonial administration. After the ship had docked, Hong Kong's Director of Immigration issued a press release stating:

> [T]he support we have received from the United Nations and from the governments of the United States, Canada and France has been most gratifying, and I am happy that we are now in a position to land these refugees temporarily in Hong Kong.[41]

There was no acknowledgement in this statement of the assistance provided the British government. MacLehose was warned that senior officials in London had read this as a slight on their part and warned that the minister 'would have taken it very badly'.[42] MacLehose explained that this was not his intention but there was strong hint of his displeasure in his response,

> Could not someone have rung us up and told us that no one in London could understand from our telegrams what we were about, that tempers were rising, and that a better explanation needed to be given to Ministers? It is so much more important to avoid misunderstandings developing than merely to allocate blame afterwards.[43]

He added that he found London's lack of empathy 'all very sad'.[44] He argued that all parties concerned, apart from London, were happy with the arrangement made by the Hong Kong government:

> Morale on the *Ava* is tremendously high because a reasonable and humane solution has been found. The Burmese too are delighted that the responsibility has been taken away from them . . . the Americans here are pleased with the way we and they are 'internationalizing' the problem.[45]

Special Processing Centre for Refugees: Hong Kong Excluded

Despite an uneasiness about London's positioning on the handling of refugee issue, Hong Kong needed the British government to represent the colony in the theatre of global diplomacy. The UK, although no longer a world leader, remained a significant player with substantial leverage. The development of the scheme of the Special Processing Centre in 1978 is

---

41. MacLehose to FCO, 30 July 1976, FCO40/720, TNA.
42. Cortazzi to MacLehose, 4 August 1976, FCO40/720, TNA.
43. MacLehose to Cortazzi, 18 August 1976, FCO40/720, TNA.
44. MacLehose to Cortazzi, 20 August 1976, TNA FCO40/720, TNA.
45. MacLehose to Cortazzi, 20 August 1976, TNA FCO40/720, TNA.

illustrative of the multi-faceted relationship between the sovereign and the colony.

The refugee situation in Indochina deteriorated further in 1978, with a surge in refugees from Vietnam. In that year, Vietnam witnessed the gravest food crisis in the country's history, as well as accelerated attempts at a socialist transformation. The Chinese community in Vietnam was particularly hard hit by the latter, as many had made a living as small traders in the local economy.[46] A rift between China and Vietnam also reinforced the persecution of ethnic Chinese within the territory. Hanoi's cordiality with the Soviet Union and growing aggression towards Cambodia, together with Beijing's support for Pol Pot's regime eventually culminated in China's 'punitive attacks' against Vietnam in early 1979.[47] All of these factors contributed to the spike in the outflow of refugees from late 1978. In May 1979, the monthly average of people seeking refuge overseas from Vietnam in small boats was 50,000, and many more left the country overland.[48]

For Hong Kong, the repercussions of these shifts were serious, with arrivals jumping from 1,001 in 1977 to 9,115 in 1978, and to the unprecedented high of 68,748 in 1979. These refugees mainly arrived in small fishing boats, which made it very challenging to deny them entry. The *Hong Kong Annual Report* provides a vivid account of the distressing scenes of the arrival of the small boats:

> They came in small decrepit craft, rickety junks with rotten timbers and tattered sails—anything that could be driven by motor or wind, loaded to the gunwales with desperate fugitives of all ages. Watching these frail hulks being towed into the harbor an observer could well believe estimates that for every refugee who sailed from Vietnam and arrived safely on the shores of a neighbouring territory, another refugee lost his life at sea.[49]

Lewis Davies, Secretary for Security of the Hong Kong Government, concluded on another occasion that 'tougher measures are not easily devised for smaller boat people. In that ultimate this means really towing or committing men, women, and children to their death. To argue that this is what public opinion would like would not salve my conscience in these

---

46. Ronald Skeldon, 'Hong Kong's Response to Indochinese Influx, 1975–93', *The Annals of the American Academy of Political and Social Science* 534, no. 1 (1994), https://doi.org/10.1177/00027 16294534001008.
47. Lien-Hang T. Nguyen, 'The Vietnam Decade: The Global Shock of the War', in *Shock of the Global: The 1970s in Perspective*, ed. Niall Ferguson, Charles Maier, Erez Manela, and Daniel Sargent (Cambridge, MA: Harvard University Press, 2010), 159–172.
48. FCO Background Brief: Refugees from Indochina: International Action Urged, 19 June 1979, FCO40/1100, TNA.
49. The *Annual Hong Kong Report* 1976, 4.

circumstances and I do not really think it is in the ultimate what Hong Kong really wants.'[50]

For Hong Kong, soliciting international assistance was even more difficult with the change in the background of the refugees. Some 80 per cent of the arrivals from Vietnam in 1979 were ethnic Chinese.[51] The dominant Chinese ethnicity of the new wave undermined the prospect of their relocation. Most Chinese in Vietnam did not have strong American ties. Concerns over the possible political impact of a massive intake of Chinese refugees also heightened the reluctance of other Asian countries to grant them admission. Malaysia, for example, simply rejected any intake of ethnic Chinese refugees from Vietnam on security grounds, since this might disrupt the country's delicate domestic racial balance. It was argued that '[t]he local people there feared and distrusted Malaysia's existing Chinese population; they just couldn't put up with boat loads of extra Chinese washing up on their shores'.[52] Furthermore, Vietnam's aggression in Indochina, which was backed by the Soviet Union, caused Washington to focus instead on the refugee situation in Thailand, Cambodia, and Laos. In a meeting with MacLehose in Washington on 18 June 1979, Richard Clark, the US Coordinator for Refugee Affairs, confirmed this official line. Clark revealed a candid assessment of the latest situation in Indochina in which he emphasized America's 'particular responsibility towards certain land-crossers from Laos to Thailand who had previous connections with the United States'.[53] In short, Vietnamese Chinese refugees were not Washington's top priority. Unfortunately for Hong Kong, the refugee crisis in the colony thus rapidly spiralled out of control.

Washington responded to the unremitting outflow of refugees with renewed enthusiasm for the scheme of overseas processing and pre-screening of resettlement eligibility. In addition to Guam, some of the military facilities on Wake Island, at the Subic Bay naval base, the Clark air force base, and on U-Tapao Island, were turned into temporary shelters for further processing of the refugees before they were cleared for admission into continental America. Extensive coordination among federal, state, local government, community organizations, and voluntary agencies was imperative for a smooth resettlement process, while the political need to minimize the impact of resettlement on localities suffering a high rate of

---

50. Official Report of Proceedings, 6 June 1979, Hong Kong Legislative Council, 902.
51. Skeldon, 'Hong Kong's Response'.
52. Munro to Simons, 20 June 1979, FCO40/1101, TNA.
53. Most of these refugees were originally from Vietnam. From Jay, British Embassy in Washington to FO, 18 June 1979, FCO40/1100, TNA.

unemployment was also considered.[54] Yet the capacity of these facilities was quickly swamped by the incessant influx of refugees. Washington expected more from her Asian allies.

In December 1978, Indonesia and Malaysia agreed to give serious consideration to the idea of acting as pre-screening sites, provided that there was a pledge from the international community that no refugee would remain in these facilities after a specified period of time.[55] Indonesia appeared to be even more forthcoming, and offered the UNHCR Galang Island, two hours by sea from Singapore, for the installation of facilities that formed a so-called special processing centre, with the capacity to hold 5,000 to 10,000 refugees.[56] The US government responded positively to the initiative and 'saw its main advantage as lying in the fact that it would extend the refugee "pipeline", and encourage countries of first asylum to continue to take in the boat people'.

MacLehose feared this scheme would attract more refugees into this region, but 'the high cost of maintenance in Hong Kong argue for transfer of long-term refugees to a cheaper processing centre'. Thus, he was prepared to make a financial contribution towards its establishment if Hong Kong would be allowed to transfer 500 of its refugee population to this facility. The problem was that the ASEAN counties were not prepared to allow Hong Kong this access. The Indonesian Foreign Minister made it categorically clear that this was entirely an ASEAN affair and would not accommodate refugees stranded in the colony.[57] ASEAN countries did not want to create precedent leading to requests from other jurisdictions like Macau or even China.[58] MacLehose was not easily deterred, and he placed his hopes on London to lobby on Hong Kong's behalf. The invitation to participate in the consultative meeting in Jakarta in May 1979 to discuss the prospect of setting up a special processing centre offered London a good opportunity to pursue Hong Kong's admission.

British diplomats made considerable efforts on the behalf of the colony. They managed to convince their European allies of the legitimacy of Hong Kong's request, with Germany and Italy agreeing to voice their support for

---

54. IndoChina Evacuation and Refugee Problems: A Study Mission Report Prepared for the Use of the Subcommittee to Investigate Problems connected with Refugees and Escapees of the Committee on the Judiciary, United States Senate, Congress on IndoChina Evacuation 1975, 9 June 1975, RG0342 Entry P89 Box 7, NARA, 17–18.
55. Record of a Meeting between Mr Luard, Parliamentary Under-Secretary of State for Foreign and Commonwealth Affairs, and Tan Sri Muhamed Ghazali Bin Shafie, Malaysia Minister of Home Affairs, held at the Foreign and Commonwealth Office at 10:20am on Friday, 15 December 1978, FCO40/998, TNA.
56. Visit of Mr. De Haan, Deputy High Commissioner for Refugees, to South East Asia, 26 February–19 March 1976, FCO40/1093, TNA.
57. T. J. O'Brien to Smith, 1 April 1979, FCO40/1094, TNA.
58. Obrien to British delegation to Jakarta Conference, 15 May 1979, FCO40/1095, TNA.

Hong Kong in the forthcoming meeting in Jakarta.[59] They also seized the opportunity of a meeting with Richard Holbrook, the US Assistant Secretary for East Asian and Pacific Affairs, to make the case for the colony. Holbrook agreed that Hong Kong had a particularly serious problem and found her request for admission 'a very fair proposition'. Nevertheless, Washington was not prepared to make her 'support' for Hong Kong public in Jakarta. Henry Cushing, the US Deputy Director of the Office of Refugees admitted that 'they would rather have a centre, which was less than perfect in that Hong Kong was excluded, than no centre at all'. He hoped that the launch of the Indonesian facilities would encourage others to follow, as the Philippines had begun to contemplate establishing similar facilities. For these reasons, Washington was reluctant to intervene on behalf of Hong Kong for its inclusion. Instead, the colony was also advised by the US not to press its case too hard lest it may disrupt the initiative.[60]

There was another important factor which undermined the impact of London's efforts: the UK government's poor track record in refugee intake. By May 1979, Britain had only accepted 174 Vietnamese refugees from Hong Kong.[61] London had indeed sensed the danger that over-enthusiasm for Hong Kong could draw unwelcome attention to her own track record and adjusted her strategy in Jakarta accordingly. Consequently, Lord Carrington, the Foreign Secretary, instructed the British diplomats that, while the principal objective of the delegation was to ensure that Hong Kong would have access in principle to the processing centre, the British representatives should in general lay low and if directly asked, should make it clear that the United Kingdom would not make a commitment to a new quota of refugee intakes from the Indochina region.[62] This order was dutifully followed, and the official statement of the British delegation to the Jakarta meeting unequivocally stated that 'there is no present prospect of Britain accepting further quota of refugees from this region'.[63] Unsurprisingly, these British efforts failed to secure a positive outcome for the colony. Hong Kong's request for admission into the scheme was not entertained in Jakarta, though it was agreed, as a courtesy, that the matter would be referred to the ASEAN members for further discussion.

---

59. Carrington to UK Mission in Geneva, 18 May 1979, FCO40/1095, TNA.
60. Minutes of the Meeting with Richard Holbrook, 18 May 1979, FCO40/1095, TNA.
61. Morgan to Murray, 29 May 1979, FCO40/1096, TNA.
62. Lord Carrington's Instruction for British Diplomats on UK Position in Jakarta, 11 May 1979, FCO 40/1095, TNA.
63. Statement by the British Delegate in Meeting of a Processing Centre for Indo-China Refugees, May 1979 (date not specified), FCO40/1097, TNA.

MacLehose Reaching Out

The colony was trapped in the abyss of a refugee crisis, and MacLehose was desperate. During the first four months of 1979, a total of 20,204 refugees arrived; only 2,612 departed for resettlement elsewhere.[64] By May 1979, there were 58,000 refugees in Hong Kong awaiting resettlement (see Table 5.1). Worse still, Washington had moreover backed down from its promise of a monthly intake of 750 from the colony. The number was cut to 400 for April and May of 1979.[65] The US quotas were reassigned to other Asian nations including Malaysia and Thailand. MacLehose felt compelled to take up the task to reach out to the world.

Table 5.1: Vietnamese refugees situation in Southeast Asia by 1 May 1979

Country	Number of refugees
Thailand	200,000 (mainly Laotians and Cambodians)
Malaysia	75,000
Hong Kong	58,000
Indonesia	31,200
Macao	1,800
Philippines	1,600
Japan	400
Singapore	300

Source: Vietnamese Refugees: The Facts, 1979, FCO 40/1101, p. 7, TNA.

MacLehose arrived in Washington in mid-June 1979 with a hectic schedule ahead of him. He was granted meetings with almost all of the top US officials involved in the Indochina refugee crisis. Among these were Warren Christopher (US Deputy Secretary of State), Richard Holbrook (Assistant Secretary for East Asian and Pacific Affairs), and Richard Clark (US Refugee Coordinator). MacLehose made the precarious situation in Hong Kong very clear: the colony had not only been hit by the influx of refugees from Vietnam, but there was also a steady stream of illegal immigrants from China. Many of these Vietnamese refugees were third- or fourth-generation ethnic Chinese. They did not see themselves as Chinese and had no connection with the local population. It was thus difficult to justify to the public that Chinese illegal immigrants, who were in most cases their

---
64. D. Wilson, letter, 18 May 1979, FCO40/1095, TNA.
65. MacLehose to FCO, 18 May 1979, FCO40/1095, TNA.

relatives, had to be sent back to the mainland, while Vietnamese refugees could stay. It was vital to ensure that people in Hong Kong understood that the Vietnamese refugee crisis was a temporary one, the Governor pleaded.[66]

MacLehose stressed that Hong Kong should not be penalized for its humane approach. The exodus of refugees from Vietnam since 1978 had triggered the rise of a more restrictive approach from most Asian countries. The Malaysian Prime Minister, Hussein Onn, for example, had made it clear that Malaysia would take firm measures to prevent the further arrivals of 'boat people', and added that 'Malaysia is not prepared to be left with the residue of refugees and that if they are not accepted for resettlement after a responsible time, the Malaysian government will send them away'.[67] In an earlier exchange with the Hong Kong Government, Chas Freeman, US State Department China Country Director designate, offered a very candid assessment of the situation:

> [a]nother slightly 'pernicious' reason why it had not hitherto been possible to look more favourably on Hong Kong was that where ASEAN countries were concerned, the US had felt that their own readiness to offtake refugees from those countries had made it more difficult for the latter to shut their door altogether, a prospect which had not seemed a real concern in the case of Hong Kong.[68]

MacLehose tried to express that the situation was leading to the growing impatience of the Hong Kong community, including parts of the media and members of the Legislative Council, who were pressing him to take more drastic action. He stated that, 'if they saw others get preferential treatment because they were being less humane then this form of pressure would increase'.[69] In his address to the House Subcommittee on Immigration and Refugees, the Governor argued that Hong Kong's civilized policies stood in contrast to those of others in the region, but their less humane policies were rewarded with a higher US intake quota. He argued that the offtake from Hong Kong should be proportionate to the size of refugee population in the territory.[70] The audiences were sympathetic and appeared convinced of the massive scale of the problem faced by Hong Kong. Warren Christopher, for example, had shown his high regard for Hong Kong's liberal approach

---

66. Record of a Meeting in Mr Warren Christopher's Room, Department of State, Monday, 18 June 1979, FCO40/1101, TNA.
67. Notes for Supplementaries: Statement by the Malaysian Authorities, 18 June 1979, FO40/1100, TNA.
68. P. J. Weston, British Embassy in DC to A. M. Simons, FCO, US Policy Towards South East Asia, 18 June 1979, FCO40/1100, TNA.
69. Record of a Meeting in Mr Warren Christopher's Room, Department of State, Monday, 18 June 1979, FCO40/1101, TNA.
70. Meeting between MacLehose and Poul Hartling in Geneva, 25 June 1979, FCO40/1102, TNA.

and stated that 'if all behaved in the same way there would be no problem'.[71] MacLehose came away from these visits optimistic that Hong Kong would be supported. He believed that the US policy makers were now aware of the urgency of the problem and that they might encourage the US to play a more vigorous role in promoting collective international action.[72]

The Governor was very wrong. Kind words from the American politicians were not followed by deeds. Upon his return to Hong Kong, MacLehose was told that there would not be any immediate change in the quota for Hong Kong, while those for Malaysia and Indonesia continued to increase substantially. The Governor found 'such discrimination in favour of inhumane treatment' disturbing and intolerable. He decided to use Richard Clark's visit to Hong Kong in late June to vent his exasperation. The meeting was nothing like a typical courtesy call between seasoned diplomats. Instead, 'it was a fairly hard-hitting exchange on both sides.'[73] MacLehose fired off with his assessment of the explosive situation in Hong Kong, since the patience of the local community was wearing thin. He reiterated the fact that the Hong Kong people found it hard to understand the American logic in intake quota allocation, which they saw as a reward for hardline approaches. He went on to highlight that the refugees' patience was also stretched to breaking point, as evidenced by growing unrest in refugee camps. Clark tried to justify the American policy by stating that since most of the arrivals in Hong Kong were from North Vietnam and a high proportion of this group were ethnic Chinese, it was inevitable that fewer of them would be eligible for admission to the US under the existing scheme, in which ties with America were the principal criteria. The Governor responded with a sharp rebuttal and stated that it was important to recognize that the Chinese in Vietnam were as much genuine refugees as others. They were being severely discriminated against, and resettlement programmes were supposed to serve all refugees.[74]

Then it was Clark's turn on the offensive. The Ambassador challenged the Governor with a question: 'what had the United Kingdom done?' Clark cornered the Governor by asking him if he was satisfied with the United Kingdom's programme but not with the American one. MacLehose pointed out that whatever Britain did was scarcely relevant, as it was essential that the intake quota should be proportional to the actual burden shouldered

---

71. Record of Meeting between MacLehose and US Senior Officials in Washington, 18 June 1979, FCO40/1101, TNA.
72. Meeting between MacLehose and members of the House Subcommittee on Immigration and Refugees, 20 June 1979, FCO40/1101, TNA.
73. MacLehose to FCO, 29 June 1979, FCO40/1102, TNA.
74. Record of Meeting between MacLehose and Ambassador Clark, 29 June 1979, FCO40/1103, TNA.

by the colony. He queried whether that the quotas for Hong Kong were kept low because of the United Kingdom. Clark frankly admitted that there was very strong feeling in the United States about the contributions made by other countries, and that the number of refugees taken by the United Kingdom had been and would continue to be a significant factor for the administration and Congress in apportioning the US quota for Hong Kong. In short, the take-home message for the Governor was, 'if the United Kingdom did more, the US would take more from Hong Kong'.[75]

Thatcher: Putting Vietnam on the Defensive

Thatcher's defeat of James Callaghan on 3 May 1979 marked a major shift in the British government's strategy in tackling the refugee crisis. The 'low-key' approach of the Labour government was discarded, with Thatcher preferring international effort to address the issue. A more proactive British approach was on the horizon. Margaret Thatcher's 1979 initiative in calling for a United Nations meeting on the refugee crisis provided an opportunity to alter international diplomacy regarding the refugee crisis.

Central to Thatcher's approach was holding Vietnam responsible for the crisis. The Thatcher administration decided to explore all possible economic leverages against Vietnam and a rigorous review of all existing British schemes of loans, aid, and trade deals with the socialist regime was launched. For Thatcher, Washington's accommodating approach towards the refugee crisis, including the idea of expanding the processing centre scheme was misguided. It would only, she argued, provide the Vietnamese authority with an opportunity to 'pass the responsibility to others for members of their own population for which they had no longer any use'.[76] The new government was also lukewarm towards the new initiative of the Orderly Departure Scheme—the Vietnamese government's promise to regulate and control the outflow of those who wanted to leave the country, in return for the assistance of the UNHCR and the United States, which it was argued, would 'permit and even encourage the continuing outflow and take pressure off Vietnam to reverse policies which cause it'.[77]

For Thatcher, Vietnam's misconduct had to be condemned. Within a month of taking office, the Vietnamese Chargé d'Affaires was summoned to the FCO and his government's corrupt, inhumane, and extortionate

---
75. MacLehose to the FCO, 29 June 1979, FCO40/1102, TNA.
76. Carrington meeting Tan Sri Ghazali, Malaysian Minister of Home Affairs, 2 July 1979, FCO40/1102, TNA.
77. R. P. Flower, South East Asian Department, FCO to Murray, Geneva Meeting on Refugee: Orderly Departure, 16 July 1979, FCO40/1104, TNA.

refugee trafficking were called out. The Prime Minister exclaimed that the British government would take a very serious view of Vietnamese government action.[78] Yet for Thatcher, calling out Vietnam had to be an international effort, 'to stir the conscience of the world'.[79] ASEAN countries which had been severely affected by the overflow of Vietnamese refugees agreed with Thatcher's hardline approach. General Kriangsak Chamanan, the Prime Minister of Thailand, echoed Thatcher's concerns regarding Vietnam's threat to regional as well as global stability and agreed that it was 'imperative that this (refugee) problem should be solved not only insofar as where these displaced persons may be but also at its source'.[80] Thatcher also found strong support from Lee Kuan Yew, who had an even more elaborate view of Vietnam's culpability. Lee, in a response to Thatcher, wrote:

> People and leaders throughout the world must be told, again and again, that it is the government of the Socialist Republic of Vietnam which has actively promoted this massive migration, causing havoc to the countries of Southeast Asia ... We must put them on the defensive. Their leaders are not mad, irrational men like Idi Amin. They had cold, calculating minds, which, whilst incapable of compassion to their own people, are nevertheless most acute in computing cost-benefits. Only the threat to becoming outcasts in the international community will force them to rethink and revise their present strategy. Until then they will push out refugees by the thousands each week.[81]

Thatcher even tried to enlist help from China. Concerned with Vietnam's aggression in Indochina and towards Cambodia in particular, Beijing embraced any initiative that would help to corner Hanoi. China was herself a victim of the exodus from Vietnam as there were more than 230,000 refugees stranded in her territory by mid-1979. Ke Hua, Chinese Ambassador to London, believed that Hanoi had heavily profited from this 'second slave trade'. The Ambassador agreed with Britain that 'there was nothing to be done except to expose them and their attitude'.[82]

If the villainy of Vietnam needed to be exposed on a global platform, and there was no more appropriate stage than a United Nations conference. Margaret Thatcher opined that the situation was desperate, and she found it regretful that most of the member states of the United Nations had done little to help. She thus demanded that a conference must be held under the auspices of the UN so that 'the international community could

---

78. Cortazzi meeting Vietnamese Chargé d'Affaires, 24 May 1979, FCO40/1096, TNA.
79. Meeting of Peter Blaker, FCO and Poul Hartling, UNHCR, 18 June 1979, FCO40/1101, TNA.
80. Office of the Prime Minister, Thailand to British Prime Minister, 14 June 1979, PREM-19-129, TNA.
81. Lee Kuan Yew to Thatcher, 5 June 1979, PREM-19-129, TNA.
82. Carrington meeting Ke Hua, Chinese Ambassador, 7 June 1979, FCO40/1100, TNA.

be brought to a proper realization of its responsibilities'.[83] At a meeting in Downing Street, she lectured Kurt Waldheim, the newly appointed UN Secretary General:

> Vietnam was continuing to confiscate the wealth and possessions of those whom they were throwing out and was shooting at them as they left. This is was a question not of a shouting match but of sheer barbarism. It should be pilloried publicly... It was essential that the United Nations should be seen to stand for something and to condemn barbarism.[84]

Washington, however, did not share Thatcher's enthusiasm for this strategy of politicization. The State Department argued that the politics of the conference could only deter some countries from resettling refugees, and it might also give them an excuse to wash their hands of their resettlement duties, since they could claim they had done their part by joining the chorus of condemnation of Vietnam.[85] With the strategic concerns of the Soviet Union's growing presence in Indochina and the possibility of pushing Vietnam even closer to the Russians, the US administration had reservations with Britain's proposed approach. Washington, however, did not dismiss the idea completely, as a UN conference would internationalize the issue, providing a platform to consolidate global support for the Orderly Departure Scheme, she proposed and of using holding centres for refugees.[86] Thus, if political and humanitarian issues could be separated, Washington would not stand in the way.

The United Nations adopted a similarly pragmatic stance. Like Washington, the UN was uncomfortable with Thatcher's political agenda of using the conference to attack socialist Vietnam. In a letter to Thatcher, Kurt Waldheim made it clear that the conference would have a humanitarian purpose, generating support for measures designed to ameliorate the plight of refugees.[87] On another occasion, he reiterated his reservations to Thatcher and argued that the proposed meeting would degenerate into a shouting match and that a political debate would simply lead to sterile confrontation.[88] However, instead of flatly rejecting Thatcher's call for a United Nations response, Waldheim skilfully made use of this occasion to enlist commitments from member nations. The United Nations listed three

---

83. Thatcher to the UNHCR, 31 May 1979, FCO40/1097, TNA.
84. Note of the Prime Minister's Discussion with the United Nations Secretary General, Dr Kurt Waldheim at 10 Downing Street, on Thursday 12 July 1979 at 1700 Hours, PREM-19-130, TNA.
85. Jay (Washington) to FCO, 18 June 1979, FCO40/1100, TNA.
86. British Embassy (Peking) to Assistant Political Advisor, Hong Kong Government, 12 June 1979, FCO40/1100, TNA.
87. From FCO to UK Mission in Geneva, 3 July 1979, PREM-19-130, TNA.
88. Note of the Prime Minister's Discussion with the United Nations Secretary General, Dr Kurt Waldheim, at 10 Downing Street, on Thursday 12 July 1979 at 1700 Hours, PREM-19-130, TNA.

conditions as prerequisites for convening the conference. First, Western countries, including Britain, should promise, preferably before the conference, to take a total of 200,000 refugees from the ASEAN area. Second, ASEAN countries should be prevailed upon to grant unlimited first asylum to refugees and to accept a sizable share for resettlement. And lastly, Britain and other countries should urge Latin American countries to accept a significant number.[89] The ball was now back in Thatcher's court.

Hong Kong's Desperation

Thatcher's proactive approach was never intended to increase Britain's financial donations or refugee intake. In June 1979, the Prime Minister made her stance clear in her first major meeting with heads of the developed world in the Tokyo Economic Summit Meeting. She insisted on the revision of the joint statement to include the following paragraph: 'that the Governments represented at the meeting, while taking full account of the social and economic circumstances in their own countries, would as part of an international effort, significantly increase their contribution'. She supplemented the amendment with an indication that the UK could admit more refugees, but not a substantial number. President Carter of the United States was not impressed and believed that the words 'taking full account' were an escape clause. President Valéry Giscard d'Estaing of France also viewed the new UK position as restrictive and argued that, if France were to take account of social and economic circumstances, it would not accept no further refugees at all. In the end, Thatcher conceded to remove the word 'full' from her proposed amendment.[90]

The Prime Minister was also seriously considering reducing British obligations regarding rescues on the high seas. Under the Heath government, the government had promised to provide refuge of last resort for refugees picked up by British ships at sea, if they were not accepted by any other country. The Thatcher administration decided to end this open-ended commitment and would only consider Britain's residual obligation on a case-by-case basis.[91] The Prime Minister also explored the prospect of Britain's withdrawal from the existing international convention concerning refugees and rescue at sea, and only stopped short of denouncing these

---

89. Murray to FCO, 6 July 1979, FCO40/1103, TNA.
90. Economic Summit Meeting in Tokyo 28/29 June 1979: Record of the Second Session in the Akasaka Palace on 28 June at 1605, Margaret Thatcher Foundation.
91. Note of the Secretary of State's Meeting with the General Council of British Shipping (GCBS) held at 1700 on Tuesday 5 June 1979, PREM-19-129, TNA.

obligations due to the strong reservations of the FCO and the Attorney General.[92]

In a sense, Thatcher's approach had been counter-productive as the call for a United Nations conference had again drawn attention to the British government's poor track record. The Home Office tried hard to defuse their mortification by reiterating the British record in humanitarian causes: Britain had settled a large number of migrants from tyrannical regimes after the Second World War, including 50,000 people who had left East Africa since colonial independence in circumstances analogous to those of the Vietnamese boat people who were admitted to the country in 1972.[93] Yet the fact remained that Britain's contribution to the alleviation of the Vietnamese refugee crisis had been hugely inadequate. According to the UN figures, out of a total of 235,801 Indochinese refugees who had been resettled around the world by July 1979, only 2,750 had been accepted by Britain. Britain's cash contribution to the UN programme for Indochinese refugees was even more embarrassing and had contributed nothing to the overall total of USD 50 million donated by the international community during this period.[94] The UN wanted Britain to settle 10,000 refugees in exchange for the convening of a conference in Geneva.

Hong Kong was desperate for any assistance from the international community, and welcomed Thatcher's initiative in calling for a UN conference. During their meeting in Washington, MacLehose expressed his 'personal view' to Christopher Warren, that the two matters of resettlement and political pressure on Vietnam were better separated in the prospective UN conference, a line that was in direct contrast to the sovereign's position.[95] Nevertheless, it was soon apparent to MacLehose that the prospect of the event was very much hinged upon Britain's acceding to the UN request for a new intake quota. MacLehose's direct encounters with top US officials simply confirmed his reading of the situation: that Washington was not happy with Britain's long-standing tepid response to its appeal for contributions to the refugee crisis, and that this could hinder further attention and support from the UN and even more importantly, from the United States.[96] The Governor aired his frustration with London in unequivocal terms,

---

92. Letter from Private Secretary, Office of the Prime Minister, 29 May 1979, and Law Officers' Department to the Office of Prime Minister, 30 May 1979, PREM-19-129, TNA.
93. Munro to Shepherd, 2 July 1989, FCO40/1103, TNA.
94. Macinnes to FCO: UN Meeting on Indochinese Refugees, 13 July 1979, PREM-19-130, TNA.
95. Record of a Meeting in Mr. Warren Christopher's Room, Department of State, Monday, 18 June 1979, FCO40/1101.
96. P. J. Weston (British Embassy in Washington) to A. M. Simons (Southeast Asian Dept, FCO): US Policy towards South East Asia, 18 June 1979, FCO40/1100, TNA.

'the Americans would not take more refugees from Hong Kong unless the British did more; and unless the Americans did more, no one else would'.[97]

It was, of course, no small challenge to convince the Iron Lady. The Prime Minister appeared unapologetic about the limited British contribution. Thatcher contended that comparisons between the British record in receiving refugees and the numbers taken in by other countries was invalid, since she believed that the United Kingdom had already granted entry with full citizenship to nearly 2 million migrants after the Second World War. She refused to accept the distinction between refugees and immigrants.[98] Britain, it was claimed, should also be given credit for Hong Kong's liberal approach towards the refugees.[99] In short, Britain had already done her part and should not be criticized. Thatcher was not swayed.[100]

Yet not everyone in Whitehall was as optimistic as the Prime Minister about the prospect of a UN conference without further British concessions. MacLehose found an ally in Lord Carrington, the British Foreign Secretary. They both underlined the difficulty which might arise if Britain's initiative was not backed up with a contribution, either in the form of a refugee intake or financial support.[101] Other senior officials concurred. Peter Blaker, the Foreign Minister, argued that the promise of a £1 million donation to the UNHCR's cause for the Indochina refugees for the year 1979 was highly inadequate, since it was embarrassingly dwarfed by the estimated budget of more than £20 million shouldered by Hong Kong for this year alone. London should offer of £ 5 million if she wanted to escape fierce criticism in the conference, Blaker opined.[102]

London, however, procrastinated over setting a new quota. The delay gave rise to rumours that the intention of the British government was to phase in the intake of 10,000 over an extended period of three years, instead of the twelve months requested by the United Nations. MacLehose was furious and called this 'distasteful and disappointing' if proven to be true. He was certain that this would upset the Americans as well as many other countries participating in the conference.[103] Unfortunately, the rumours were not entirely unfounded. The Home Office did in fact suggest to the Prime Minister that, while Britain should be able to absorb 10,000 more refugees, the annual intake would be at best set at the level of 3,000

---

97. Office of the Lord Privy Seal to Home Office, 4 July 1979, FCO40/1103, TNA.
98. Note for the Record, 14 June 1979, PREM-19-129, TNA.
99. Note of the Prime Minister's Discussion with United Nations Secretary General, Dr Kurt Waldheim, at 10 Downing Street, on Thursday 12 July 1979 at 1700 Hours, PREM-19-130, TNA.
100. Letter from Private Secretary, Prime Minister's Office, 15 June 1979, FCO40/1101, TNA.
101. Wall, FCO to Office of Prime Minister, 15 June 1979, PREM-19/789, TNA.
102. Blaker to Secretary of State, 6 July 1979, FCO40/1103, TNA.
103. MacLehose to FCO, 14 July 1979, PREM-19-130, TNA.

to 4,000 arrivals.[104] Lord Carrington found this arrangement difficult to sell and argued that if Britain could not come forward with a significant offer, there would be a damning international and domestic response. Thus, he counter-proposed that the intake should be phased over two years, although he suggested that the additional number of refugees should be taken from Hong Kong only, and that any Vietnamese boat people rescued on the high seas by UK-registered ships should be subtracted from the overall total. Thatcher eventually consented to this proposal but added that the pledge by the previous administration of an intake of 1,500 should also be subtracted from the 10,000 quotas, reducing the new promised intake to 8,500.[105] Unaware of the details of these deliberations in the British cabinet, MacLehose was in agony. To secure London's consent, the Governor desperately and generously suggested that, while Hong Kong would accept the imposed intake quota of 10,000, the colony was prepared to go the extra mile to gain London's support:

> Would it help if the UK and HK pledges were merged into a single British pledge of 20,000? This would leave room for Hong Kong to take rather more than half if you ran into domestic difficulties. I have sounded the senior member who thinks we could get this through ExCo. Our problem is so vast that to accept one or two thousand more would be a reasonable price to ensure the UK's position remained unassailable, and thus assisted the success of the conference, and the removal of the bulk of the refugees from us.[106]

The Geneva Conference, 1979

Thatcher finally conceded to the UN request for a new intake commitment of 10,000, although with the numbers from previous unused pledges redacted and the period of implementation still ambiguous. The UN conference was eventually held in Geneva on 20–21 July 1979. It was attended by delegations from seventy-two countries, plus representatives of many inter-governmental and non-governmental agencies. The resettlement issue was the dominant concern of the event, as requested by the United States. The major positive consequence of the conference was that it overshot its own goals in in securing contributions from the global community. Commitments to refugee intake by participant countries exceeded the original target of 200,000 and reached a total of 260,000 (see Table 5.2).

---

104. Home Office to Prime Minister, 9 July 1979, PREM-19-130, TNA.
105. Note for the Record: Vietnamese Refugees, 9 July 1979, PREM-19-130, TNA.
106. MacLehose to FCO, Personal from Governor: UN Conference on Indo-Chinese Refugees, 3 July 1979, PREM-19-130, TNA.

Table 5.2: Quota of extra intake for Indochinese refugees agreed at Geneva Conference 1979

Country	Number of persons	Country	Number of persons
Argentina	4,000–5,000	Italy	1,000
Australia	14,000	Japan	500
Austria	580	Luxembourg	55
Belgium	2,000	Monaco	25
Brazil	26	Netherlands	1,360
Canada	30,000	New Zealand	1,050
Denmark	500	Norway	3,000
Finland	100	People's Republic of China	10,000
France	10,000	Spain	1,000
Germany, Federal Republic of	10,000	Surinam	750
Greece	150	Sweden	2,000
Iceland	30	Switzerland	2,000
Ireland	100	United Kingdom	10,000
Israel	200	United States of America	161,000
		Total	260,000 (rounded)

Source: Note on Technical Meeting on Resettlement, held at UNHCR Headquarters, Geneva, Monday 23 July 1979, FCO 40/1105, TNA.

Washington seized the opportunity of the conference to set a vision of how the situation could be ameliorated. The solution, in the view of the United States, must comprise increased contributions from the international community, engagement with Vietnam, and the setting up of overseas refugee holding centres. The idea of mega holding facilities for 150,000 refugees in isolated areas of South-East Asia was expounded. Based on the Galang Island experience in Indonesia, these facilities were to serve as the first buffer against the sudden massive population inflow to the resettlement countries, and would also to help encourage the countries of asylum to open their doors to refugees. While refugees awaited permanent settlement in these holding facilities, they would be screened for their eligibility to be resettled. In return, the operational expenses of these facilities

Humanitarianism Outsourced 135

would be met by the United States and the UNHCR. The intention was that refugees should leave these facilities 'within a reasonable period of time' and thus the host countries had no need to worry about a refugee residue.[107] Washington also took the opportunity to elaborate on her new initiative in engaging with Vietnam, the Orderly Departure Scheme. Under this arrangement, American personnel were allowed to carry out the task of screening people in Vietnam. Vietnam also did its part by agreeing to a moratorium on the unorganized exodus and declared 'that for a reasonable period of time it will make every effort to stop illegal departures'.[108] The Americans believed that such an arrangement would moderate the pace of the outflow of Vietnamese, of which most were ethnic Chinese that Saigon was determined to expel, and thus help alleviate the pressure on countries in the region as well as the international community at large. This American framework for the global division of responsibility in tackling the refugee crisis was thus fully confirmed in the Geneva Conference.

For Thatcher, the outcome was satisfying. Lord Carrington, leader of the British delegation, believed the event had met the primary objective of the Prime Minister: to pile up pressure on Vietnam. In his speech to the Conference, he dutifully conveyed the main message of Thatcher and pulled no punches in attributing the humanitarian crisis to Saigon:

> It is not the practice for British ministers to comment on the internal affairs of other countries. But I am bound to wonder what lies behind this exodus, and why tens of thousands of men, women, and children, perhaps as many as the whole population of Geneva—have died in the South China Sea because they could not, or would not, continue living in their own country. They have been driven out by no natural disaster. One can only conclude that they have left because the policies of the Vietnamese government made it impossible for them to remain. And their fate, caused by the policies of the Vietnamese government, is now the international concern of us all.[109]

Carrington was particularly pleased with the strong-worded speeches of the Americans, Canadians, Australians, and Chinese against Vietnam, which rendered futile the Vietnamese attempt to 'portray themselves as the hapless victims of a problem beyond their control'. The Conference's success in raising an extra USD 190 million for the UNHCR and a pledge of a total intake of 260,000—almost double the commitment secured before

---

107. US Department of State: The UN-Sponsored Meeting on Indochinese Refugees at Geneva, RG59, P16 Box 15, NARA.
108. Barry Stein, 'The Geneva Conferences and the Indochinese Refugee Crisis', *The International Migration Review* 13, no. 4 (1979): 716–723.
109. Speech by the Secretary of State for Foreign and Commonwealth Affairs, the Right Honourable the Lord Carrington, at Geneva on Friday 20 July 1979, FCO40/1105, TNA.

the event—helped to alleviate the pressure on Hong Kong and London. Most importantly, the British government saw the success of the event as justifying her gracious retreat on this matter. 'I think we can now afford to lower our profile on the whole issue of Vietnam refugees, leaving it as far as possible to others to maintain the pressure on Vietnam,' Carrington suggested to the Prime Minister.[110]

Conclusion

The Geneva Conference proved to be another false dawn. Hong Kong benefited from the pledges of participant countries and in 1980 the number of refugees stranded in the territory fell. The total number awaiting resettlement however remained higher than 10,000 for the next five years. In fact, right after the conclusion of the Conference, the rising tensions at the Thailand and Cambodia border in late 1979 once again led the Americans to shift their attention away from Hong Kong. To demonstrate support for Thailand, Washington decided to speed up the refugee intake from there. The colony was therefore informed the US could no longer resettle 2,000 per month as originally planned, although the Americans promised they would support the idea of granting the colony access to the refugee processing facilities on Batan Island in the Philippines. London raised no objection as Whitehall shared US concern about Vietnam's aggression against the Beijing-backed Pol Pot regime.[111] In fact, Britain was busy rekindling the debate on its commitment to take in 10,000 refugees from Hong Kong at the same time. Ever since the start of the programme, London's determination to honour the pledge within twelve months, as demanded by the United Nations, was dubious. Within the first three months after the Conference, only 302 refugees in Hong Kong were resettled in Britain, whereas Canada had taken up 2,384 during the same period. There was a slight increase in November, but London was reluctant to take more than 500 a month.[112] The colony was told that March 1981 was a more realistic deadline for Britain to fulfil her quota.[113] The resumption of the exodus of Vietnamese in the mid-1980s presented a further challenge for the colony.

---

110. Carrington to Prime Minister: Geneva Conference on Refugees in Indo-China, 24 July 1979, FCO40/1105, TNA.
111. 'Anglo-American Discussion on Southeast Asia in the Foreign and Commonwealth Office on Friday, 16 November, 1979 at 10.30 am', FCO 40/1109, TNA. and 'Call on Minister of State Mr. Peter Blake MP, by Mr. Richard Holbrooke in the Foreign and Commonwealth Office on Friday, 16 November 1979 at 12 noon', FCO40/1109, TNA.
112. HK to FCO: UK Vietnamese Resettlement Programme, 20 November 1979, FCO40/1109, TNA.
113. William Whitelaw (Home Secretary) to Prime Minister, 28 December 1979, FCO40/1100, TNA.

Hong Kong was forced to resort to a more repressive approach in handling the ever-expanding population of Vietnamese stranded in the territory, creating closed camps and voluntary repatriation, which made the colony vulnerable to international criticism and pressure.[114] The refugee issue was never really solved until the mid-1990s.

The refugee saga of 1975 to 1979 is illustrative of the vulnerability and precariousness of the colony in the theatre of world politics. Despite having to accommodate an inflow of illegal immigrants from the mainland, Hong Kong was unilaterally assigned by Washington as port of first asylum for the Vietnamese refugees. Its compliance was, however, not always rewarded by assistance. Notwithstanding these challenges, Hong Kong put up a spirited fight to make its voice heard during this trying time. Punching above his weight, MacLehose confronted the big players in theatres of global diplomacy in Washington, Geneva, and many other venues. To gain sympathy in international stage, Hong Kong turned to London. The dialogue with the sovereign on this matter uncovers a multi-faceted relationship. London was not enthusiastic, but at the same time not entirely indifferent to Hong Kong's plea. British diplomats conveyed the concerns of the colony whenever the opportunity arose, providing a degree of leverage for Hong Kong, an influence over decision makers in North America and Europe, as well as South-East Asia. The sovereign's commitment to defend Hong Kong's interests was, however, constrained by the need to placate Washington. On many occasions, London's 'firm support' for Hong Kong's decision was compromised when the US objected. The key strategic interest of London was in preserving a relationship of cordiality with Washington. Furthermore, Britain's ability to represent Hong Kong was hindered by its reluctance to make any major commitment to refugee intake and financial assistance. 'What had the United Kingdom done?' this rhetorical question had been regularly used by UN representatives, senior officials in Washington, or ambassadors from all over the world to reject Hong Kong's demands for support. London was a leverage, but it was also a liability for the colony's pursuit of its agenda. The sovereign's moral obligation towards her colony appeared irrelevant when the colossal financial and political cost of accepting thousands of refugees was at stake. Humanitarian concerns were best outsourced.

---

114. Henry Litton, 'The Vietnamese Boat People Story: 1975–1999', *Alternative Law Journal* 26, no. 4 (2001), https://doi.org/.10.1177/1037969X0102600406; S. Alex Cunliffe, 'Vietnamese Boat People in Hong Kong: Policies and Prescriptions', *The Pacific Review* 4, no. 3 (1991): 272–276; Roda Mushkat, 'Refuge in Hong Kong', *International Journal of Refugee Law* 1, no. 4 (1989): 449–480.

# 6
Asserting Local Concern
Land Leases in the New Territories and the Future of Hong Kong

Introduction

29 March 1979 was a date of historic significance. MacLehose was invited by the Chinese Ministry of Foreign Trade to visit Beijing, making him the first colonial governor given the opportunity to make an official visit to China since 1949. Yet the significance of the event goes beyond this fact. He was granted an audience with the Chinese Vice-Premier Deng Xiaoping. This encounter marked the commencement of the dialogue between Britain and China over the future of Hong Kong. In the press conference held upon his return, the main message relayed by the Governor to the anxious public was Deng's line of 'investors should put their hearts at ease'. Unknown to the local population, there had been an audacious attempt made by MacLehose during the trip to tackle the issue of business confidence, as it related to the looming challenge of 1997. In Beijing, the Governor proposed that the Hong Kong government should grant new land leases in the New Territory beyond July 1997, with the tacit consent of Beijing. The essence of this legalist attempt was to separate the short-term problem of business confidence from the long-term issue of the future of Hong Kong.

In the end, this plan failed miserably, and the Chinese government eventually branded it 'unnecessary and inappropriate'. Beijing was not at this point ready to engage with British officials over the fate of Hong Kong, but MacLehose's suggestion had accelerated the process which Chinese and British governments formulated the future policies. Expecting to leave the colony by mid-1979, the governor felt obliged to address a 'technical aspect' of the future of Hong Kong. This is a story of a colonial administrator trying to assert local concerns into the agenda of policy makers at the very top level.

Hong Kong: Valuable but Not a Vital Interest

Sovereignty over Hong Kong had always been a contentious issue between China and Britain. Whereas Britain maintained the legitimate claim on the basis of the three treaties signed by the Qing government in the nineteenth century, both the Nationalist and Communist governments denied the validity of these agreements and saw the eventual recovery of the territory integral of China's political programmes. The ascendancy of China in the post-war years and the anti-imperialist stance of the United States further complicated matters. In short, Hong Kong was an asset, but not a vital interest, and Britain was not prepared to hold on to the colony at all costs.

The economic value of the colony was cherished by London. In a top-level communication about whether Britain should hold on to Hong Kong in face of the imminent Communist takeover of China in 1949, the financial importance of maintaining the colony was agreed on among the senior officials in the Ministry of Defence and Treasury:

> It is certain that there is nothing which can take the place of Hong Kong in the foreseeable future as a rallying-point for financial and economic order in the Far Eastern region. Sterling is the traditional currency of Far Eastern trade, and the loss of Hong Kong would be very serious to the prospect of re-establishing economic stability in that area, to the share of the sterling area in any such establishment, and to the position of sterling itself as a world trading currency.[1]

Another assessment conducted by Colonial Office in 1957 as part of a general cost-benefit analysis of colonial dependencies also warned that the loss of Hong Kong would deprive British industrialists, traders, bankers, and shipowners of a crucial base in the Far East, and incalculable British capital investments associated with those occupations would have to be written off as well. The colonial government's ability to pay its own way and balance the budget without significant aid from London was also noted.[2]

Politically, the colony also gained symbolic significance as a proof of the benevolence of British imperial rule. 'Hong Kong is an outpost of good government, justice and individual freedom in the Far East and a sanctuary for refugees; it is a shop window for the British way of life in that part of the world,' stated a Colonial Office document titled, *Hong Kong: Value and Cost to the United Kingdom 1957–1959*.[3] Another cabinet study in 1959 argued that it served as 'a visible demonstration of achievements under British rule'

---

1. S.A.C. (49) 5, 6 and 7, 19 May 1949, T236 (4274), TNA.
2. Extract from Colonial Office Paper: Future Constitutional in the Colonies: Economic and Financial Considerations/The Special Position of Hong Kong, 1957, T236 (4274), TNA.
3. Hong Kong: Value and Cost to the United Kingdom, February 1957, CO1030/859, TNA.

and showed 'the western determination to resist communist expansion'.[4] The role of the colony as an intelligence outpost for the US also aligned with American Cold War agenda in South-East Asia, and helped cement the relationship between Britain and the US.[5]

There were, however, costs in holding on to the colony. Hong Kong's industrial success had made the colony Britain's competitor in the domestic and overseas markets by the 1950s. Certain British industries, such as textiles, clothing, and toys, were severely challenged by Hong Kong exports, and the British obligation to offer preferential treatment led to demands of UK and overseas industries for protection. Nevertheless, economic concerns were dwarfed by the threat of China. Britain was under no illusions about Beijing's ultimate intention of recovering the sovereignty of Hong Kong. During the war years, the Nationalist government nourished the expectation that all parts of Hong Kong would be returned to China after the victory of allies. In 1942, the Nationalist even went further to test Britain's resolve. Emboldened by the American anti-imperialist stance, Chiang Kai-shek demanded the termination of the New Territories Lease of 1898 during the negotiations about the abolition of extra-territoriality with the British government. Notwithstanding American sympathy towards the Nationalist cause, the British government responded that it 'would not regard the maintenance of British sovereignty over the Colony as a matter beyond the scope of . . . discussion' during the reconstruction in the Far East after the war, although no commitment to the retrocession of Hong Kong to China was mentioned.[6] London eventually refused to accede to Chiang's demand, and the Treaty to Relinquish Extra-Territoriality was signed in 1943 with no mention of the fate of Hong Kong, although the Nationalist government insisted on the right to raise the issue at a later date.

Another incident occurred towards the end of the war in 1945. As the Allied Supreme Commander of the China Theatre, Chiang Kai-shek believed he was entitled to accept the Japanese surrender of Hong Kong, since he held that the colony was within China. Britain, however, informed Chiang that 'irrespective of the confines of an operational theatre, wherever a Sovereign power has sufficient forces available, it should resume its authority and accept the Japanese surrender there'.[7] British Admiral Cecil Harcourt's frantic dash to Hong Kong to accept the Japanese surrender in

---

4. Cabinet Study of Future Policy: Hong Kong 1960–1970, n.d., CAB21/5127, TNA.
5. Nancy Tucker, *China Confidential: American Diplomats and Sino-American Relations, 1945–1996* (New York: Columbia University Press, 2001).
6. Kit Ching Lau Chan, 'The Hong Kong Question during the Pacific War (1941–1945)', *The Journal of Imperial and Commonwealth History* 21 (1973): 56–78.
7. Pares to Williamson: Sovereignty over Hong Kong, 27 June 1980, FCO40/1162, TNA.

1945 attested to London's concern about the Chinese territorial claim over the colony.[8]

Unfortunately for London, the Chinese Communists were no less nationalistic. Like the Nationalists, the Communist regime saw the colony as a perpetual affront to China's dignity and contended that Hong Kong was inalienable Chinese territory. This was an 'outstanding' issue in the regime's relations with Britain. In March 1963, Beijing expounded the Chinese government's attitude towards Hong Kong for the first time and in the most conspicuous manner, an article in the *People's Daily* noted that,

> such questions as those of Hong Kong and Macao relate to the category of unequal treaties left over by history . . . As a matter of fact, many of these treaties concluded in the past either have lost their validity, or have been abrogated or have been replaced by new ones.[9]

During the Cultural Revolution, the *People's Daily* published another article on Hong Kong in August 1967, which reiterated the assertion that Hong Kong has been Chinese territory since time immemorial. This was preceded by the remarks of Zhou Enlai made to Kenneth Kaunda, the Zambian President two months earlier:

> The destiny of Hong Kong will be decided by our patriotic countrymen in Hong Kong and the 700 million Chinese people and definitely not by a handful of British imperialists.[10]

Breaking out of her self-imposed diplomatic isolation in the early 1970s also allowed China a wider array of leverages for registering this territorial claims. After being admitted into the United Nations in 1971, Huang Hua, the then Chinese Foreign Secretary, wrote to the UN Committee on Decolonization and argued that, since Hong Kong and Macao belong to the 'category of questions resulting from the series of unequal treaties left over by history', they should not be considered as colonial territories.[11]

Britain's Hong Kong policy had always been underscored with a sense of vulnerability. A Cabinet study on the future of Hong Kong in 1959 vividly portrayed this sense of the colony's fragility. It argued that it was extremely doubtful that Hong Kong was defensible, even with nuclear weapons, against an all-out attack by China. The British government was convinced that if the colony was attacked, it was unlikely that the US would commit to

---

8. Lau Chan, 'The Hong Kong Question'.
9. Webb to McLaren, Chinese Statements on the Status of Hong Kong, 30 March 1979, FCO40/1058, TNA.
10. Webb to McLaren, Chinese Statements on the Status of Hong Kong, 30 March 1979, FCO40/1058, TNA.
11. Webb to McLaren, Chinese Statements on the Status of Hong Kong, 30 March 1979, FCO40/1058, TNA.

defend the territory. Moreover, major reinforcement of British forces was militarily and financially untenable. China was also capable of inflicting damage on the colony with indirect influence and could easily bring the colonial government to its knees by cutting off food supplies or mobilizing supporters in local trade unions. In short, it would be impossible to maintain stability and essential public services if China was determined to apply pressure on the colony. As a cabinet study of 1959 noted, 'we have been able to keep Hong Kong for a hundred years because China has been weak. She is now strong and getting stronger.'[12]

Fortunately, Communist China developed a pragmatic policy towards Hong Kong despite her nationalistic rhetoric on the issue of sovereignty. In effect, China granted the colonial government de facto recognition by referring to it as the 'British administration in Hong Kong'. Beijing's preferred tactic was to maintain the status quo in Hong Kong, since the colony could be used as an economic and political window to the outside. This message was reiterated on numerous occasions from the 1940s onwards. 'Long-term planning and full utilization' as Beijing called it, was the regime's official policy towards Hong Kong. 'It would not be in China's interest if Hong Kong were taken back now,' Zhou Enlai told a group of journalists and film makers from Hong Kong in 1965. A similar message had been reiterated by Liao Chengzhi and other senior officials over the years.[13]

Consequently, Britain's position on the future of Hong Kong was founded on two presumptions. Firstly, there was a consensus on the fate of the colony: 'sooner or later, we must expect to lose it,' the 1959 Cabinet study concluded.[14] This view was shared by Robert Black, Governor of Hong Kong between 1958 and 1964. The Governor opined,

> we must not delude ourselves that the Chinese regard the present relative calm as more than a tactical pause or that their long-term objectives have in any way changed. These must remain the recovery of Hong Kong and the total elimination of British and American influence here: in the long run nothing less than this is reconcilable with national pride or party dogma.[15]

A Cabinet study conducted in the aftermath of the 1967 Riots in 1969 assigned even greater salience to the 1997 divide. It argued that 'it is inconceivable that any communist Chinese government would "negotiate" an

---

12. Cabinet Study of Future Policy: Hong Kong 1960–1970, n.d., CAB21/5127, TNA.
13. David Trench to Secretary of State for the Colonies, Chinese Attitudes towards Hong Kong, 11 August 1965, FCO40/1674, TNA.
14. David Trench to Secretary of State for the Colonies, Chinese Attitudes towards Hong Kong, 11 August 1965, FCO40/1674, TNA.
15. Governor of Hong Kong to the Secretary of State for the Colonies, Hong Kong: Review of Political and Economic Development, 27 May 1964, FO371/175888, TNA.

extension of the Hong Kong lease . . . there is no real prospect of any solution that does not provide for the resumption of Chinese sovereignty over Hong Kong'.[16] In another FCO paper on the future of Hong Kong produced in 1971, a similarly gloomy view prevailed,

> the Chinese government may well take the view in 1997, when they will be presented with a clear-cut choice, that for reasons of national prestige and to safeguard their claims to be in the forefront of anti-colonialism they must reclaim the Colony, despite the economic benefits which would then be denied to them.[17]

Alec Douglas-Home, the Foreign Secretary at the time, concurred. 'We should not underestimate the possibility that before 1997 national pride will overcome economic realism,' he warned.[18]

Secondly, an eventual negotiated withdrawal from Hong Kong was the best deal for Britain. For London, a forced retreat in response to China's hostility was unimaginable. The danger of leaving millions of Hong Kong citizens behind with no satisfactory arrangement made for them by China was genuine, and the difficulty of moving British assets out of the colony was also a major concern. Furthermore, it would be challenging to maintain internal security once any hint of a unilateral British retreat was noticed by the locals. London's ultimate aim was to persuade China of the need for a jointly agreed policy for Hong Kong's future and to seek an eventual amicable settlement with the regime, hopefully with some role for the British in Hong Kong beyond 1997. But before this fateful day arrived, Britain should strive to convince Beijing that maintaining the status quo in Hong Kong was in the best interest of both countries.

Surviving China: Strategies of London

There were three discernible components of the British attempt to reinforce Beijing's desire to maintain status quo in Hong Kong. First and foremost, Britain needed to refrain from provoking China on the issue of sovereignty over Hong Kong. The British government had been very cautious in making public assertions of sovereignty over the colony in the post-war years. In face of occasional pressure from Parliament to clarify the status of Hong Kong, British governmental officials always refused to make bold assertions on this matter. For example, when asked about the government's stance on

---

16. Cabinet Ministerial Committee on Hong Kong, 'Hong Kong: Long Term Study', 28 March 1969, FCO40/160, TNA.
17. The Future of Hong Kong, 1971, FCO40/331, TNA.
18. Memorandum by the Secretary of State for Foreign and Commonwealth Affairs, Alec Douglas-Home, 13 December 1971, CAB148/117, TNA.

the colony whilst she was under unprecedented pressure during the 1967 Riots, Lord Shepherd, Minister of State for Foreign and Commonwealth Affairs, stated in the House of Lords that Her Majesty's Government 'would not consider any abrogation of their responsibility to the people of Hong Kong'. In 1976, Lord Goronwy-Roberts replied to a parliamentary question with another carefully phrased implicit assertion of British sovereignty, that 'the government would continue to administer the territory (of Hong Kong) in the interests of those who live there'. Governor Robert Black also tried to dissuade Jeremy Bray's motion for a debate in Parliament in 1963 by saying that public debate on the future of the colony 'could bring nothing but harm for Hong Kong'.[19]

To avoid provoking China, self-determination was another taboo topic. The British government had been extremely cautious in reiterating the 'special situation' of Hong Kong in any discussion on decolonization and the development of self-government. Although the Labour Party included Hong Kong among the thirty-three smaller dependent territories that should have the right of self-determination in its Manifesto on Colonial Policy in 1957, such a right, it was stated, 'can only legitimately be exercised when democracy has been firmly established and thus all the people have an equal opportunity to share in the decision'.[20] In effect, this option of self-government was ruled out for Hong Kong given London's unwillingness to introduce constitutional democracy in the colony. This was also the case when the Committee of Twenty-Four of the United Nations was charged to discuss and make recommendations about all remaining non-self-governing territories in 1964. The British delegation made sure that the general recommendations were not applicable to Hong Kong.[21] In a 1967 Cabinet paper on the future of dependent territories conducted, Hong Kong was classified among the 'special problem territories', for which 'for obvious international reasons', independence or constitutional progress towards internal self-government would not be considered.[22]

Britain's feeble reaction to China's aforementioned request to remove Hong Kong from the United Nations list of colonial territories in 1972 further attests to London's accommodative approach towards Beijing on this matter. China's request was eventually granted by the General Assembly of the United Nations, and this effectively deprived the people of Hong

---

19. Robert Black to the Secretary of State for the Colonies, Personal for Wallace, 7 April 1963, CO1030/1674, TNA.
20. Secretary of State for the Colonies to Sir A. Grantham, 19 June 1957, CO1030/708, TNA.
21. Robert Black to Higham, 6 May 1964, FO371/175888, TNA.
22. Cabinet Defence and Oversea Policy Committee, The Outlook for the Dependent Territories: Memorandum by the Ministry of State for Commonwealth Affairs, 2 March 1967, FCO40/494, TNA.

Kong of the opportunity for self-determination. London simply responded with a notice claiming the decision would have no implication for British legal position in Hong Kong, and the United Kingdom would cease to supply them with information on Hong Kong, as the future of the territory was no longer within the jurisdiction of the UN Special Committee.[23]

The second component of Britain's strategy to maintain the status quo was to bolster the economic value of Hong Kong to China. This had always been seen as leverage for deterring China's immediate takeover of the colony. Hong Kong provided China with a window to the outside world. The colony helped to connect China, in her self-imposed isolation, to the global economy. Hong Kong was a market, a trading platform, a source of goods and foreign exchange, and a conduit through which China maintained its access to South-East Asia and beyond. Its port facilities and aviation networks, understanding of the logic of capitalism, and access to global economy were cherished by the Chinese communists who were still hamstrung by the burden of central planning and Party dogma. 'Hong Kong under Chinese ownership will no longer be the powerhouse it is today,' a Cabinet Committee argued in 1971.[24] The economic card was thus the trump card prolonging the British role in Hong Kong's survival. Reflecting on the 1967 Riots, the most serious challenge to British authority in Hong Kong in the post-war years, a Cabinet Committee paper came to this conclusion:

> The Chinese recognize that the events of 1967 showed they could not achieve dominance except by the use of violence to a degree which would have gravely impaired Hong Kong's value to them. This price they were not prepared to pay.[25]

The same document argued that the strength of the Hong Kong economy was also important for improving Britain's bargaining position the eventual negotiations with China over the future of the colony:

> We consider finally what initiative we may possess in bringing the Chinese to negotiations or an understanding about Hong Kong when the time seems right, bearing in mind that at any time China could make our position in the Colony impossible and force us to withdraw on their terms. The initiative would seem to be in our hands only to the extent that: (a) the economic value of Hong Kong might be so important to China that they

---

23. Patricia Dagati, 'Hong Kong's Lost Right to Self-Determination: A Denial of Due Process in the United Nations', *New York Law School Journal of International and Comparative Law* 13, no. 1 (1992): 153–179.
24. The Future of Hong Kong, 1971, FCO40/331, TNA.
25. Cabinet Ministerial Committee on Hong Kong, 'Hong Kong: Long Term Study', 28 March 1969, FCO40/160, TNA.

would be prepared to treat with us to preserve this so far as possible after our departure, (b) the settlement of Hong Kong's future could be linked with a desire by China for a détente in its international relations.[26]

Such calculations underpinned the British strategy for preparing for these prospective negotiations and it was translated into a detailed blueprint for social reform. The 1976 Planning Paper on Hong Kong, discussed in Chapter 4, suggested that '[a] maximum degree of economic progress and tranquillity in the Colony, and international respect for it, must be achieved during the run-up to the proposed attempt to negotiate about its future with the Chinese in the mid-1980s'.[27]

The third dimension of Britain's strategy was to show the commitment to Hong Kong before China opened up a conversation about its future. 'Since we have no alternative but to stay in Hong Kong, we must, without provoking the Chinese, show the world that we intend to stay here,' the British government argued in her analysis in 1959.[28] This was the key to maintaining local confidence in the British authority in Hong Kong. Without this, London argued, its rule in the colony would be untenable. Britain should be prepared to stand up for her position in the colony when it was directly challenged by the Chinese Communists, the paper contended:

> The overwhelming majority (of local population) are politically inarticulate, and wish only to trade and survive. But they do not want to be on the losing side, and once confidence starts to slip, in however small a way, the process will be cumulative and there will be an increasing tendency to make terms with the other side. If there seemed to be a possibility of the Chinese Communists taking control in the near future, many of the local population, if not actively assisting, would at least do nothing to oppose them. Any signs of weakening of will on or part would have most damaging consequences.[29]

Less than a decade later, Britain's will to stay was put to the most severe test. During the 1967 Riots, the colonial government was confronted with the full mobilization of the communist machinery in the territory and sustained pressure from Beijing. While this full-scale fallout was rare, occasional altercations between the colonial government and the Chinese authorities were not uncommon. The colonial administration was fully aware of the Communist strategies of infiltration and sabotage in the colony and was prepared to assert its authority in containing the spread of subversive

---

26. Cabinet Ministerial Committee on Hong Kong, 'Hong Kong: Long Term Study', 28 March 1969, FCO40/160, TNA.
27. Planning Paper on Hong Kong, 1976, FCO40/704, TNA.
28. Cabinet Study of Future Policy: Hong Kong 1960–1970, 1959, CAB21/5127, TNA.
29. Cabinet Study of Future Policy: Hong Kong 1960–1970, 1959, CAB21/5127, TNA.

activities. Beijing was certainly not pleased to see her agents and supporters harassed or persecuted by the colonial authorities, and Hong Kong's defence was that the crackdowns were not targeted at the Communists only. That is, the containment policy was extended to the American-backed Taiwanese agents in Hong Kong as well. As Steve Tsang put it, this 'neutrality approach' was central to the survival of colonial rule.[30] It was argued that, in one sense, this could in fact help to prevent Hong Kong from becoming a base for subversion against China and thus serve the interests of Beijing. Naturally, this balancing act required colossal effort and shrewd political judgement. It is an understatement to say that the colonial government was in a precarious position.

When the 'Conditions Are Ripe'

British officials had constantly debated the best time to discuss the matter of the future of Hong Kong with China. The 1969 'Long Term Study' identified four possible scenarios of retreat from Hong Kong:

(a) To abdicate the position in Hong Kong by unilateral action;
(b) To accept indirect Chinese influence over the way in which we administer Hong Kong with a view to the ultimate transference of control;
(c) To approach China formally with a view to negotiating our withdrawal; or,
(d) To approach China informally about an eventual withdrawal at a suitable agreed date.

Options (a) and (b) were seen as non-starters. The third option was viable but 'there could be no drawing back if the terms were unacceptable and British position in Hong Kong could not survive abortive negotiation', which would put London in a very disadvantageous bargaining position. The issue must thus be handled with extreme caution. The preferred interim strategy was option (d): an informal sounding out with China about British intentions to retreat from Hong Kong, pursuing through a reliable intermediary with the utmost secrecy. The paper envisaged that the British side could relay its intention to leave Hong Kong and their concern with the orderly transfer of power to China. To this end, London would endeavour to avoid disruptive moves such as the development of a representative and accountable government in the colony. In return, Britain would not accept humiliation and disorder and insisted on its obligation to protect those to whom it

---

30. Steve Tsang, 'Strategy for Survival: The Cold War and Hong Kong's Policy towards Kuomintang and Chinese Communist Activities in the 1950', *The Journal of Imperial and Commonwealth History* 25, no. 2 (1997): 294–317.

had a duty.[31] The study did not commend immediate action, however. The prevailing radicalism in China and its tensions with the outside world in the late 1960s obviously did not present a favourable environment for such a delicate communication. There was no specific time frame suggested for the initiation of this contact, but the report stated that the initiative should be taken not later than the early 1980s.[32] The FCO paper, 'The Future of Hong Kong' produced in 1971 shared this analysis but added that the approach was more urgent a matter. The paper warned that 'the nearer we approach to 1997 the greater is the danger of loss of confidence in Hong Kong', which could lead not only to a breakdown in administration, but might also erode business confidence. It envisaged that when investment fell off and the industrial machine ran down, Hong Kong could quickly turn into a financial liability to Britain. The 1997 problem could potentially come to the surface by the mid-1970s, when the government had to make a decision on the renewal of franchises for utilities such as telephone and electricity services. Again, no immediate action was recommended, but FCO officials were instructed to review the situation annually from then onwards.[33]

The debate within the FCO over the right moment to sound this out with China continued throughout the early 1970s. In 1973, Percy Cradock, who served as Head of Assessment Staff of the Cabinet Office, argued that the time was right for making an initial contact with Beijing, the Anglo-Chinese relationship at the time being good.[34] Yet Alec Douglas-Home, the Foreign Secretary, remained indecisive. While the Foreign Secretary agreed with Cradock that the present climate in terms of relationship between the two countries was favourable, but he was concerned about the consequences of premature engagement with China. Douglas-Home had not completely abandoned hope that the British might stay beyond 1997, and he did not find 1973 to be a particularly promising moment to wrangle a favourable deal. He believed that China was not yet prepared to talk, and his personal encounter with Zhou Enlai certainly affected his judgement. Zhou told him in their meeting in Beijing in November 1972 that China would not use force to take back Hong Kong, and its future was a matter that should be settled through negotiation at some future date, but that 'there was no need to discuss it now'. The same message that 'this was a matter for the future' was relayed to Douglas-Home again by Ji Pengfei, the Chinese

---

31. Cabinet Ministerial Committee on Hong Kong, 'Hong Kong: Long Term Study', 28 March 1969, FCO40/160, TNA.
32. Cabinet Ministerial Committee on Hong Kong, 'Hong Kong: Long Term Study', 28 March 1969, FCO40/160, TNA.
33. Memorandum by the Secretary of State for Foreign and Commonwealth Affairs, Alec Douglas-Home, 13 December 1971, CAB148/117, TNA.
34. Cradock to Stuart, 3 January 1973, FCO40/424, TNA.

Foreign Secretary, the following June.[35] Besides, he also saw the danger of an earlier negotiation: public knowledge of an agreement with China on British a retreat twenty-four years before 1997 could destroy local confidence immediately and make the British position in Hong Kong untenable. The uncertainty of the succession of leadership and the outcome of the factional struggle in the aftermath of the death of Mao Zedong and Zhou Enlai also reinforced this wait-and-see approach. In the 1976 Hong Kong Planning Paper, it was stated explicitly that 'there is nothing or little that can be done until the next generation of Chinese leaders has emerged, and their policies established'. The document acknowledged that this policy was 'not without risk' and the assumption of continuing tranquillity of China would be difficult to defend publicly when the Hong Kong community started to worry about the future. However, it was the 'least risk policy and the one best suited to present circumstances', the paper concluded.[36]

MacLehose: Buying Time for Negotiation

When MacLehose arrived in Hong Kong, he generally agreed with this approach. He was no stranger to the deliberations over the long-term future of the colony. As Political Advisor to Governor Robert Black in the 1960s, he had been involved in the many discussions on this matter and was aware of the colonial officials and Whitehall's analysis of the Hong Kong issue. For example, in an exchange with the Colonial Office over the 1963 *People's Daily* article about China's position on Hong Kong, he believed that the combination of military deterrence and commercial advantage should continue to influence China in favour of not disturbing the status quo in Hong Kong.[37] Upon his imminent return to the colony in 1971, MacLehose further elaborated his view on the handling of Britain's relationship with China in the document Guideline for the Governor Designate. MacLehose prepared this document for the FCO himself, and in it were listed the policy priorities of his governorship. He argued that the economic utility of Hong Kong to China was the key to the colony's survival, and with China's hunger for foreign exchange, the status quo was unlikely to be disrupted in foreseeable future. For him, Hong Kong's future remained obscure, and as Governor all he could do was to ensure that 'the advantage China obtains (from Hong Kong) are maximized and the disadvantages and loss of face

---

35. Webb to McLaren, Chinese Statements on the Status of Hong Kong, 30 March 1979, FCO40/1058, TNA.
36. Planning Paper on Hong Kong, 1976, p. 11, FCO40/704, TNA.
37. MacLehose to Higham (Colonial Office), 2 April 1964, CO1030/1674, TNA.

are minimized'.[38] In his review of his first year of Governorship, he reiterated this belief:

> The most obvious benefit the Chinese Government derives from Hong Kong is financial and economic. And though this factor may not be conclusive, it is one to which the present leaders of China obviously give great weight in deciding to accept the status quo.[39]

Based on this reasoning, MacLehose preferred a delayed negotiation. In another report to London in 1972, the Governor spelt out his plans for preparing for the definitive negotiations with China:

> I assume that our objectives should be ... to gain 10 or 15 years in which Hong Kong can have time to grow and prosper in confidence, suppress its warts and wrinkles, and become as hard for China to absorb as possible, and in which post Mao/Zhou China can emerge and show its credentials as a negotiating partner.[40]

To achieve this, the Governor pledged that Hong Kong needed 'to tackle the domestic problems of the Colony so vigorously during the next 10 years that they would be eliminated to a point at which Western standards there was nothing to be ashamed of anywhere, and by Chinese standards much to spur civic pride and a sense of achievement everywhere'.[41]

Beneath MacLehose's strategy of development and reform lies a sense of cautious optimism that Britain could secure via negotiation a 'special status' for Hong Kong after 1997. In exchange with the FCO right before the commencement of his governorship in October 1971:

> I do not dissent at all from the conclusion that we should negotiate, at the right time, for the best terms that we can term that we can get, not even excluding renewal of the Lease. For my part I think that the best we could hope for would be some form of special status for Hong Kong under which sovereignty would return to China, but Hong Kong might be defined as a special administrative district to be managed in a way that would facilitate the continued residence of foreigners.[42]

---

38. Guideline for the Governor Designate, Hong Kong: Paper C: Hong Kong and China, 1976, FCO40/329, TNA.
39. 'Who Benefits from Hong Kong?' The Governor of Hong Kong to the Secretary of State for Foreign and Commonwealth Affairs, 11 October 1973, FCO40/439, TNA.
40. MacLehose, Hong Kong in the New Sino/British Dialogue: Summary, 5 May 1972, FCO21/1023, TNA.
41. MacLehose, Hong Kong in the New Sino/British Dialogue: Summary, 5 May 1972, FCO21/1023, TNA.
42. MacLehose to Wilford, 27 October 1971, FCO40/331, TNA.

MacLehose further articulated his vision for Hong Kong's future shortly after he took up the office of Governor. His plans and the ways in which he believed he could contribute to this prospect warrant extended quotation:

> They [the Chinese] might see merit in some continuing arrangement for Hong Kong whereby a special regime was established that nominally removed the colonial stigma, but preserved for China some of the economic and other material and political benefits of the present status, saved them from having to absorb a population with such different standards of living and attitudes of mind, and on the other hand preserved for foreigners a tolerable trading base, some security for investment and acceptable living conditions while concentrating them in a single area where they did not affect life in the rest of China . . . I believe that the more undeveloped and discontented Hong Kong is the less likelihood there would be of this or a similar concept being adopted, and conversely the evolve the colony the more attractive such a half-way house might appear to the Chinese leadership, assuming it was prepared to compromise at all . . . But I think that this is the best contribution the Hong Kong Government can make to achieving a satisfactory settlement, and for this it would need about 10 years.[43]

MacLehose: Separating Land Lease Issue from Sovereignty Controversy

However, by mid-1978, with the expectation of finishing his tenure as the Governor in about a year's time, MacLehose felt obliged to raise an issue concerning the future of Hong Kong. While he maintained the view that it was still too early to approach China for clarification of British position in Hong Kong beyond 1997, and 'the time when that will happen is still a few years off', he saw the urgency of a 'legal problem': the right of the Hong Kong government to grant lease in New Territories beyond the end of June of 1997. The gist of the problem was that thousands of land leases in the New Territories would expire three days before 1 July 1997, when the lease of the New Territories signed between the British and the Qing governments in 1898 ran out. The Governor contended that the approaching expiry date, and, even more importantly, the inability of the Hong Kong government to grant new leases extending beyond 1997, would deter major investments and thus create problems in terms of confidence, unless some solution could be found. The urgency of the issue had certainly been reinforced by the Governor's audacious housing programme. In 1972,

---

43. MacLehose, Hong Kong in the New Sino/British Dialogue: Summary, 5 May 1972, FCO21/1023, TNA.

the Governor pledged to house 1.8 million people in his ten-year public housing programme. Central to the success of this vision was the creation of new towns. The Special Committee for Land Production was established in 1977 to identify possible sources of land and consequently, the potential of developing New Territories was raised.[44]

For MacLehose, this was a technical problem that could be separated from the question of Hong Kong future. He took the initiative to detail his proposal to FCO colleagues in a letter in July 1978.[45] The solution proposed by MacLehose was for the Hong Kong government to issue future land leases in the New Territories without a fixed term, valid 'for so long as Her Majesty may administer the Territories', and to convert the existing leases into indeterminate leases of the same kind. The solution would require new legislation in Hong Kong as a lease of indefinite term was unknown in the Common Law system. This needed to be backed by an Order in Council in the United Kingdom. This was necessary for two reasons. It could help to reduce the risk of appeals to the legislation in the local courts and enhanced the position of the Hong Kong government against these possible legal challenges. Yet the main concern was political. The Order would demonstrate London's full support for this action. For MacLehose, the appeal of the proposal for Beijing was that it did not require any positive action on the part of the Chinese. He argued that 'all they would need to do would be to raise no objection . . . and perhaps to allow us to say in public that they had not objected'.[46]

FCO officials, who were always concerned with the nature and timing of an eventual approach to the Chinese, showed great interest in MacLehose's initiative. Antony Rushford, Deputy Legal Adviser of FCO, did not share the Governor's view that the Hong Kong government could not legally grant leases extending beyond the expiry date of the New Territory Lease.[47] Nevertheless, FCO officials appreciated MacLehose's tactic of obliterating the significance of 1997 and focusing only on the legal and administrative aspect of the issue, and they also saw the merit of the solution that required no action on the part of the Chinese government other than not objecting to the steps taken in Hong Kong. They also shared MacLehose's emphasis on the importance of securing China's consent to the proposed legislation.[48]

---

44. Maurice Yip, 'New Town Planning as Diplomatic Planning: Scalar Politics, British-Chinese Relations, and Hong Kong', *Journal of Urban History* (2020): 1–20.
45. Deny Roberts to McLaren, 6 July 1978, FCO21/1632, TNA.
46. McLaren to Murray and Cortazzi, 14 March 1979, FCO40/1058, TNA.
47. Rushford to Gardner, 17 August 1978, FCO21/1632, TNA.
48. Gardner to MacLehose, 8 September 1978, FCO21/1633, TNA.

A key question remained: was it a right time to make a move? China's changing political outlook played a role in MacLehose's reasoning and helped to persuade London of the validity of his approach. Deng Xiaoping, who was perceived as a pragmatist and a moderate, was now firmly in charge and a purge of radicals from the party-state machinery was in full swing. The concern with the succession of leadership was thus no longer an issue. Deng's embrace of modernization and economic development would also enhance the strategic value of Hong Kong. Similarly, China was developing a different approach to her relationship with the West. The normalization of relationship with the United States in 1972 was followed by elevation of diplomatic relationships with the United Kingdom. Beijing's friendly overture to Taiwan further confirmed its new image as a rational player in global politics. Robin McLaren of Hong Kong and General Department concurred, 'Anglo/China relations are now excellent, and the atmosphere in Peking is certainly more conductive to a frank discussion about the future of Hong Kong.'[49] Percy Cradock shared a similar view. The British Ambassador to Beijing believed that with Deng Xiaoping at the height of his power, the next one or two years were likely to be as good as the British could get. He suggested to take 'the next favourable opportunity to approach the Chinese'.[50]

The possibility of a visit by the Governor to Beijing appeared as a favourable opportunity. The Governor was invited to visit Beijing in 1979 by Chinese Minister of Foreign Trade, Li Qiang, and this presented an opening for MacLehose's initiative. David Owen, the British Foreign Secretary, was convinced by the Governor's approach and the timing and agreed that the Governor should accept the invitation and sound out the Chinese about the idea. The imminent departure of the Governor was a consideration, as the Foreign Secretary believed that the British government should 'exploit to the full the period during which Sir Murray MacLehose remains in office',[51] as the Governor was a very experienced China hand and well respected in Hong Kong and in Britain. David Owen also appeared optimistic about the viability of this approach, as he wrote to MacLehose:

> I think we should aim to make substantial progress if we can by combining yours and my visits at a time of greatly improved relations. The decisiveness of the present Chinese Government in many areas at present might make it possible to reach agreement faster than we expect.[52]

---

49. McLaren to Murray, 29 January 1979, FCO40/1058, TNA.
50. Cradock to FCO, 4 January 1979, FCO21/1734, TNA.
51. Walden to Far East Department, 26 January 1979, FCO21/1734, TNA.
52. Owen to Hong Kong, 14 March 1979, FCO40/1058, TNA.

The Governor's proposal was also endorsed at the very top level of the British government. 'The Prime Minister has been informed and is content,' MacLehose was told.[53]

Approaching Deng Xiaoping

After securing approval from within the Whitehall, the Governor, together with Cradock and other FCO officials, set to work hammering out the strategy for presenting these ideas in Beijing. It was agreed that the dialogue should start with the possible contribution which Hong Kong could make to China's modernization program and general economic development. The Governor could illustrate this with the collaboration and joint projects between Hong Kong and Guangdong in recent years and expand on how each could help the other. Following these amicable economic accounts, the Governor would introduce the proposed solution to the land lease issue, with four key messages to be delivered when explaining the rationale of the proposal:

(a) Something must be done quite soon if the more valuable types of long-term investment were not to be deterred;
(b) The Hong Kong government would have to find an answer fairly soon if the right sort of development was to continue;
(c) The answer would have no impact on China's well-known position on Hong Kong; and,
(d) The essence of the action would be to stop issuing leases drafted to expire on 29 June 1997, and substitute a validity for 'as long as the Crown administers' the territories; existing leases with a terminal date would be similarly amended. It would require a simple piece of legislation.[54]

In order not to overdramatize the occasion, David Wilson, the Political Adviser to the Governor, was instructed to touch base with officials of the New China News Agency (NCNA) in Hong Kong and offer hints about the Governor's intention to discuss land leases in the New Territories during his prospective visit to Beijing.[55]

MacLehose was treated as a VIP during this visit. He was granted meetings with Huang Hua, the Chinese Foreign Secretary, Liao Chengzhi, the Director of the Office of Hong Kong and Macao Affairs, and most importantly, Deng Xiaoping, the de facto top leader of Communist China. The

---
53. McLaren to Murray and Cortazzi, 14 March 1979, FCO40/1058, TNA.
54. MacLehose to FCO, Handling of Leases Problem during Visit to Peking, 12 February 1979, FCO40/1058, TNA.
55. MacLehose to FCO, 19 March 1979, FCO40/1058, TNA.

Chinese officials were in a mood to show their goodwill to the Governor and revealed enthusiastically their appreciation of the Hong Kong government and their continued willingness to engage with the colonial administration. The Governor was delighted at this unequivocal expression of the Chinese leaders' desire for increased trade, tourism and investment, and willingness to cooperate with Hong Kong in these areas. He also took comfort in the Chinese officials' acknowledgement of the current strength of Hong Kong's economy and the importance of maintaining business confidence to sustaining its vitality.[56] The British side's 'economic card' argument was officially vindicated by the top level of Chinese government.

Deng Xiaoping was also in the mood to share his preliminary views on the future of Hong Kong. Deng's vision of Hong Kong's future was one under Chinese sovereignty with some political changes, but he stressed that any arrangement and discussion would respect the special status of Hong Kong. This special status would guarantee that economic life and security of investment would not be affected. He went on to draw analogies with Taiwan and Macao. China had affirmed its respect for Taiwan's special status and would not change its social system or affect its living standards, and he argued that the administration in Taiwan would enjoy local autonomy and even maintain its own armed force under Chinese sovereignty. Deng stressed that policy would also apply to Hong Kong and Macao. He explained that 'China needed Hong Kong and the policy was beneficial to socialist construction.'[57]

Yet MacLehose was more concerned with the immediate future of Hong Kong and was eager to propose his 'practical solution' to the land lease issue to Deng. MacLehose told Deng that the long-term future of Hong Kong was a matter between the Chinese and British governments, but that there was however an immediate problem of individual leases in the New Territories that could not wait. MacLehose explained painstakingly that this matter was not related to China's underlying position on Hong Kong, but that if the problem could be solved, a solution would attract investment and thus would be beneficial to China and Britain. Deng's only immediate comment on the proposal was that he disliked the phrase 'for as long as Her Majesty may administer the Territories' and suggested that the mention of British administration should be avoided. However, he emphasized that the Governor should tell investors that they should 'put their hearts at ease' and concluded that in this century—and even at the beginning of next—Hong

---

56. MacLehose to McLaren, Visit to China and the Leases, 10 April 1979, FCO40/1058, TNA.
57. Beijing to FCO, Personal for Cortazzi: New Territories Leases, 3 April 1979, FCO40/1058, TNA.

Kong would still remain a capitalist territory while China was developing its socialist system.[58]

Deng's message did little to allay the anxiety of local businesses. For example, members of the newly created Advisory Committee on Diversification under the Financial Secretary, which was comprised of local business elites and was assigned with the task of exploring the economic prospects of Hong Kong, found Deng's message futile for sustaining confidence and the economic development that hinged on it. In a secret assessment, they concluded that 'there was a growing body of opinion that it was now an opportune moment for Britain and China to commence preliminary dialogue about sovereignty and the longer the delay the more perplexed and vexed people would be'.[59]

MacLehose and other British officials had mixed feelings. On the one hand, Deng's official acceptance of the status quo and the economic contribution of Hong Kong was appreciated. The Governor was particularly impressed with the initiative of Yang Shangkun in meeting him when he was on his way back to Hong Kong. Yang was a close ally of Deng Xiaoping and was now in charge of Guangzhou. MacLehose took this as a move by China towards the consolidation of Hong Kong-Guangzhou collaborations. The term 'special status' and the continuation of capitalism were also mentioned for the first time at the top level, and this would leave room for the speculation about Britain's role after 1997. However, the Governor found Deng's general assurance rather empty:

> [m]oreover the value of an economic assurance cannot be separated from an economy's political framework. There are memories of the swings of the political pendulum in China, and it is far from accepted here that political stability has been achieved. Much would depend on how far in the future a political change was envisaged.[60]

His major disappointment, of course, was the ambiguity of Deng's response to his proposal. He believed that Deng did not fully understand that his ideas were related to the immediate problem about leases in New Territories rather than to long-term Chinese claims of sovereignty over Hong Kong. The Governor argued that this was partly due to Deng's lack of briefing in advance since his specific request for a meeting with Liao Chengzhi before Deng was rejected. As the Director of the Office of Hong Kong and Macao Affairs, Liao was regarded as the most knowledgeable

---

58. Beijing to FCO, Personal for Cortazzi: New Territories Leases, 3 April 1979, FCO40/1058, TNA.
59. Sze-yuen Chung, *Hong Kong's Journey to Reunification: Memoirs of Sze-yuen Chung* (Hong Kong: Chinese University of Hong Kong Press, 2001), 31–32.
60. MacLehose to McLaren: Visit to China and the Leases, 10 April 1979, FCO40/1058, TNA.

person on Hong Kong matters in the Chinese government, and he should have been able to grasp the gist of MacLehose's proposal and the attendant issue. Liao's briefing for Deng may have made all the difference, the Governor believed.

Percy Cradock, who also attended the meeting with Deng, was relatively more upbeat, describing the meeting was 'on the whole a good one'. He was not surprised by Deng's refusal to give a clear answer to the proposal and took comfort in the fact that there was no immediate negative response.[61] The Ambassador had a more nuanced understanding of the ambiguity in Deng's position. He believed that Deng was not yet certain when Beijing would resume sovereignty over Hong Kong, and preferred to keep his options to himself since he was now fully preoccupied with the task of luring Taiwan back to the motherland. Cradock was certainly more aware of the sensitivity of the issue in hand, and was more sympathetic to Deng's apprehension about the implications of MacLehose's proposal:

> While we are doing nothing to which the Chinese need object, we are in fact paving the way for a continuation of the political situation beyond 1997. We are affecting the Chinese position though not contradicting it.[62]

Cradock, in other words, saw the implications of the proposal beyond a simple solution to the immediate problem of land leases in the New Territories, and questioned whether it could be so easily decoupled from the British role in Hong Kong beyond 1997. Cradock was right. According to Zhou Nan, who later headed the Chinese delegation for the Sino-British negotiations, Deng Xiaoping was concerned that consent to MacLehose's proposal as providing a licence for the British to rule Hong Kong beyond 1997.[63]

In reality, it was very doubtful whether the British legal distinction between territories ceded in permanence (that is, Hong Kong Island and Kowloon Peninsula south of Boundary Street), and the territory leased under the 1898 Treaty, would have much relevance for the Communists, since they had never recognized the authority of the three 'unequal treaties'. In fact, it was hard to imagine how the colony could survive economically and socially if the New Territories were returned to China. In his 1971 conversation with Malcolm MacDonald, a British MP, Zhou Enlai pinpointed the interdependence of the two parts of the colony and argued

---

61. Cradock to FCO, 30 March 1979, FCO40/1058, TNA.
62. Cradock to McLaren, Visit to China and the Leases, 23 April 1979, FCO40/1059, TNA.
63. Daoyi Zhong et al., ed., *Oral History by Zhou Nan* (Hong Kong: Joint Publishing Company Ltd, 2007), 239.

that 'Hong Kong would not be a viable administrative or economic unit without the New Territories.'[64]

'Unnecessary and Inappropriate'[65]

In the face of a lack of clear agreement from the Chinese side, the British decided to play a wait-and-see game and to give the Communist officials more time to digest and evaluate the proposal. Cradock suggested that the Chinese government needed more education. Yet the Ambassador warned that this should be mostly done at an ambassadorial level in Beijing or the colony since 'any more high-level approach would give the exercise too much political content and detract from our presentation of it as a piece of legal housekeeping designed simply to maintain investment in the interests of both sides'.[66] MacLehose agreed but wanted to set a time frame for the whole process. Unaware of the prospect of an extension of his governorship, MacLehose apparently wanted to get the job done before he left office. He thus saw his last annual speech to the Legislative Council on 10 October 1979 as the ideal occasion for the official announcement of his legislative plan for the land lease issue. He noted that 'no similar opportunity will occur before I leave'. His idea was to include a public announcement of British legislative intentions by adding the proposal to the legislative schedule of the Council for the coming year. This would look like a routine legislative practice since it would come as part of a general programme rather than in dramatic isolation. This would also give Beijing ample time to decide whether to agree or to object to the proposal.[67]

In July 1979, Cradock took the initiative and approached Song Zhiguang, the Chinese Assistant Foreign Secretary. Cradock passed Song a prepared note detailing the rationale and implications of the British proposal and conveyed the 'deadline' suggested by MacLehose. Once again, it was stressed that the British 'had no intention to pre-judge in any way what particular course of action with regard to the future of the territory might be pursued by either a present or a future Chinese government'.[68] This was followed up via David Wilson's meeting with Li Jusheng, the Second Director of the NCNA in Hong Kong. Li was aware of the dialogue between Cradock and Song in Beijing and admitted that the Chinese side 'now had

---

64. Webb to McLaren, Chinese Statements on the Status of Hong Kong, 30 March 1979, FCO40/1058, TNA.
65. Cradock to FCO, 24 September 1979, FCO40/1060, TNA.
66. Cradock to McLaren, Visit to China and the Leases, 23 April 1979, FCO40/1059, TNA.
67. MacLehose to FCO, 3 May 1979, FCO40/1059, TNA.
68. Speaking Note on New Territories-Left with Chinese Assistant Foreign Minister, Song Zhiguang, by the British Ambassador on 5 July 1979, FCO40/1060, TNA.

a better understanding of what was intended than when the Governor had spoken to Deng', but replied that the matter was complicated and they would need time to examine it further. Li, however, promised that they would reply sometime in August.[69] Yet come August there was still no reply. Nevertheless, the knowledge that the Chinese side was now giving the issue serious consideration convinced MacLehose to reconsider the 'deadline'. He argued that,

> we know the Chinese are giving our proposal serious consideration and have not dismissed it out of hand. We believed it to be in their interest as much as ours, and in no way to prejudice their position or freedom of action with regard to Hong Kong. But it does involve both time and a major effort on the part of the Chinese to come to see this, considerable courage to recommend it, and a decision at the highest level to authorize it. All this or attempt to hustle, it will not help the answer we wish.[70]

In addition, the Chinese premier Hua Guofeng was due to visit London in late 1979, and this appeared to be a better occasion for both sides to exchange views on this matter. Thus, MacLehose suggested that, if by mid-September, the Chinese had still not responded, he would inform Wang Huang, the First Director of the NCNA, that the government legislation empowering land leases with no fixed term would aggravate the uncertainty of the situation and exacerbate the spike in land price, and so he would not include the proposal in the legislative schedule in October as originally planned.[71]

The new administration under Thatcher was however less enthusiastic about MacLehose's approach idea than the Callaghan government. Since the 'setback' in Beijing, the Governor's proposal had been re-evaluated within the FCO. William Quantrill of the Hong Kong and General Department of the FCO contended that 'we might now be on the wrong track in continuing to pursue the idea of indeterminate lease as a solution to the New Territories lease problem'. He argued that the new legislation required would attract more attention than it might otherwise do. Based on the experience of other former colonies, Quantrill argued that 'it has never been held to invalidate leases and contracts extending beyond the point at which the change of political sovereignty is to take place: it is taken for granted that the new government will assume the obligations of its predecessors', and the new government would be perfectly entitled to repudiate any obligations which she did not want to maintain.[72] The Governor's proposed

---
69. MacLehose to FCO, 30 July 1979, FCO40/1060, TNA.
70. MacLehose to McLaren, 30 August 1979, FCO40/1060, TNA.
71. MacLehose to McLaren, 30 August 1979, FCO40/1060, TNA.
72. Quantrill to McLaren, 9 May 1979, FCO40/1059, TNA.

legislation was therefore deemed as unnecessary. More damagingly, the Governor had also lost ministerial support for his proposal. Michael Havers, the Attorney General of the Thatcher administration who came to the office in May 1979, suggested that it might be better to wait until 1997 and then to draw up a further Treaty if the Chinese were so inclined.[73] Unlike his predecessor, Lord Carrington, the new Foreign Secretary was also not very enthusiastic. He had made it clear to his subordinates in the FCO that he had some doubts about whether the solution proposed by the Governor and the Ambassador would in fact achieve its objective of inspiring new confidence in the business community. Moreover, even a close advisor to the Governor had withdrawn his support for the proposal.[74] Yuet-Keung Kan, the senior unofficial member of Executive Council who was present at the meeting with Deng Xiaoping in March 1979, told Lord Carrington that he thought that 'the Governor was making too much of his proposed solution to the lease issues, and that this solution would not convince Hong Kong public opinion'.[75] This was an important shift with MacLehose sensed that his initiative may have failed.

Unfortunately, MacLehose was right. On 24 September 1979, Cradock was summoned to Song Zhiguang, who dutifully read out a memorandum from the Chinese Foreign Ministry to the Ambassador. The memorandum firstly reiterated the special status of Hong Kong. It stated that Hong Kong's special circumstances would be considered and the confidence of investors would not be damaged when the time to address the future of the colony finally came. It added that the statement of Deng Xiaoping in the March meeting should be a powerful enough assurance to allay the concerns of these investors. For these reasons, the Chinese government would not accept MacLehose's proposal:

> The Chinese government considers as unnecessary and inappropriate the legal steps that the British side now proposes to take regarding the term of administration of the New Territories by the Governor of Hong Kong and the question of lease for land in the New Territories. Therefore, the Chinese government urges the British side to desist from taking the proposed actions, for the repercussions therefrom would adversely affect the interests of both the Chinese and British sides.[76]

The British side was understandably disappointed but conceded that it was unwise to go ahead with the legislation. 'I do not think we were wrong on that score, but we evidently underestimated Chinese sensitivity on any

---

73. McLaren to Cortazzi, 19 July 1979, FCO40/1060, TNA.
74. A Note by Walden, 5 July 1979, FCO40/1060, TNA.
75. A Note by Walden, 5 July 1979, FCO40/1060, TNA.
76. Cradock to FCO, 24 September 1979, FCO40/1060, TNA.

question touching on the future of Hong Kong,' Robin McLaren concluded.[77] Cradock believed that Beijing had seen the British approach in a wider context, and that any attempt to isolate the land lease issue from that of sovereignty was futile. He argued that 'they will be unwilling to take action in respect of Hong Kong that could upset their Taiwan planning or weaken their position in relation to the Taiwan authorities. The essence of their position on Taiwan is that sovereignty must not be conceded', adding that 'the Chinese almost certainly see the only way ahead as one requiring some form of recognition of Chinese sovereignty'.[78] Cradock attributed this failure to Beijing's desire to sweep the problem 'under the carpet of generalities of goodwill'. The British, on the other hand, had tried 'to get them to lift the carpet' in an attempt to make progress.[79] MacLehose accepted that his effort was a fair but failed attempt, but he did not agree that Deng's remarks had settled the confidence issue and that his proposal was therefore unnecessary. He insisted that economic pressures would emerge in three to four years' time, which would prove the Chinese wrong.[80] The proposal officially died when Carrington informed the Chinese premier, Hua Guofeng, during their meeting in London on 1 November 1979, that the British government would not pursue the legislation 'since any proposal had to be acceptable to both sides'.[81]

The Tin Shui Wai Project: A False Dawn

One lesson which the British learned from the setback was that China did not want to be 'pushed'. Cradock came to the conclusion that the Chinese preferred to keep their options open and resented that the British seemed to be taking the lead on the future of Hong Kong and expecting China to acquiesce.[82] While MacLehose concurred with the view that Beijing wanted more time to ponder their next move on the Hong Kong matter, he argued that 'as time passes pressure will mount on them from their own trading organizations and business contacts in Hong Kong to solve the problem'.[83] Sooner or later, he expected Chinese officials would have to reveal their intentions:

---

77. McLaren to Benjamin, 9 October 1979, FCO40/1060, TNA.
78. Cradock to FCO, 5 October 1979, FCO40/1060, TNA.
79. Cradock to MacLehose, 8 April 1980, FCO40/1162, TNA.
80. MacLehose to FCO, 9 October 1979, FCO40/1060, TNA.
81. Records of Second Plenary Discussion between the Prime Minister and Premier Hua Guofeng: 1 November 1979, FCO40/1061, TNA.
82. Cradock to FCO, 24 September 1979, FCO40/1060, TNA.
83. MacLehose to FCO, 27 September 1979, FCO40/1060, TNA.

There could be other and less obtrusive ways of handling this problem if the Chinese wish to take the initiative (our proposal was designed to enable them to keep out it) and I should be surprised if sooner or later and through one channel or another we do not get hints of what possibilities the Chinese have in mind.[84]

The Governor was particularly intrigued by a conversation which he had with Wang Kuang, the First Director of NCNA, shortly after Beijing's rejection of his proposal. Wang raised the issue of the impact of Deng's assurance on business confidence and admitted that he had the impression that the Vice-Premier's words had not put the hearts of the Hong Kong people at ease. The problem of the New Territories leases was complicated, and would be addressed politically, or, as the British had suggested. He argued however that neither solution was practicable at present. There was however a third approach: economic cooperation. Wang suggested that business collaboration between Hong Kong and China would improve prosperity on both sides and render the problem of assurance less important. Upon the Governor's request for clarification, Wang confirmed that investment in real estate in both Hong Kong Island and the New Territories would also be counted as economic cooperation.[85]

The expectation of hints from China and this conversation with Wang may explain the British misreading of the significance of the Tin Shui Wai Project. On 7 January 1980, the Secretary for the New Territories received a formal request for permission to develop a new town in Tin Shui Wai from the Luen Tak Company. The land known as Tin Shui Wai was probably the largest plot of developable land in New Territories, comprising about 486 hectares (1,200 acres). It lay to the north of Ping Shan, Yuen Long, and included almost all the land in that area between the road leading to Lau Fo Shan and the sea. The proposed project was a massive new housing initiative accommodating more than 200,000 residents with all the necessary amenities, and because most of the land was designated for agricultural use at time of application, government approval was required. The project was important not only for its scale, but was also for its completion date. It was unlikely that the construction could be concluded before the mid-1980s, so it required the granting of land use beyond 1997. What made the case even more interesting was the background of the investor. The largest shareholder of Luen Tak turned out to be China Resources, a Chinese state-owned enterprise. By late October 1979, China Resources had spent in the region of HKD 500 million to acquire a 50–55 per cent share of Luen Tak.

---

84. MacLehose to FCO, 27 September 1979, FCO40/1060, TNA.
85. Record of Part of a Conversation between H E the Governor and Mr Wang Kuang, First Director NCNA at dinner at Government House on 1 November 1979, FCO40/1061, TNA.

The other significant shareholder was Li Ka-shing, who had recently been invited to sit on the board of China's International Trust and Investment Corporation, a de facto sovereign fund of the Chinese government. David Wilson believed that China Resources was in it 'purely to make money'. Nevertheless, 'an official Chinese organization owning and trying to develop a large tract of land in the New Territories is a novel concept to put it mildly,' the Political Advisor reminded his FCO colleagues.[86] Meanwhile, British inklings of the potential significance of the project were further raised by Gordon Wu of Trafalgar Holdings, one of the local companies involved in the project. Wu made an approach to David Akers-Jones, the Secretary for the New Territories and made two suggestions. Firstly, he suggested that the payment of the land development premium should be spread over twenty years, that is, stretching beyond 1997. In addition, he claimed that there was no need to set the expiry date of the lease to three days before 30 June 1997 as usual, since China Resources were confident that the status quo of Hong Kong would outlast that date. Wu insisted that these messages were relayed on the instruction of China Resources.[87]

The Hong Kong government responded to these developments with great interest. Reflecting on the setbacks in 1979, the Governor still believed that it was right for him to raise the issue of the New Territories land lease with Deng Xiaoping in Beijing. Since his attempt in 1979 had been rejected categorically, it was unwise for the British to make another approach, but the Governor argued that a Chinese agreement to a solution was still imperative to economic stability of the colony. MacLehose believed that 1982 would be a potentially critical year, as fifteen years was the standard for mortgage agreements, and 'if confidence in the value of land leases in the New Territories began to fade, not only would investment dry up, but property developers would rapidly redeploy their cash flow overseas, with consequent damage to the value of Hong Kong dollar'.[88] MacLehose also believed that one year after he had raised the land lease issue to Deng, Beijing should be able to understand the distinction between the long-term problem of Hong Kong's future and the short-term issue of the New Territories land leases. The significance of the latter, which was his primary concern, increasingly began to be shared by the local business sector, including those with connections to China. Businesses had expressed their uneasiness to the Bank of China and the NCNA and urged the Chinese and British governments to reach an agreement on the issue.[89] MacLehose was

---

86. Wilson to Hong Kong and General Department (FCO), China Resources Purchase of Land in Hong Kong, 25 January 1980, FCO40/1162, TNA.
87. Wilson to Clift, Hong Kong and General Department, 5 June 1980, FCO40/1062, TNA.
88. MacLehose to Cradock, 22 February 1980, FCO40/1163, TNA.
89. MacLehose to Cradock, 22 February 1980, FCO40/1162, TNA.

therefore even more confident than before that hints about China's position would soon emerge.

With these presumptions in mind, it is easy to understand the Governor's assumption that the Tin Shui Wai project was the initiative of the Chinese government:

> There are indications that the Chinese are themselves seeing land purchase in the New Territories as a way of boosting confidence and eroding the significance of 1997. China Resources is involved in the major land development at Tin Shui Wai and it is possible that within the next one or two months they may suggest a 20-year lease. Whether they do or don't, this is the sort of eventuality we must now be ready for and consequently must clear our minds quickly on the complex legal issues involved.[90]

Ian Orr, the Acting Political Adviser, also wrote that 'we are interested in the political implications of the involvement by China Resources. We think it possible that these have been carefully considered on the Chinese side but unfortunately we have no information about the level at which this may have been done.'[91]

FCO officials also took a serious interest in these developments. While agreeing with MacLehose's suggestion that they should not 'risk another rebuff', Edward Youde, Deputy Under-Secretary for Asia and the Far East at the time, saw great potential in the Tin Shui Wai project for resuming the discussion with China:

> It may be that they (the Chinese) will not be prepared to examine practical solutions in any detail until they see clear signs of business confidences slipping in Hong Kong; that might not be until the late 1981 or even 1982. Much the most satisfactory course for us would be to use concrete cases (e.g. Tin Shui Wai) to build up an arrangement which would allow for land leases to run beyond 1997. That would probably lead naturally into a discussion on various possible types of determinate or indeterminate leases, and possibly the question of the need for legislation in Hong Kong.[92]

A detailed strategy, in fact, had been hammered out in a meeting between the Governor, various senior colonial officials, and Richard Clift of the Hong Kong and General Department of the FCO in late November, for rekindling the discussion on the required legislation for land lease approval beyond 1997. According to the plan, David Akers-Jones was instructed to offer two proposals to China Resources concerning their land deals: (a) a lease beyond 1997 with no terminal date, and (b) a lease of seventy-five years

---

90. MacLehose to Donald, 7 July 1980, FCO40/1162, TNA.
91. Orr to Pierce, 27 October 1980, FCO40/1164, TNA.
92. Youde to MacLehose, 26 November 1980, FCO40/1164, TNA.

with an option for a further seventy-five years (as on Hong Kong Island). If China Resources took the bait and showed interest in either option, Akers-Jones should explain the British legal requirements and implications of each. Most importantly, it should be highlighted that the possible legal challenge could be avoided by action from London. If they were still interested, the Secretary should confirm whether they were speaking with the authority of the Government of Beijing. If the answer was affirmative, Akers-Jones should suggest that both parties should take time to reflect on the proposals and report back to their respective governments.[93]

While the British remained hopeful, this unfortunately turned out to be a false dawn. During the meeting with Edmund Lau of the Hong Kong and Yaumatei Ferry Company, Liao Chengzhi expressed his annoyance with the involvement of China Resources in Tin Shui Wai development. Liao revealed that the Chinese leadership had never been consulted on this matter.[94] David Wilson responded to this development by approaching Li Jusheng, the second Director of the NCNA. Li confirmed that China Resources did not have the Chinese government's backing and stressed his hope that the Hong Kong government would not try to use the 'small question of local leases as a way of dealing with the large question of the future of Hong Kong'.[95] Shortly afterwards, China Resources responded to Akers-Jones' overture by dissociating itself from all long-term land leases. Tin Shui Wai was a normal project, they claimed, and they had not thought about the lease and would continue the project in accordance with the normal practice of the Hong Kong government.[96] Gordon Wu still tried to convince the government of the backing of Beijing for this project with a story of his audience with senior officials of the Hong Kong and Macao Office in Beijing during the Christmas period. David Wilson, by then, was fed up with Wu, whom he touted as 'a brilliant entrepreneur who quickly erases from his mind anything which fails to fit with his own scheme'.[97] The saga was over, as Wilson concluded:

> Whatever the truth about the approaches made to us allegedly on behalf of China Resources, it seems that, at the political level, the Chinese do not at present wish to use this opportunity to deal with the lease issues in an indirect manner.[98]

---

93. Clift to Donald, Future of Hong Kong and New Territories Leases, 2 December 1980, FCO40/1164, TNA.
94. Wilson to Clift, 17 January 1981, FCO40/1286, TNA.
95. Donald to McLaren, 5 February 1981, FCO40/1286, TNA.
96. Wilson to Clift, 27 January 1981, FCO40/1286, TNA.
97. Wilson to Clift, 23 February 1981, FCO40/1286, TNA.
98. Wilson to Clift, 17 January 1981, FCO40/1286, TNA.

Conclusion

Compared with the other crises faced by MacLehose, the New Territories land issues was an existential one affecting Britain's position in Hong Kong after 1997. As a Political Adviser in the 1960s, he was well educated on the precarious nature of sovereignty in Hong Kong and the colony's vulnerability. He shared his predecessors and other FCO officials' judgement that negotiations with China were inevitable and believed that it was his responsibility to prepare Hong Kong for the ultimate encounter. Through robust social policies, investment in infrastructure, and institutional reforms, he was confident that he had improved the bargaining position of the British by making a prosperous, stable, and thus more valuable Hong Kong for Beijing. The economic card had always been seen as the best leverage that Britain had for the 1997 negotiations. However, the Governor did not always act in full accordance with the script. Prompted by his perception of the immediate developmental needs of Hong Kong (space for housing projects, imminent renewal of franchises of major utilities, and most importantly the anxiety of the business sector), he saw the urgency of approaching China in 1979, years ahead of the British expected negotiations in the mid-1980s. MacLehose played a key role in this early approach. He initiated discussions about the pressing need to sort out the legal complications related to the land lease in the New Territories beyond 1997, and he was heavily involved in hammering out the solution. He argued that the forthcoming visit to Beijing was the opportune moment to start the conversation. Most importantly, the Governor was the one who sold the idea to Deng Xiaoping.

This audacious attempt to insert Hong Kong's local agenda into the very top level of Anglo-Chinese diplomacy was unfortunately a failure. It ended with a categorical rejection from the Chinese side, who branded the Governor's initiative 'unnecessary and inappropriate'. With hindsight, the Governor's tactic of separating the lease issue in the New Territories land from the larger question of the future of Hong Kong was rather naïve. The attempt to present this problem as a legal one did not have much mileage among the Chinese officials. Beijing was enthusiastic about expanding cross-border collaboration and recognized the value of Hong Kong for its modernization programme, but was never solely driven by economic concerns. Politics always dominated Chinese leaders' thinking, particularly when the issue of sovereignty was at stake. MacLehose's approach probably came too soon. By 1979, the priority of Chinese leaders was reunification with Taiwan, not Hong Kong. According to Zhou Nan, the Chinese Vice Foreign Minister who was heavily involved in the Anglo-Chinese negotiation over Hong Kong, Deng Xiaoping only ordered Liao Chengzhi to work out a general strategy for handling the matter of Hong Kong's future after the meeting with MacLehose. Subsequently, there were rigorous exchanges among the Ministry of Foreign Affairs, the Hong Kong and Macao Affairs Office, the New China News Agency, and the Ministry of Foreign Economic Relations and Trade, and a 12-Point Programme was finally produced in 1982.[99]

MacLehose had obviously misread the situation, but so had the other 'Old China hands', with Percy Cradock, Edward Youde, and David Wilson all believing 1979 was not a bad time to start the conversation with Beijing. China however, remained elusive, despite the emergence of a more moderate and sensible leadership after the death of Mao. 'Reforming China' almost sounded oxymoronic, with inherent contradictions and incoherence aplenty. The government's embrace of capitalism was guarded with distaste for individual freedom and institutional certitude, its willingness to engage with the global economy was counteracted by scepticism against Western values and lifestyles, and its façade of pragmatism was regularly punctuated by Party dogma and rhetoric. The challenge of figuring out China's intentions was further compounded by the long-standing British tradition of accommodating Beijing's concerns about the Hong Kong matter. The British government, after all, would not hold on to the colony at all costs, and was not prepared to launch into chaos to defend Hong Kong's interests. This had been its stance on Hong Kong since the 1940s and was probably still the foundation of the British position on the eve of its negotiations with China. The Governor's 1979 approach was a failed attempt to pursue the colony's interest. Still, MacLehose's courage and determination against all odds to defend the territory's interests in maintaining business confidence and economic stability were forces to be reckoned with. Neither should his role in making substantial progress in the colony's social and economic developments and thus offering the British a solid platform for bargaining with Beijing be overlooked.

The 1979 approach was a significant part of Britain's learning curve on China's position on Hong Kong. For a very long time, London had been evasive on the 1997 issue and had taken extreme caution not to provoke China over sovereignty of the colony. None of the countless in-house studies were followed by any attempt to initiate conversation with China on these matters. MacLehose's ice-breaking effort, however, helped to push London into the uncharted zone of the British role in Hong Kong beyond 1997. Cradock believed that even by the late 1970s, London probably did not share the colony's anxiety about the uncertain future of the territory. He recalled that 'it was not yet the most urgent or the dominating issue

---

99. Daoyi Zhong et al., ed., *Oral History by Zhou Nan* (Hong Kong: Joint Publishing, 2007), 240.

in Sino-British relations and there was no clear view of the likely terms of any such settlement'.[100] MacLehose's initiative in 1979 probably accelerated the tempo of the dialogue between the two sovereigns. His historic meeting with Deng Xiaoping in 1979 also helped to ascertain the new Chinese leadership's thinking on the future of Hong Kong. London also noted that the meeting confirmed that 1997 was the terminal date and that British concession on sovereignty was the prerequisite for any dialogue. For the first time also, the fate of Hong Kong was on official record, linked to the future of Taiwan. This link was significant because it guaranteed a special status for Hong Kong after 1997. The model of 'One Country, Two Systems', though it had not yet been named as such, was already on the horizon amid the land lease discussions. This glimpse of China's pragmatism and her recognition of Hong Kong's economic value were positive signs for London which probably emboldened Thatcher to make a move in 1982. Still basking in the glory of Britain's victory in the Falklands War, the Prime Minister was optimistic and confident when she went to meet Deng Xiaoping and proposed some form of tenancy agreement or management contract for extending the British rule in Hong Kong. As Chi-Kwan Mark argued, Thatcher saw the engagement with China essential to her project of 'Global Britain' and believed Britain would, via its continued presence in Hong Kong after 1997, play a part in Chinese learning of the norms of the global capitalist system.[101] However, her spectacular tumble in front of the People's Hall in Beijing marked the commencement of the protracted and tortuous negotiations over the future of Hong Kong between 1982 and 1984.[102]

MacLehose's foresight on the future arrangements for Hong Kong proved to be prophetic. A special administrative district under the sovereignty of China was the best the British could get, as the Governor-designate predicted in late 1971.[103] Yet it is even more important to remember his warning against blind optimism about the bestowment of special status. As he cautioned in 1980, 'it may take time before they (the Chinese) realise that, for many years to come at least, essential elements of a successfully capitalist Hong Kong will be UK management and UK law and a currency separate to China's and the confidence of investors that all these will continue'.[104] The Governor's concerns were apparently heeded by the

---

100. Percy Cradock, *Experiences of China* (London: John Murray, 1994), 163.
101. Chi-Kwan Mark, *Decolonisation in the Age of Globalization: Britain, China, and Hong Kong, 1979–89* (Manchester: Manchester University Press, 2023).
102. Gary Ka-wai Cheung, *Secrets from the British Archives: Hong Kong and Its Post-colonial Future* (Hong Kong: City University of Hong Kong Press, 2023).
103. MacLehose to Wilford, 27 October 1971, FCO40/331, TNA.
104. MacLehose to Donald, 7 July 1980, FCO40/1162, TNA.

British team during the Sino-British negotiations over the future of Hong Kong. A promise to preserve most of the pre-1997 British-style pro-market economic institutions and practices were included in the eventual Joint Declaration. The jury is, however, still out on whether Beijing fully understood what it would take to sustain capitalist Hong Kong in economic as well as socio-political terms.

7
Final Remarks

Introduction

At a press event a few months before his anointment as the first head of the Hong Kong Special Administrative Region (HKSAR) government, and still basking in the exuberance of his electoral victory in late 1996, Tung Chee-Hwa, the Chief Executive-select, found it hard to swallow a provocation from a foreign journalist who asked him whether he had ever said 'no' to China. Generally seen as an even-tempered man, Tung reacted quite out of character and retorted by asking when a British Governor had ever stood up to London. Chris Patten was not impressed. 'Where has he been all these years?' the last Governor ridiculed Tung's rhetorical question. 'There was a time when Lord MacLehose used to be described as the second most unpopular foreign leader in the FCO after Dom Mintoff,'[1] Patten added.[2]

Like many of his predecessors, MacLehose stood up to London on countless occasions. The story told in the preceding pages, however, is not just about how the Governor resisted and heroically battled with the sovereign. Rather, it is about how a royal agent could navigate all the obligations and constraints inherent in his role as the Queen's servant in the territories and find a balance between his potentially conflicting responsibilities towards the home government and the local community. It is an account of bargaining as well as of collaboration and persuasion in a tense environment. Ultimately, it is the tale of how autonomy was earned, stretched, and

---

1. Dom Mintoff was the Maltese Prime Minister who played a key role in Malta's independence from the British Empire and the creation of the Maltese republic. His relationship with London had been tense; one of his political ambitions was to rid the island of all military bases and to eventually force Britain to pay for its right to station troops on Maltese soil. He was also hated by British diplomats for his failure to show deference to Britain. 'Dom Mintoff obituary', *The Guardian*, 21 August 2012.
2. Chris Patten, *The Hong Kong Diaries* (Hong Kong: Allen Lane, 2022), 436.

defined under imperial rule. The episodes revisited here shed new light on the complexity of the colonial order, with relevance for understanding 'One Country, Two Systems', a scheme which has only just reached its halfway point.

The Long 1970s: A Call for Action

During the 1950s, the colonial administration was hesitant and inactive on domestic issues. Governors before David Trench saw no urgency to invest in public services and build up institutions, despite the glaring signs of the growing inadequacy of the local community in addressing various social ills. Their reticence seems even more ridiculous when the steady development of the colony's economy and the consequent swelling of the public purse in the post-war years is considered. They were equally evasive when it came to handling corruption. Colonial officials were not unaware of the prevalent socio-economic dislocation and growing frustrations within the local community, but they lacked the drive to attack these issues face-on and were content with modest responses and limited reforms at the margin. David Trench, who never enjoyed a particularly strong rapport with the local society, was an unsung hero of social reform. Under his leadership, the colonial government started to conduct meticulous reviews of social service provisions, and long-term initiatives finally took off. He also gave anti-sleaze efforts the final push and passed the Prevention of Bribery Ordinance, which was a game changer in the battle against corruption. Even so, most of his reviews did not deliver results until after the outbreak of the 1967 Riots. Even in his crusade against corruption, Trench stopped short of making the ultimate decision to create an independent institution detached from the police establishment. Yet the most glaring evasion concerns the fate of the colony. The sovereignty issue of Hong Kong was like Voldemort in the Harry Potter stories—no one dared or wanted to raise it in any conversation. Notwithstanding the hostility of the Communist regime towards the 'unequal treaties', London's approach was not to provoke Beijing on this matter, and if a response was necessary, to try to be as pragmatic and flexible as possible. The colony was seen as an asset, but not as indispensable or deserving of military intervention if threatened. The prospective negotiations over the future of Hong Kong became visible concerning the aftermath of the 1967 Riots, but there was still no concrete action plan by the late 1960s.

MacLehose inherited a range of these unsettled issues, chronic uncertainty about 1997, and half-baked reforms that did not fully address the various problems. The 1967 Riots had however served as a wake-up call for the colonial administrators, and sweeping demands for reforms under the carpet was no longer an option. The Governor was further prompted to invest in social services and infrastructure because these interventions would consolidate the colony's role as an industrialized economy and a regional financial hub. There were, however, many unexpected developments along the way. For example, it was the embarrassing escape of Peter Godber which pushed the Governor to make the final leap in his crusade against corruption and create the ICAC. He also did not anticipate the Labour government's strong interest in welfare conditions in Hong Kong and its disregard for the convention of ruling the colony at arm's length.

The biggest surprise, nevertheless, was the rise of China. MacLehose arrived at a time when the Cultural Revolution had already lost momentum, with the moderate wing of the Chinese leadership reasserting their grip. This was soon followed by the seismic shift in China's diplomacy and its desire to engage with the world. The ascendence of Deng Xiaoping paved the way for a pragmatic approach in China's economic development. An ideological straitjacket of Maoism was replaced by an embrace of market economy, via the creation of Special Economic Zones in the coastal region. Deng's China was ready to embark on the journey to the Open Door Policy and capitalist reforms. This was an opportunity for Hong Kong, as the colony could serve as a platform for relaying foreign capital and business knowhow to China. Beijing was particularly keen to consolidate the economic partnership between Hong Kong and Guangdong.

A new China presented various challenges for MacLehose. A materialistic China could be friendly and pragmatic, yet growing confidence could also make it more assertive. Huang Hua's request to delist Hong Kong from the category of a colony in the United Nations in 1972 illustrates this shift. More importantly, an improved Anglo-Chinese relationship also made negotiations about the colony's future a more material prospect. When compared with the revolutionary regime under Mao, London saw the stable and moderate leadership of Deng as a more manageable audience for dialogue and exchange. With the clock ticking, MacLehose assigned greater salience to the 1997 issue than his colleagues in London. Hong Kong needed to brace itself for the ultimate dialogue and he wanted the socio-economic development of the colony to create preconditions for prospective negotiations. He was emboldened by the role of Hong Kong in China's modernization programme, and worked on the assumption that Beijing would have much to learn from the colony—a poster boy for capitalism. A new China, therefore, represented opportunities as well as challenges for Britain and Hong Kong. The re-engagement both nurtured a degree of confidence but also bred anxiety among colonial administrators.

On the subject of 1997, MacLehose made a move with his idea of separating the legal issue of land leases in the New Territory from the political future of the colony and he raised this idea when he met Deng Xiaoping in 1979. While the policy process of Communist China remained opaque, it would be wrong to label this a misjudgement, but the Governor failed spectacularly on this occasion, and then misunderstood the significance of the Tin Shui Wai project. However, it was his initiative that instilled the process with a sense of urgency and accelerated the negotiations between the two sovereigns. It helped to deliver the eagerly awaited agreement over the future of Hong Kong by the mid-1980s, right before local anxiety reached breaking point.

The paradigmatic shifts witnessed by MacLehose were not confined to Hong Kong's changing relationship with China and domestic development. The 1970s was a period of major realignment within global politics with major efforts to reduce the tension between the United States and the Communist camp. The Nixon administration altered the containment approach against the Soviet Union and China and the US strategic priority shifted to Indochina. Desperate to overcome Communist insurgency, Washington committed to neutralizing the role of the two dominant Communist powers in Vietnam. A split within the Communist camp and the rise of pragmatism in China, provided the US with the scope to adopt new policies. The military operation, however, did not proceed as planned, with the US eventually forced to retreat in disgrace from Vietnam. Hanoi soon discovered a new tactic for destabilizing international powers, allowing people to leave and take up the status of refugees. This was partly triggered by the fear of authoritarian rule, but it was also a result of Hanoi's anti-Chinese stance. The resultant humanitarian crisis was a global challenge. The US administration was determined to share the bill with other developed countries. Notwithstanding the reconfiguration of world politics in the twilight years of Cold War, a golden rule of British diplomacy lingered: when Washington made a request, London must reckon. Britain in effect subcontracted its obligations to support the US to Hong Kong. The colony was pressurized to shoulder a disproportionate share of coping with refugees. MacLehose stood up for Hong Kong as best he could, but this episode confirmed the harsh reality that there was always a limit to the colony's defiance.

Motivating Metropolitan Intervention

The book attempts to map out the relationship between the metropolis and the colony. More specifically, it intends to answer these questions: 'when would London get involved in the colony's business?' and 'how far could the colony push back?' While there is a long tradition within the British Empire of respecting the man on the spot,[3] it is erroneous to think that the colony as free from the interference of the sovereign. From the four cases discussed, it is evident that London was motivated to get involved whenever its interests were at stake. The level of metropolitan intrusion was largely determined by two variables: the cost of reticence and the exigence of the issue. The former refers to the actual or potential impact of a colonial development on London. Tangible and immediate costs such as incurring financial burden or damaging the British economy would lead to the close monitoring of Hong Kong affairs and London interfering in colonial governance in ways that eroded Hong Kong's political autonomy. For example, the prospect of extra expenses for supporting refugee intake and threat to the balance of trade triggered intervention from Whitehall. Yet in most cases, it was political pressure on the British government that prompted metropolitan policy responses. Parliamentary interest in and British media attention on colonial affairs, especially scandals (such as the escape of Peter Godber) were embarrassments and irritations for the Foreign Secretary and FCO officials were always alert to the imperative of protecting the reputation of their bosses. The escalation of these awkward moments into a full-fledged crisis must be avoided, even if this meant quarrels with the governor and colonial officials. While some political pressures could peter out quickly, other concerns were more fundamental and had a lasting effect on the calculations of British officials. For instance, the rise of the Labour Party in the 1970s meant that its ideological outlook defined London's disposition and policies towards the colony via a renewed commitment to welfarism and social reforms.

Nevertheless, it was the geostrategic calculation of London that appeared to be the most important factor in shaping its proclivity towards the colony. London had striven to maintain a working relationship with China even during her most radical years, and Beijing's moderate turn in the 1970s gave further weight to the China factor, with the economic potential of this gigantic market looming large. Britain's 'special relationship' with the United States was, however, the ultimate concern of her diplomacy. Leveraging American influence by making Britain useful to Washington was London's primary method of maintaining global relevance. The tiny colony of Hong Kong should never undermine the sovereign's relationship with these two powers.

---

3. Robert Bickers, 'Loose Ties that Bound: British Empire, Colonial Autonomy and Hong Kong', in *Negotiating Autonomy in Greater China: Hong Kong and Its Sovereign before and after 1997*, ed. Ray Yep (Copenhagen: Nordic Institute of Asian Studies, 2013), 29–54.

London's decision to get involved in the colony's affairs was also affected by the exigence of the issue. This concerns London's perception of the urgency and necessity of intervention in the colony's affairs. This was in turn determined by two factors: confidence in the colony's ability to solve the problem in hand and its disposition to comply and cooperate with the sovereign. Central to these was London's trust in the colonial governor. There were several mechanisms in place that would guarantee the loyalty of this official. With the exception of Chris Patten, all governors were transferred from the British bureaucracy or the colonial service, and their common career trajectory and socialization should ensure a considerable degree of similarity in temperament, values, and general outlook with their colleagues in Whitehall. The presence of a political adviser, a seconded officer from the FCO, would also provide London with an on-the-spot monitor for the colony. The convention of bestowing lordship on a retiring governor should also help to entice compliance from the man on the ground. MacLehose was experienced in diplomacy with a rich knowledge of the culture, etiquette, hidden rules, and personal networks with former colleagues in the foreign ministry. FCO officials certainly found him more approachable than David Trench, yet he was however not always a kindred spirit. The Scot may have been more tactful and diplomatic in handling the officials in London, but as seen in the preceding discussion, he could also be an irritation to them. Nevertheless, London's confidence that the colony has been well run did not rest solely on its perception of the governor's characters, but it also hinged on its assessment of the overall capacity of the local administration. Here are some key questions which London asked when deciding whether immediate intervention was necessary: Does the colony have a plan to clean up its own mess? And does it have the resources to get the job done? For example, the creation of the ICAC in 1974 was a masterstroke in defusing the pressure on both Hong Kong and London and bought the colony more time and autonomy to handle the embarrassment of Peter Godber's flight. Similarly, despite London's strong desire to push a rigorous reform programme onto the colony, this programme was, after all, financed by the colony's money. The fiscal independence did, in a way, put a brake on London's encroachment.

London's desire to intrude into local affairs, was also affected by the firmness of the colony's pushback, which showed how willing Hong Kong was to comply and cooperate with the sovereign. This was a delicate issue, since a certain degree of firmness from the governor could give the colony more room for manoeuvre, yet it could also backfire and provoke a strong response from the metropolis. The case of the altercations over social reform is illustrative of this. The open defiance of the Governor as well as the Financial Secretary aroused London's suspicions about the colony's commitment to the reform agenda. Consequently, an elaborate monitoring scheme was put in place. A detailed plan for implementation which defined the pace and scope of the reforms was imposed, and a regular and comprehensive reporting arrangement was required. Even the idea of creating the post of a second political adviser as extra leverage for this monitoring had been considered. London's perception of the incongruence of interests between the sovereign and the colony surely motivated this intervention.

Based on these considerations, the London–Hong Kong relationship exemplified in the four cases under review can be categorized into four patterns that vary in terms of level of intervention, as summarized in Figure 7.1 below.

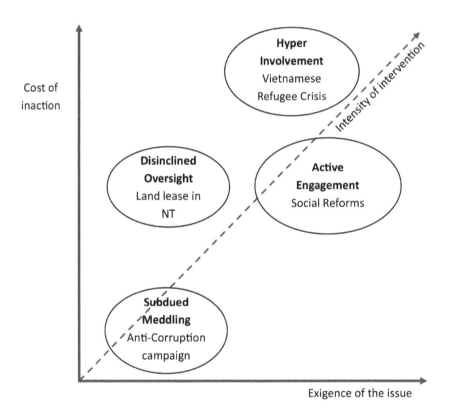

Figure 7.1 Patterns of London's involvement

Hyper Involvement: For example, the Vietnamese refugee crisis. This is a case where the fundamental interests of the sovereign were at stake. London was hard pressed to respond to the American request for greater contribution and was under tremendous pressure to increase refugee intake. In a sense, London and Hong Kong were trapped in a zero-sum situation where the colony's accommodation of refugees was an escape route for the sovereign. London played an active role in delivering the American vision of the global solution to the humanitarian crisis and ensuring that the assigned role for Hong Kong in this scheme would be materialized, even at the expense of the colony. Meanwhile, London was also determined to minimize the impact of refugee intake on the homeland economy and British society and was entangled in heated exchanges with Hong Kong on this matter. This particularly became the case when Margaret Thatcher came to power, at a time when the exodus of refugees had resurged in the late 1970s. Thatcher's preference for a more proactive mode of tackling the crisis reinforced this sense of urgency. For London, the colony was a useful piece in the global chess game and had to be deployed for the sake of her overall plan. Despite the Governor's diplomatic initiatives, the resolution of the global humanitarian crisis primarily hinged upon bargaining and cooperation among sovereign states. At times, London's support for amplifying the colony's voices was crucial. This dependence would however invite further involvement of the sovereign in the handling of refugees crisis in Hong Kong.

Active Engagement: For example, social reforms and the Hong Kong Planning Paper. This is another case where London was highly motivated to get involved in the colony's affairs. The ideological disposition of the Labour government, together with the domestic pressure from the left (unionists) and the right (British manufacturers) created sustained pressure for social reforms in the colony. The Wilson and Callaghan administrations took a rather exceptional approach in handling the whole matter. London chose to dictate a detailed blueprint for the implementation of its visions in the colony, the Hong Kong Planning Paper, and supplemented it with a comprehensive reporting and monitoring mechanism. MacLehose was not entirely against the idea of expanding the role of the government in social development; in fact, he regarded this as a crucial step for maintaining stability and an integral part of the preparation for the prospective negotiations over the future of Hong Kong with Beijing. However, he and Philip Haddon-Cave found the pace and scope of the reforms unrealistic. Their relentless pushback trapped the colony and London in a vicious cycle of mutual distrust and further intrusion. Nevertheless, at the end of the day, implementation of the social reform programmes was fundamentally a domestic affair, and, even more importantly, it was billed by local finances. The financial independence of the colony has enhanced Hong Kong's bargaining power vis-à-vis London. MacLehose was also aware of the limits of resistance and always managed to deliver considerable progress in social services. His half-baked improvements were not exactly what London wanted, but seasoned politicians and officials in Whitehall probably reckoned that this was not a bad deal, given that the option of flooding the colony with financial resources and strings was simply a non-starter.

Indecisive Oversight: For example, land leases in the New Territories. The future of Hong Kong was supposed to be a matter of monumental importance for Britain. London had prepared for the worst-case scenario of eventual withdrawal from Hong Kong, but there remained hope among Whitehall officials for finding a creative way to retain the most valuable possession of the post-war Empire. China appeared more pragmatic and open after the conclusion of Cultural Revolution, and a new chapter of the Anglo-Chinese relationship was on the horizon with the reform-minded Deng Xiaoping now in charge. By 1979, the British government, nevertheless, appeared not yet ready for the ultimate negotiation with Beijing. However, MacLehose, the man on the spot, had a different sense of urgency and he saw the necessity of immediate action before local confidence collapsed. He felt obliged to address the issue of land lease in the New Territories before he left. He proposed the idea of separating the technical issue of the land leases from the political problem of 1997 and got the support from the very top of the British hierarchy. David Owen, the Labour Foreign Secretary, was supportive but he may have underestimated the gravity of the challenge and wrongly believed that the issue could be solved within a few months. With Beijing's objection to the Governor's suggestion and the change of government in Britain, London soon became resigned to a wait-and-see approach in further engagement. FCO officials neither encouraged nor discouraged MacLehose's further probing and approaches, maintained the veto power over the colony's overtures to Beijing, and became involved in the process whenever MacLehose or Percy Cradock believed London's intervention was instrumental to a breakthrough in the discussions. The Thatcher government however did not view the issue of Hong Kong's future as a priority and did not have an elaborated game plan until 1982. In short, London preferred a back seat and was content with a general oversight of the whole process in 1979. During this brief period of indecisiveness, the Governor played a key role and enjoyed considerable room for making initiative. He may have failed in his attempt to secure China's consent to his proposed solution in 1979, but he managed to get his concerns heard at the very top levels in Beijing and London.

Subdued Meddling: For example, the Anti-Corruption Campaign. This is a case where London showed minimal interest in the affairs of Hong Kong. Here, the main concern of British officials was to avoid embarrassment for politicians, and they were involved in the dialogue with Hong Kong mostly due to the controversy over the failure of Peter Godber's extradition. They saw the anti-sleaze campaign as primarily a domestic issue of the colonial administration, and were prepared to extend maximum freedom for Hong Kong in dealing with it. London chose not to exercise the royal prerogative on behalf of the Queen to repeal the local anti-bribery legislation, which they believed was inconsistent with the principles of the Common Law system. Yet the saga of Godber's escape to Britain attracted unwanted attention from the British public. The growing interest of the media and the opposition soon translated to pressure for the FCO and the Hong Kong government. The prospect of investigation into the colony's corruption was particularly alarming for the latter. London's intervention was rendered less necessary with MacLehose's pre-emptive strike in creating the ICAC and the good fortune of finding a Crown witness for Godber's extradition to Hong Kong. The Governor demonstrated his ability to clean up his own mess, and London was happy not to get involved. The sovereign's interest waned swiftly when the attention of the homeland public shifted elsewhere. Even during the crisis situation of police mutiny in 1977, London maintained its passive role on this matter.

The Repertoire for Making the Hong Kong Case

The scope of the colony's autonomy was not, however, defined merely by the intentions and interests of the sovereign. It is best described as a process of co-production. While London may have had a dominant role in defining the limits of the colony's manoeuvres, there was always room for initiative from the periphery and space for contention and bargaining. The Governor, as the front man of the local administration, played a key role in determining Hong Kong's success in pursuing its own agenda. He was the chief spokesman for Hong Kong for both British and international audiences, and the pilot who helped the colony navigate through the maze of British bureaucracy and parliamentary politics. The negotiations between London and Hong Kong may have frequently resulted in heated debates and altercations between FCO officials and the Governor behind the scenes, yet the latter never shied away from making his disagreement with London's unfair treatment publicly known. MacLehose's case shows that the governor's experience, charisma, skills, and stature in the British establishment had material significance. Like most of his predecessors,

MacLehose believed that enacting his primary role as the Queen's agent in Hong Kong meant sternly defending local concerns. When the Governor perceived that the interest of the colony was under threat, he lobbied hard with arguments and facts, put pressure on the sovereign with hints of local fury and resentment, or even threatened to resign.

Four tactics are particularly noteworthy:

Leveraging local sentiment. As an alien ruler, London was fully aware of the importance of gaining the acquiescence of the local population. The importance of public sentiment was reinforced by the colony's unique constitutional development. Unlike other British possessions, democracy was a non-starter in Hong Kong. The presence of a hostile Communist regime ready to exploit any sign of local unrest compounded the situation further. In a sense, these were blessings in disguise, since the public opinion of Hong Kong people was used to justify concession. As argued by Florence Mok, this was particularly the case in the 1970s when the colonial government was highly motivated to keep tabs on the public mood.[4] Views of the unofficial members of the Executive and Legislative Council were always used as a proxy of public sentiment. The resistance of the business sector was cited as the justification for rejecting London's suggestions for tax increases and radical social reforms, investors' concerns about long-term deals was leveraged to warrant immediate probing on the land lease issue with Beijing, and London was asked to arrange the extradition of Peter Godber due to the potential escalation of public resentment. The Governor, as the man on the ground, was justified in his claim to have a better sense of the local mood than his counterparts in London.

Exploring opportunities in the legal framework. Rule by law was instrumental to colonial governance. Legality offered some degree of certitude and a sense of fairness for the governed. It formed a key element of public discourse on the propriety of governmental action and defined the rule of engagement between the colony and London. MacLehose viewed the powers entrusted to the governor in the colonial constitutional documents of the Royal Instructions and Letters Patent as a contract between the colony and the sovereign and a basis for his relationship with London. For example, he successfully requested the use of the legal power entrusted in him to dismiss corrupt officers under the provision of 'Queen's displeasure', which greatly expedited the cleanup of the police force. During the Peter Godber crisis, MacLehose also confronted the FCO on the legal ground that the latter's refusal to extradite Godber on the grounds of a lack

---

4. Florence Mok, *Covert Colonialism: Governance, Surveillance and Political Culture in British Hong Kong, c. 1966–1997* (Manchester: Manchester University Press, 2023).

of double criminality was unsound, since the sovereign had chosen not to exercise her royal repeal against colonial legislation when the Anti-Bribery Ordinance was passed in 1970. In his attempt to commence the dialogue on Hong Kong's future with Deng Xiaoping in 1979, he also found that the instrument of Order in Council in the British Parliament was a method by which to commit London to the attempt and lend credibility to his adventurous move.

Reaching out to the world. The four cases discussed here show the fact that while engagement with London was inevitable, the colony enjoyed freedom with some leeway to make its case to the global audience. The case of the Vietnamese refugee crisis is illustrative of this. While the colony cherished the intermediation of London in articulating its plea for support to the world, MacLehose also took initiatives to engage foreign leaders directly. He approached the United Nations relentlessly with his demands for a better deal for Hong Kong and made painstaking efforts to present his case for Hong Kong to senior officials and politicians in Washington. This was enabled by Hong Kong's unique position within global capitalism and geopolitics, and his experience as a seasoned diplomat seems also to have helped. These initiatives may not have delivered what MacLehose had hoped, but it extended a narrative to a global audience about Hong Kong's situation in a way that counteracted the version presented by Britain, whose interests were not always aligned with the colony's concerns. To a certain extent, these engagements translated into pressure on London to modify her stance on Hong Kong.

Knowing when to give and take. Notwithstanding the imperative to defend Hong Kong's interests, the governor never lost sight of the subordinate status of the colony. It was crucial that he knew when to stop pushing his case. MacLehose was, for example, adamant that none of the ringleaders of the police mutiny in 1977 should not be let off. Nevertheless, when the proceedings against the Yaumatei syndicate revealed the complexity of the situation and the process and heightened London's concerns about backlash against the possible failure of prosecution, he accepted a more selective approach in apportioning punishment and contented himself with a milder retribution for the officers concerned. Even amid heated altercations with London, MacLehose was always aware of the importance of demonstrating his subservience. Thus, while he opted to rigorously defend the fiscal conservatism of Philip Haddon-Cave and resisted the radical reforms proposed by London, he never lost sight of the significance of delivering some progress, even if his reforms were not fully consistent with what the metropole had actually demanded. The half-baked results of these attested to the Governor's respect for London's concern, and proof of his loyalty. Similarly, while MacLehose fought viciously for a higher refugee intake from Britain and pulled no punches in uttering his bitterness on this matter publicly, behind the scenes he offered to take London's share of the intake quota if Britain agreed to concede to the UN's demands and make the Geneva Conference possible. Convincing your superior that you are part of the establishment and trustworthy seemed to be one of the central tenets of Hong Kong's approaches in handling London.

A Lesson for the Hong Kong Special Administrative Region

China's resumption of sovereignty over Hong Kong in 1997 marked the beginning of a new chapter. The jury is still out on whether the novel idea of 'One Country, Two Systems' can maintain the city as a liberal and capitalist haven under the Communist Party leadership. The Basic Law passed by the National People's Congress in 1990 promises, at least on paper, a high degree of autonomy for the newly created HKSAR and reveals great respect for the freedom of Hong Kong's citizens. There were queries at the onset about whether this mini constitution premised on Beijing's understanding of the situation of colonial Hong Kong in the 1980s could really accommodate the growing vibrancy of civil society in the HKSAR and the changing aspirations of local citizenry after 1997. The incessant political disturbances and confrontations over the last ten years have certainly reinforced the arguments of those more sceptical about these safeguards. Is there any lesson that our analysis here can teach us about interactions between the centre and the local region after 1997?

When compared with the colonial government, it is more challenging for the HKSAR government to manage its relationship with the sovereign for various reasons. Firstly, the Chinese state had a different persona with stronger motivation to become entangled in the local scene. This is based in part on an emotional attachment of the Chinese leaders to the new order. The return of Hong Kong is a matter of great national pride to Beijing, as it marks the victorious eradication of a century-long humiliation. Yet this honour could only be upheld if Beijing managed to maintain stability and prosperity in Hong Kong after the reunification. The anxiety to prove that life remains there after the British thus became an integral part of the sovereign's psyche.[5] Beijing has shown little hesitation when becoming

---

5. Anthony Cheung, 'New Interventionism in the Making: Interpreting State Interventions in Hong Kong after the Change of Sovereignty', *Journal of Contemporary China* 2 (2000): 291–308. Zhu Rongji, the Chinese premier also made the following statement during his visit to Hong Kong in 2002: 'if we make a mess of Hong Kong after 1997, we will be sinners in history!', accessed 22 December 2022, https://www.youtube.com/watch?v=JvBtPQ30WTE

embroiled in local developments. The stimulation package for reviving the Hong Kong economy in the aftermath of the SARS epidemic in 2003 attests to this determination to intervene. Secondly, Communist China prefers a public display of authority. The centralism inherent in the authoritarian order entails a strong expectation of subordination and reverence for one's superiors on the part of the local administration. For Beijing, it is necessary for this pattern of relationship to be overtly displayed and perceived. The classic case is Premier Zhu Rongji's theatrical criticism of Tung Chee-hwa and his cabinet in 2001. In a room flooded with cameras and journalists, a stern-faced Zhu Rongji warned the Tung government they must reflect seriously on their own limitations and avoid the proclivity of inaction.[6] London officials did, of course, present their fair share of directives and comments on the colony's affairs before 1997, yet when compared to the Chinese leaders' deliberations, the British approach was far more discrete and subtle, with most exchanges conducted behind the scenes. The public display of authority of the Chinese leaders is not only embarrassing, but it significantly circumscribes the local administration's room for manoeuvre. Thirdly, Beijing's siege mentality with respect to China's relationship with the West also strengthens its commitment to intervene in Hong Kong, and even manifest itself as a conspiracy theory that Hong Kong has been used as a base for anti-China activities. Beijing's sense of insecurity was heightened with the outbreak of the Occupy Movement in 2014 and the Anti-Extradition Bill Protest in 2019. It was this concern about the proliferation of subversive and secessionist activities in Hong Kong that eventually led to the proclamation of the National Security Law in Hong Kong in 2020. Beijing felt compelled to assert its authority in the territory during the so-called new Cold War era.

Today, Beijing's will to intervene is supported by the wide array of leverages for involvement and control at Beijing's disposal.[7] The velocity of the economic integration between Hong Kong and the mainland has been accelerating since the early 1980s. The flows of capital, goods, and tourists across the border are now major sources of growth for the Hong Kong economy, and mainland immigrants constitute the main drive behind local population growth. This extensive socio-economic integration is reinforced by elaborated political linkages. Thousands of local elites are absorbed into all levels of the People's Congress and the Chinese People's Political

---

6. Press Release of Hong Kong SAR Government, 5 September 2001, accessed 22 December 2022, https://www.info.gov.hk/gia/general/200109/05/0905176.htm
7. Ho-fung Hung, *City on the Edge: Hong Kong under Chinese Rule* (Cambridge: Cambridge University Press, 2022).

Consultative Conference and Hong Kong chapters of state-sponsored mass organizations like the All-China Federation of Youth have proliferated rapidly in recent years.[8] Meanwhile, mainland entrepreneurs have been aggressively acquiring control of local media businesses since 1997. Jack Ma of the Alibaba group now owns the influential English newspaper the *South China Morning Post*, and in 2016, mainland media mogul Li Ruigang, also confirmed his role as chairman of Hong Kong Television Broadcasting, the media company that commands the largest market share of television business in Hong Kong.[9]

Most importantly of all, Beijing has established an elaborate mechanism of official representation in the HKSAR after 1997. The Liaison Office of the Central People's Government has functioned as the focal point of communication between Hong Kong and Beijing and has been regularly subject to allegations of its involvement in elections, voting in the Legislative Council, and even the operation of the HKSAR government.[10] As foreign affairs and defence are outside the realm of the autonomy of the HKSAR, the Office of the Commissioner of the Ministry of Foreign Affairs and the People's Liberation Army Hong Kong Garrison are installed in the territory. Yet, it is the creation of a national security agency that the locals find most alarming. Immediately after the passage of Hong Kong's National Security Law on 30 June 2020, Office for Safeguarding the Central People's Government of the People's Republic of China in the HKSAR was founded. Housed right opposite Victoria Park, a site of great symbolic importance to local defiance against authoritarianism where annual vigils for the June 4 Incident were held before they were banned in 2020, the agency is staffed by mainland officials with the responsibility of supervising and directing the HKSAR government on the implementation of Hong Kong's National Security Law. The breadth and width of the Chinese authorities' integration and penetration into the local political economy after 1997 are beyond the imagination of the British colonial rulers. Such all-inclusive and far-reaching machinery could greatly facilitate Beijing's intrusion into the domestic affairs of Hong Kong if the Chinese leaders see the need to do so.

---

8. Samson Yuen and Edmund Cheng, 'Deepening the State: The Dynamics of China's United Front Work in Post-Handover Hong Kong', *Communist and Post-communist Studies* 53, no. 4 (2020): 136–154.
9. Francis Lee, 'Changing Political Economy of the Hong Kong Media', *China Perspectives*, no. 3 (2018): 9–18.
10. Kevin Carrico, *Two Systems, Two Countries: A Nationalist Guide to Hong Kong* (Oakland: University of California Press, 2022), and Ching Kwan Lee, *Hong Kong: Global China's Restive Frontier* (New York: Cambridge University Press, 2022).

Final Remarks

When contemplating intervening in Hong Kong's business, Beijing should take a lesson from the preceding discussion. The four cases studied here have uncovered the essence of the relationship between the sovereign and the colony before 1997: local governance was not sustained simply by Hong Kong's subordination to the metropole, and allowing for pushback and different approaches from below were central both to the local administration's maintenance of authority and to that of the sovereign. The Governor was an agent of the British monarch, but he was also the leader of the Hong Kong community. He was accountable to London, but also needed to respond to local concerns. His accountability was not expressed in electoral terms, yet the lack of a democratic mandate merely reinforced the importance of the governor being aware of local sentiment. He had to be seen as someone who cared, and, most crucially, as a leader with the courage to stand up for Hong Kong, if necessary, even this would be seen as defiance against the sovereign. The story here reminds us that the formal constitutional structure of imperial control did not provide a full picture of the London–Hong Kong relationship. Whereas London enjoyed extensive powers, allowing veto against local initiatives, and could legislate for Hong Kong, the metropole did not simply rule by fiat or command most of the time. The relationship, in essence, was characterized rather by bargaining and persuasion. Hong Kong became a cosmopolitan city with world-class infrastructure and a thriving economy before 1997, and in addition to the grit and talent of the local population, the fact that the local government was allowed to conduct business in the way they saw best for Hong Kong was decidedly a key ingredient of this success. This 'defiance' from below was thus not a threat and challenge to sovereignty, but a pathway to effective governance. In order to serve the interest of the sovereign, it is imperative that local administrations serve local interests as well.

To a certain extent, this is no different from the trajectory of central–local relationship in post-reform China. Accommodation of local conditions holds the key to the progress of the post-Mao marketization. Central leaders' pragmatism towards local differences and concerns has taken various guises. Test points, experimental zones, pilot schemes, or provisional methods all imply tolerance for non-conformity with national policy and the appreciation of spontaneity from below. This room for local autonomy, however, must be earned. Central to this bargaining process has been the ability of the local units to demonstrate that autonomy will bring prosperity. As Qian and Weingast coined it, China operates on a system of 'market-preserving federalism' under which the economic vitality of different regions has secured them the freedom to run these social and economic developments in their own ways, despite the formal structure of the unitary system of the People's Republic of China.[11] Yet the reform story also unearths the importance of the local leaders. It entails more than their courage to stand up for local interests, but also requires the skill and knowledge to navigate the command structure and bureaucratic maze of the supervising authority, the ability to present cases in best possible light, the knowhow for making domestic and external alliances, the acumen for balancing the potentially conflicting concerns of the local community and the metropole, and most importantly, the faculty for maintaining the superior's trust despite all altercations and debates. There are parallels between MacLehose story and the many success stories of local reformers in post-Mao reforms.

Final Words

This book does not attempt to debunk the popular perception of MacLehose as a hero. Hong Kong should be grateful for all the reforms and progress made during his era that transformed the socioeconomic landscape of the city and paved the way for the further development of Hong Kong as a world-class city. This is an account with a modest aim to reiterate the imperative of situating the MacLehose era within a wider context. We need a historical perspective highlighting the context under which developments unfolded, and how he rode the momentum of change which had been set in motion before he came to the scene. It is also essential for us to see the development under his governorship in a global perspective. The MacLehose story reminds us how Hong Kong responded to the challenges and opportunities of a world order which was rapidly being reconfigured in the 1970s. Most importantly, the coloniality of Hong Kong needs to be restated. The Hong Kong story is ultimately about how local administration managed the sovereign. As the MacLehose story tells us, the sovereign could hinder, undermine, or even sacrifice local interests for its own agenda and priorities, but Hong Kong could also use the sovereign's power to advance its interests, including on the world stage. To read the history of colonial rule as an account of subordination and to believe that loyalty is the most important attribute of a local agent in serving national interests is a mistake of monumental proportions.

---

11. Yingyi Qian and Barry Weingast, 'China's Transition to Market: Market-Preserving Federalism, Chinese Style', *Journal of Economic Policy Reform* 1, no. 2 (1996): 149–185. See also Chenggang Xu, 'The Fundamental Institutions of China's Economic Reforms and Development', *Journal of Economic* 49, no. 4 (2011): 1076–1151, and Sebastian Heilmann, *Red Swan: How Unorthodox Policy-Making Facilitated China's Rise* (Hong Kong: Chinese University of Hong Kong Press, 2018).

Bibliography

Archival sources

The National Archives, Kew, Surrey, UK

CAB 21	Cabinet Office and Predecessors: Registered Files (1916–1965)
CAB 134	Cabinet: Miscellaneous Committees
CAB 148	Cabinet Office: Defence and Overseas Policy Committee and Sub-Committees
DEF 13	Ministry of Defence: Private Office, Registered Files (All Ministers')
FCO 21	Foreign and Commonwealth Office: Far Eastern Department and Successors
FCO 40	Foreign and Commonwealth Office: Hong Kong Department
FO 371	Foreign Office: Political Department
PREM 19	Prime Minister's Office: Correspondence and Papers, 1979–1997

National Archives and Records Administration, College Park, Maryland, US

RG 59	Department of State
RG 342	US Air Force Commands, Activities and Organization

Public Records Office, Kwun Tong, Hong Kong

HKRS742-15-22

Bodleian Library, University of Oxford, UK

Interview with Lord MacLehose of Beoch, MSS.Ind.Ocn.s.377
Interview with Sir David Trench, Mss.Ind.Ocn.348
Interview with Arthur Frederick Maddock, Mss. Ind. Ocn.441

Churchill Archives Centre, Churchill College Library, Cambridge, UK

British Diplomatic Oral History Programme

Margaret Thatcher Foundation

Economic Summit Meeting in Tokyo 28/29 June 1979: Record of the Second Session in the Akasaka Palace on 28 June at 1605.

Library of Legislative Council, Hong Kong

Address by H.E. the Governor, *The Legislative Council Debates Official Report*, 1972, 1976, 1977, and 1979.
Minutes of Legislative Council.
The Budget for 1976–1977, 25 February 1976, Official Report of Proceedings, Hong Kong Legislative Council.
The Budget for 1977–1978, 2 March 1977, Official Report of Proceedings, Hong Kong Legislative Council.

Newspapers

Guardian (UK)
Ming Pao (Hong Kong)
South China Morning Post (Hong Kong)
Sunday Times (UK)
Tai Kung Pao (Hong Kong)
Wah Kiu Yat Po (Hong Kong)

Printed Primary Sources

Aims and Policy for Social Welfare in Hong Kong. Hong Kong: Government Printer, 1964.
Annual Report of ICAC, 1974–1980. Hong Kong: Government Printer, 1974–1980.
Chung, Sze-yuen. *Hong Kong's Journey to Reunification: Memoirs of Sze-yuen Chung*. Hong Kong: Chinese University of Hong Kong Press, 2001.
Cradock, Percy. *Experiences of China*. London: John Murray, 1994.
First Report of the Commission of Inquiry under Sir Alastair Blair-Kerr. Hong Kong: Government Printer, 1973.
Lugard, Frederick. *The Dual Mandate in British Tropical Africa*. London: Forgotten Books, 2012.
McGregor, Jimmy. 'Fighting the "Vermin of Society"'. In *Hong Kong Remembers*, edited by Sally Blyth and Ian Wotherspoon, 148–157. Hong Kong: Oxford University Press, 1996.

Monnery, Neil. *Architect of Prosperity: Sir John Cowperthwaite and the Making of Hong Kong.* London: London Publishing Partnership, 2017.
Parkinson, Cosmo. *The Colonial Office from Within.* London: Faber & Faber, 1947.
Patten, Chris. *East and West: The Last Governor of Hong Kong on Power, Freedom and the Future.* London: Pan Macmillan, 1998.
Patten, Chris. *The Hong Kong Diaries.* Hong Kong: Allen Lane, 2022.
Report on the Feasibility of a Survey into Social Welfare Provision and Allied Topics in Hong Kong. Hong Kong: Government Printer, 1966.
Review of Policies for Squatter Control, Resettlement and Government Low-cost Housing, 1964. Hong Kong: Government Printer, 1964.
Second Report of the Commission of Inquiry under Sir Alastair Blair-Kerr. Hong Kong: Government Printer, 1973.
Tucker, Nancy. *China Confidential: American Diplomats and Sino-American Relations, 1945–1996.* New York: Columbia University Press, 2001.
Zhong, Daoyi et al., ed. *Oral History by Zhou Nan.* Hong Kong: Joint Publishing, 2007.

Secondary Sources

Atwell, Pamela. *British Mandarin and Chinese Reformers.* Hong Kong: Oxford University Press, 1985.
Bates, Robert H. *Toward A Political Economy of Development: A Rational Choice Perspective.* Berkeley: University of California Press, 1988.
Bickers, Robert. 'Loose Ties That Bound: British Empire, Colonial Autonomy and Hong Kong'. In *Negotiating Autonomy in Greater China: Hong Kong and Its Sovereign before and after 1997*, edited by Ray Yep, 232–254. Copenhagen: Nordic Institute of Asian Studies, 2013.
Carrico, Kevin. *Two Systems, Two Countries: A Nationalist Guide to Hong Kong.* Oakland: University of California Press, 2022.
Carroll, John. *Canton Days: British Life and Death in China.* Lanham, MD: Rowman & Littlefield, 2020.
Carroll, John. *A Concise History of Hong Kong.* Lanham, MD: Rowman & Littlefield, 2007.
Carroll, John. *Edge of Empire: Chinese Elites and British Colonials in Hong Kong.* Cambridge, MA: Harvard University Press, 2005.
Cell, John. *British Colonial Administration in the Mid-Nineteenth Century.* New Haven, CT: Yale University Press, 1970.
Cell, John. 'Colonial Rule'. In *The Oxford History of the British Empire: Volume IV, The Twentieth Century*, edited by Judith Brown and W. M. Roger Louis, 232–254. Oxford: Oxford University Press, 1999.
Chan Lau, Kit Ching. 'The Hong Kong Question during the Pacific War (1941–1945)'. *The Journal of Imperial and Commonwealth History* 21 (1973): 56–78.
Cheung, Anthony. 'New Interventionism in the Making: Interpreting State Interventions in Hong Kong after the Change of Sovereignty'. *Journal of Contemporary China* 2 (2000): 291–308.

Cheung, Gary Ka-wai. *Secrets from the British Archives: Hong Kong and Its Post-colonial Future.* Hong Kong: City University of Hong Kong Press, 2023.

Chin, Angelina. *Unsettling Exiles: Chinese Migrants in Hong Kong and the Southern Periphery during the Cold War.* New York: Columbia University Press, 2023.

Chiu, Stephen Wing Kai, and Tai Lok Lui, eds. *The Dynamics of Social Movement in Hong Kong.* Hong Kong: Hong Kong University Press, 2000.

Clayton, David. 'Buy British: The Collective Marketing of Cotton Textiles, 1956–1962'. *Textile History* 41 (2010): 217–235.

Cosemans, Sara. 'Undesirable British East African Asians. Nationalities, Statelessness and Refugeehood after Empire'. *Immigrants & Minorities* 40, no. 1–2 (2022): 210–239.

Cullen, Michael. *The Statistical Movement in Early Victorian Britain: The Foundations of Empirical Social Research.* Brighton: Edward Everett Root, 2017.

Cunliffe, S. Alex. 'Vietnamese Boat People in Hong Kong: Policies and Prescriptions'. *The Pacific Review* 4, no. 3 (1991): 272–276.

Dagati, Patricia. 'Hong Kong's Lost Right to Self-Determination: A Denial of Due Process in the United Nations'. *New York Law School Journal of International and Comparative Law* 13, no. 1 (1992): 153–179.

Darwin, John. *The Empire Project: The Rise and Fall of British World-System 1830–1970.* Cambridge: Cambridge University Press, 2009.

Darwin, John. 'Hong Kong and British Decolonization'. In *Hong Kong's Transition, 1842–1997*, edited by Judith M. Brown and Rosemary Foot, 16–32. Basingstoke: Macmillan, 1997.

Darwin, John. *Unfinished Empire: The Global Expansion of Britain.* London: Penguin, 2012.

Della Porta, Donatella, and Alberto Vannucci. *Corrupt Exchanges: Actors, Resources, and Mechanisms of Political Corruption.* New York: Aldine de Gruyter, 1999.

Downey, Bernard. 'Combatting Corruption: The Hong Kong Solution'. *Hong Kong Law Journal* 6, no. 1 (1976): 63.

Duara, Prasenjit. *Culture, Power, and the State: Rural North China 1900–1942.* Stanford, CA: Stanford University Press, 1988.

Faure, David, ed. *A Documentary History of Hong Kong: Society.* Hong Kong: Hong Kong University Press, 1997.

Fellows, James. 'The Rhetoric of Trade and Decolonization in Hong Kong, 1945–1984'. PhD diss., Lingnan University, 2016.

Goodstadt, Leo. *Uneasy Partners: The Conflict between Public Interest and Private Profit in Hong Kong.* Hong Kong: Hong Kong University Press, 2005.

Hamilton, Peter. '"A Haven for Tortured Souls": Hong Kong in the Vietnam War'. *The International History Review* 73, no. 3 (June 2015): 565–581.

Hampton, Mark. 'British Legal Culture and Colonial Governance: The Attack on Corruption in Hong Kong, 1968–1974'. *Britain and the World* 5, no. 2 (2012): 228–229.

Hampton, Mark. *Hong Kong and British Culture, 1945–1997.* Manchester: Manchester University Press, 2016.

Bibliography

Havinden, Michael, and David Meredith. *Colonialism and Development: Britain and Its Tropic Colonies, 1850–1960*. London: Routledge, 1993.

Heilmann, Sebastian. *Red Swan: How Unorthodox Policy-Making Facilitated China's Rise*. Hong Kong: Chinese University of Hong Kong Press, 2018.

Hung, Ho-fung. *City on the Edge: Hong Kong under Chinese Rule*. Cambridge: Cambridge University Press, 2022.

Hyam, Ronald. *Understanding the British Empire*. Cambridge: Cambridge University Press, 2010.

Jones, Carol, and Jon Vagg. *Criminal Justice in Hong Kong*. London and New York: Routledge-Cavendish, 2007.

Jones, Catherine. *Promoting Prosperity: The Hong Kong Way of Social Policy*. Hong Kong: Chinese University of Hong Kong Press, 1990.

Ku, Agnes, and Pan Ngai, eds. *Remaking Citizenship in Hong Kong: Community, Nation and the Global City*. New York: Routledge, 2006.

Laidlaw, Zoe. *Colonial Connections, 1815–45: Patronage, the Information Revolution and Colonial Government*. Manchester: Manchester University Press, 2005.

Lam, Kit Chun, and Pak Wai Liu. *Immigration and the Economy of Hong Kong*. Hong Kong: City University of Hong Kong Press, 1998.

Lary, Diana. 'Review of *Elusive Refuge: Chinese Migrants in the Cold War*, by Laura Madoko'. *Pacific Affairs* 90, no. 4 (2017): 793–795.

Lau, Siu Kai. *Society and Politics in Hong Kong*. Hong Kong: Chinese University of Hong Kong Press, 1982.

Law, Wing Sang. *Collaborative Colonial Power: The Making of the Hong Kong Chinese*. Hong Kong: Hong Kong University Press, 2009.

Lee, Ching Kwan. *Hong Kong: Global China's Restive Frontier*. New York: Cambridge University Press, 2022.

Lee, Francis. 'Changing Political Economy of the Hong Kong Media'. *China Perspectives*, no. 3 (2018): 9–18.

Lethbridge, Henry. 'Corruption, White Collar Crime and the ICAC'. *Hong Kong Law Journal* 6, no. 2 (1976): 169.

Lethbridge, Henry. J. 'The Emergence of Bureaucratic Corruption as a Social Problem in Hong Kong'. In *Hong Kong: Stability and Change*, edited by H. J. Lethbridge, 214–237. Hong Kong: Oxford University Press, 1978.

Litton, Henry. 'The Vietnamese Boat People Story: 1975–1999'. *Alternative Law Journal* 26, no. 4 (2001). https://doi.org/.10.1177/1037969X0102600406.

MacMillan, Margaret. *History's People: Personalities and the Past*. Croydon: Profile Books, 2015.

Mark, Chi-Kwan. 'Crisis or Opportunity? Britain, China, and the Decolonization of Hong Kong in the Long 1970s'. In *China, Hong Kong, and the Long 1970s: Global Perspectives*, edited by Priscilla Roberts and O. A. Westad, 257–277. London: Palgrave Macmillan, 2017.

Mark, Chi-Kwan. *Decolonisation in the Age of Globalization: Britain, China, and Hong Kong, 1979–89*. Manchester: Manchester University Press, 2023.

Mark, Chi-Kwan. *The Everyday Cold War: Britain and China, 1950–1972*. London: Bloomsbury Academic, 2017.

Mark, Chi-Kwan. 'Lack of Means or Loss of Will? The United Kingdom and the Decolonization of Hong Kong, 1957–1967'. *The International History Review* XXXI (March 2009): 45–71.

Mark, Chi-Kwan. 'The "Problem of People": British Colonials, Cold War Powers, and the Chinese Refugees in Hong Kong, 1949–62'. *Modern Asian Studies* 41, no. 6 (2007): 1145–1181.

Mattausch, John. 'From Subjects to Citizens: British "East African Asians"'. *Journal of Ethnic and Migration Studies* 24, no. 1 (1998): 135.

Miners, Norman. *Hong Kong under Imperial Rule, 1912–1941*. Hong Kong: Oxford University Press, 1988.

Mok, Florence. *Covert Colonialism: Governance, Surveillance and Political Culture in British Hong Kong, c. 1966–1997*. Manchester: Manchester University Press, 2023.

Mushkat, Roda. 'Refuge in Hong Kong'. *International Journal of Refugee Law* 1, no. 4 (1989): 449–480.

Nasar, Saima. 'When Uganda Expelled Its Asian Population in 1972, Britain Tried to Exclude Them'. *New Line Magazine*, 12 August 2022.

Nguyen, Lien-Hang T. 'The Vietnam Decade: The Global Shock of the War'. In *Shock of the Global: The 1970s in Perspective*, edited by Niall Ferguson, Charles Maier, Erez Manela, and Daniel Sargent, 159–172. Cambridge, MA: Harvard University Press, 2010.

Osterhammel, Jürgen. *Colonialism*. Princeton, NJ: Markus Wiener Publishers, 2005.

Palmier, Leslie. *The Control of Bureaucratic Corruption*. New Delhi: Allied Publishers, 1985.

Persson, A., Bo Rothstein, and Jan Teorell. 'Why Anti-Corruption Reforms Fail—Systemic Corruption as a Collective Action Problem'. *Governance: An International Journal of Policy, Administration, and Institution* 26, no. 3 (2013): 449–471.

Qian, Yingyi, and Barry Weingast. 'China's Transition to Market: Market-Preserving Federalism, Chinese Style'. *Journal of Economic Policy Reform* 1, no. 2 (1996): 149–185.

Richards, Thomas. *The Imperial Archive: Knowledge and the Fantasy of Empire*. London and New York: Verso, 1993.

Roberts, Priscilla. 'Introduction: China and the Long 1970s: The Great Transformation'. In *China, Hong Kong and the Long 1970s: Global Perspective*, edited by Priscilla Roberts and O. A. Westadpp. 1–30. London: Palgrave Macmillan, 2017.

Roberts, Priscilla. 'Prologue: Cold War Hong Kong: The Foundations'. In *Hong Kong in the Cold War*, edited by Priscilla Roberts and John Carroll, 15–25. Hong Kong: Hong Kong University Press, 2016.

Rose, Richard, and Phillip L. Davies. *Inheritance in Public Policy: Change without Choice in Britain*. New Haven, CT: Yale University Press, 1994.

Schenk, Catherine. 'Economic History of Hong Kong'. In EH.net, *Encyclopaedia*, edited by Robert Whaples. Accessed 26 September 2022. https://eh.net/encyclopedia/economic-history-of-hong-kong/

Schenk, Catherine. *Hong Kong as an International Financial Centre: Emergence and Development 1945–65*. New York and London: Routledge, 2001.
Scott, Ian. *Political Change and the Crisis of Legitimacy in Hong Kong*. Hong Kong: Oxford University Press, 1989.
Sinn, Elizabeth. *Power and Charity: A Chinese Merchant Elite in Colonial Hong Kong*. Hong Kong: Hong Kong University Press, 2003.
Skeldon, Ronald. 'Hong Kong's Response to Indochinese Influx, 1975–93'. *The Annals of the American Academy of Political and Social Science* 534, no. 1 (1994). https://doi.org/10.1177/0002716294534001008.
Smart, Alan. *The Shek Kip Mei Myth: Squatters, Fires and Colonial Rule in Hong Kong, 1950–1963*. Hong Kong: Hong Kong University Press, 2006.
Smart, Alan, and Tai-Lok Lui. 'Learning from Civil Unrest: State/Society Relations before and after the 1967 Disturbances'. In *May Days in Hong Kong: Riot and Emergency in 1967*, edited by Robert Bickers and Ray Yep, 145–160. Hong Kong: Hong Kong University Press, 2009.
Snow, Philip. *The Fall of Hong Kong: Britain, China and the Japanese Occupation*. New Haven, CT: Yale University Press, 2004.
So, Alvin. 'The Economic Success of Hong Kong: Insights from a World-System Perspective'. *Sociological Perspectives* 29, no. 2 (April 1986): 241–258.
Stein, Barry. 'The Geneva Conferences and the Indochinese Refugee Crisis'. *The International Migration Review* 13, no. 4 (1979): 716–723.
Tsang, Steve. *Democracy Shelved: Great Britain, China and Attempts at Constitutional Reform in Hong Kong, 1945–1952*. Hong Kong: Oxford University Press, 1988.
Tsang, Steve. *Governing Hong Kong: Administrative Officers from the Nineteenth Century to the Handover to China, 1862–1997*. Hong Kong: Hong Kong University Press, 2007.
Tsang, Steve. 'Strategy for Survival: The Cold War and Hong Kong's Policy towards Kuomintang and Chinese Communist Activities in the 1950s'. *The Journal of Imperial and Commonwealth History* 25, no. 2 (1997): 294–317.
Turner, H. A. et al. *The Last Colony: But Whose?* Cambridge: Cambridge University Press, 1980.
Ure, Gavin. *Governors, Politics and the Colonial Office: Public Policy in Hong Kong, 1918–58*. Hong Kong: Hong Kong University Press, 2012.
Williams, Stephanie. *Running the Show: Governors of the British Empire*. London: Penguin, 2011.
Xu, Chenggang. 'The Fundamental Institutions of China's Economic Reforms and Development'. *Journal of Economic Literature* 49, no. 4 (2011): 1076–1151.
Yep, Ray. 'Beyond the "Great Man" Narrative: Scandals, Cumulative Reforms and the Trajectory of Anti-Corruption Efforts in Colonial Hong Kong before MacLehose Years'. *Social Transformation in Chinese Societies* 18, no. 2 (2021): 154–170.
Yep, Ray. 'The Crusade against Corruption in Hong Kong in the 1970s: Governor MacLehose as a Zealous Reformer or Reluctant Hero?'. *China Information* 27 (July 2013): 197–221.

Yep, Ray. '"Cultural Revolution in Hong Kong": Emergency Powers, Administration of Justice and the Turbulent Year of 1967'. *Modern Asian Studies* 46, no. 4 (2012): 1007–1032.

Yep, Ray. *Jingmo Geming* [Quiet revolution: The long campaign against corruption in Hong Kong]. Hong Kong: Chunghwa, 2015.

Yep, Ray, and Tai-Lok Lui. 'Revisiting the Golden Era of MacLehose and the Dynamics of Social Reforms'. *China Information* 24, no. 3 (2010): 249–272.

Yip, Ka-che. *Disease, Colonialism, and the State: Malaria in Modern East Asian History*. Hong Kong: Hong Kong University Press, 2009.

Yip, Maurice. 'New Town Planning as Diplomatic Planning: Scalar Politics, British-Chinese Relations, and Hong Kong'. *Journal of Urban History* 48, no. 2 (2020): 1–20.

Yuen, Samson, and Edmund Cheng. 'Deepening the State: The Dynamics of China's United Front Work in Post-Handover Hong Kong'. *Communist and Post-communist Studies* 53, no. 4 (2020): 136–154.

Zhang, Junfeng. *Fantan Tingbuliu* [The unstoppable anti-corruption campaign]. Hong Kong: Joint Publishing, 2010.

Index

Note: Page numbers in **bold** direct the reader to tables or other images.

Akers-Jones, David, 163–165
Australia, 4, 30, 91

Black, Robert, 23, 37, 101, 142–144, 149
Blaker, Peter, 132
Bray MP, Jeremy, 144
British Empire: administration of, *see* Foreign Office; anti-imperialism, 4; 'benevolent' imperialism', 139; 'caretake' imperialism, 49; colonial nationalism, 3–5; Colonial Regulations, 77; commercial project of, 3; decolonization, 13, 44, 144; 'dual mandate' 5; incoherence of, 2–3; 'Imperial Preference', 36–38, 140; intermediaries, reliance on, 4–5, 10; knowledge of, *see* Great Britain, British Museum; Lancashire Agreement (1959), 88–89; Manifesto on Colonial Policy (1957), 144; Ottawa Conference (1932), 37; 'responsible government', 4; self-determination, 144–145. *See also* Australia, British Malaya, Canada, Falkland Islands, Hong Kong, India, Kenya, Malta, Nova Scotia, Rhodesia, South Africa, Tanzania, Uganda, United States of America, Weihaiwei
British Malaya, 9, 22. *See also* Malaysia, Singapore

Burma: *Ava see* Hong Kong, civic and municipal matters, *Ava*, arrival of; Vietnamese refugees, attitude to, 116–117

Callaghan, James, 79, 98, 127
Cambodia: Thailand, relationship with, 136; Vietnam, relationship with, 30, 108, 120–121, 128
Campbell, Joseph, 50
Canada, 119, 136
Carnarvon, Earl of, 46
Carrington, Lord Peter, 123, 132–136, 160
Carter, Jimmy, 130
Cater, Jack, 58–59, 65–71, 74
Ceylon (now Sri Lanka), 53–54
Chamanan, Kriangsak, 128
Chamberlain, Joseph, 3, 47
Cheng Hon-Kuen, 64–65
Chiang Kai-shek, 140–141
China, civic and political matters: Basic Law, 20, 182; British ambassadors to, *see* Cradock; Cultural Revolution (1966–1976), 24–25, 32, 83, 110, 172, 178; famine, 79, 110; Foreign Secretaries of, *see* Huang Hua, Ji Pengfei, Liao Chengzhi, Song Zhiguang; Great Leap Forward, 31; Joint Declaration, 169; Kuomintang, *see* Hong Kong, China, relationship with, Kuomintang violence;

leaders of, *see* Deng, Mao, Zhou; Nationalism, 5–6, 12, 139–142; NCNA, *see* NCNA; nuclear technology, 32; 'One Country, Two Systems', 168, 171, 182; Open Door Policy, 172; People's Republic (PRC), 11, 15, 23, 28–30; Qing government, 5–6, 11–13, 139, 151; Shanghai Communiqué (1972), 23, 34; Soviet Union, relationship with, 30–33; Taiwan, relationship with Taiwan, 153, 161, 166–168; Treaty to Relinquish Extra-Territoriality (1943), 140; UN membership, 15, 23, 33, 141; US, relationship with, 153; 'utilitarian familism', 79; Vietnam, relationship with, 108–109, 128

China, economic matters: Bank of China, 163; *baojia* system, 5; China Resources, 162–165; International Trust and Investment Corporation, 163; Special Economic Zones (SEZs), 15, 172; UN embargo on trade, 13, 28–30, 37; US embargo on trade, 28, 37

China, geographical areas: Changsha, 31; Chongqing, 31; Guangdong, 154, 172; Guangzhou, 156; Hankou (now part of Wuhan), 23; Hong Kong, *see* Hong Kong; Macao, *see* Macao; Nanjing, 31; Shanghai, 15, 29; Shenyang, 31; Taiwan, *see* Taiwan; Weihaiwei, *see* Weihaiwei; Zhenbao Island, 33

China, military matters: Boxer Uprising, 91; Civil War (1927–1949), 28; People's Liberation Army (PLA), 25, 31; Red Guards, 31–32

Clark, Richard, 121, 124–127
Clift, Richard, 164
Cold War: 'special relationship', 20, 23, 33, 109–112, 140, 173–174;

Suez Canal crisis, 39; Vietnamese refugee crisis, *see* Hong Kong, civic and municipal matters, Vietnamese refugees, attitude to

Colonial Office: bribery, attitude to, 46–48, 51; Colonial Secretary, 2; *Hong Kong: Value and Cost to the United Kingdom 1957–1959*, 139; low status of, 2–3. *See also* Foreign Office

Communism: Chinese, *see* China, civic and political matters, PRC; Hong Kong, *see* Hong Kong, Communists, local; Soviet, *see* Soviet Union

Cortazzi, Hugh, 94–97, 102
Cowperthwaite, John, 35–36
Cradock, Percy: China, visit to (with MacLehose), 153–154, 157–162; Deng, attitude to, 148, 153, 157, 178; Red Guards, attacked by, 32; Song Zhiguang, meeting with, 167–168

Crane, Jim, 74
Crowson, Richard, 57
Cushing, Henry, 123
Czechoslovakia (now the Czech Republic and Slovak Republic), 22, 42

Davies, Lewis, 120–121
Deng Xiaoping: ascendance of, 153, 172; Macao, attitude to, 155; MacLehose, meeting with, 138, 154–157, 160–163, 168, 172–173, 181; reforming agenda of, 43, 153, 178; Taiwan, attitude to, 155, 166–167

Denmark: ambassador to, 23, 42; *Clara Maersk*, *see* Hong Kong, civic and municipal matters, *Clara Maersk*, arrival of

Douglas-Home, Sir Alec, 62–63, 84, 143, 148
Duara, Prasenjit, 5–6

Elliott, Elsie, 56
Ellis, Alan, 56
England, Joe, *Hong Kong: Britain's Responsibility*, 86–87
European Economic Community (EEC), 33, 37–38, 88

Fabianism, 86–70
Falkland Island, Falklands War, 168
Fellows, James, 37–38
Foggon, George, 85–87, 98
Foreign and Commonwealth Office (FCO): corruption, attitude to, 53–59, 66–69, 72, 77; Far Eastern Department, 22; Foreign Secretaries, *see* Callaghan, Carrington, Douglas-Home, Owen; 'Future of Hong Kong' (1971), 148; Godber, attitude to, 60–61; *Hong Kong Planning Paper* (1976), 79, 92–97, 100–107, 146–149, 177; 'Long Term Study' (1969), 147; merger, 3; 'old China hands' in, 1, 167; unhelpfulness of, 3, 90–97, 100–107, 112–116, 131–132, 170n1, **176**. *See also* Colonial Office
France, 22, 119, 130
Freeman, Chas, 125

Galsworthy, Anthony, 36, 100
Germany, 122–123
Godber, Peter: escape of, 172–175, 179; extradition, 60–65, 76–77, 179–181; Riots, role in, 55; scandal (corruption), 16, 20, 54–55
Goodfellow, M. A., 90
Goronwy Roberts, Lord Goronwy Owen, 66, 94–95, 98–102, 119, 144
Grantham, Alexander, 37, 101
Great Britain, civic and political matters: Board of Trade, 8; British Empire, *see* British Empire; British Museum, 8; China, exports to, 32; Chinese diplomats in, 32; Cold War, *see* Cold War; Colonial Office, *see* Colonial Office; Conservative governments, election of, 106; Cotton Board, 88; EEC, membership of, 33, 37–38, 89; Foreign Office, *see* Foreign Office; General Registry Office, 8; Joint Declaration, 169; Labour governments, election of, 1, 17, 64, 85, 89; royal family, *see* Queen Elizabeth, Prince Philip, Princess Alexandria; Sino-British Joint Declaration, 20; 'special relationship', *see* Cold War, 'special relationship'; taxation, 91; Vietnamese refugees, attitude to, *see* Thatcher
Great Britain, leaders of, *see* Heath, Macmillan, Queen Elizabeth, Thatcher, Wilson (Harold)
Great Britain, regulation: British Fugitive Offenders Act, 60–64; Commonwealth Immigrants Act (1962), 113; Registration Act (1836), 8
Great Depression, 37
Grey, Anthony, 40–41
Guam, 112, 121

Haddon-Cave, Philip: fiscal conservatism of, 98–102, 107, 177, 181; Vietnamese refugee crisis, role in, 114–115
Hampton, Mark, 52
Harcourt, Cecil, 140–141
Hastings, Warren, 8
Havers, Michael, 160
Heath, Edward, 33, 113, 114n16, 130
Ho Cheung, 42n43
Holbrook, Richard, 123–124
Hong Kong, China, relationship with: China, UN trade embargo against, 13, 28; Chinese immigrants ('mainlanders'), 26–29, 79–80, 109–110, 124–125, 184; 'Hong Kong question' (sovereignty), 13–15, 18, 23, 143–157, 163–166,

171; Kuomintang violence, 12; land leases, 18, 138, 143, 150; New Territories Lease, 140, 151–166, 173, 178; Office for Safeguarding the Central People's Government, 184; reunification, 9, 18, 81–84, 139–140, 182; Riots, *see* Hong Kong, Riots; Sino-British Joint Declaration (1984), 20; Special Administrative Region (HKSAR), 170, 182–184

Hong Kong, civic and political matters: Advisory Committee on Diversification, 156; Air Raid Precaution Department (ARPD), 50; *Ava*, arrival of, 116–118; British Garrison, 24, 34, 39–40; census (1961), 26; China Motor Bus Company, 75; civic pride, 81–84, 150; civil society, growth of, 15, 20; *Clara Maersk*, arrival of, 110–116; Communists, local, 25, 31, 80–81, 146–147; Cross-Harbour Tunnel, ix, 14; demographics, 25, 81; education, 78, 87, 98; Hong Kong and Yaumati Ferry Company, 165; housing, 25–27, 78–80, 84–87, 151–152, 162, 166; Kai Tak Airport, 55; Kin Lee Construction Company, 50; labour, 82–88, 92–93, 96; Luen Tak Company, 162; Mass Transit Railway, 14, 90; racial segregation, 48; refugees from, 13; regulation, *see* Hong Kong, regulation and policy documents; SARS epidemic, 183; social welfare, 93–95, 102–105, **103**, 171, 177; Special Processing Centre, 119–123; taxation, increasing, 5–6, 28, 180; taxation, low, 10, 17, 79, 97–98, 102; Telephone Company, 75; Trade Development Council, 89; Trafalgar Holdings, 163; Tung Wah, 19, 111; Vietnamese refugees, attitude to, 17, 106–137, **124**, 177,

181; white papers, 80; Yaumatei police station, 70, 73, 181

Hong Kong, corruption: Advisory Committee on Corruption, 53; Anti-Corruption Office, 52–55, 63–66, 179; ethnic divide, myth of, 48–51, 55; Independent Commission Against Corruption (ICAC), 14–16, 45–46, 58–59, 64–76, **66**, **68**, **75**, 172–175, 179; police corruption, 45–47, 52, 65–69. *See also* Hong Kong, policing, crime and unrest; syndicates, 69, 181

Hong Kong, economic matters: Chamber of Commerce, 37–38; economic growth and strength, 19, 28–30, 99, 145–149, 155, 166, 183–185; exports, 24, 28, 34–40, 86–88, 99, 140; Hong Kong dollar, 163; 'Hong Kong gap', 29; *mui-tsai* labour, 19; pound (sterling), value of, 35–36, 99, 139; regional financial centre, 28–29, 172; Sterling Area, 29, 34–36; Stock Exchange, 29–30; taxation, *see* Hong Kong, civic and municipal matters, taxation

Hong Kong, geographical areas: Island, 157, 165; Kowloon, 13, 47–50, 70, 157, 184; Lai Chai Kok, 27; Shau Kei Wan, 27; Tin Shui Wai, 161–165, 173; Wanchai, 64

Hong Kong, governors, *see* Black, Grantham, Lugard, MacDonnell, MacLehose, Northcote, Patten, Robinson, Trench, Youde, Young

Hong Kong, policing, crime and unrest: Anti-Extradition Bill Protest, 183; Double-Tenth Festival confrontation, 12; drugs, 48, 52, 73; extortion and blackmail, 48, 52; gambling, 46–49; Japanese Occupation, *see* Japan, Hong Kong, occupation of; June 4 Incident, 184; Occupy Movement, 183; police corruption, *see* Hong Kong, corruption; police morale, 68, 72; Police Mutiny (1977), 45–46, 70–72, 76; prostitution, 47–48, 52; Riots, *see* Hong Kong, Riots; statistics, **26**; Triads, 26, 52. *See also* Hong Kong, corruption.

Hong Kong, regulation and policy documents: Aims and Policy for Social Welfare in Hong Kong (1964), 27; *Annual Reports*, 120; *Development of Medical Services in Hong Kong* (1964), 27; Employment Ordinance, 94; Establishment Regulation 444, 52; Illegal Strikes and Lock-out Ordinances, 84; Industrial Relations Bill, 84; Misdemeanours Punishment Ordinance (1898), 47, 51; National Security Law (2020), 183–184; Police Ordinance, 72; Prevention of Corruption Ordinance (1948), 51–52; Prevention of Bribery Bill (1970), 53–54; Prevention of Bribery Ordinance (1971), 16, 45, 54–55, 60–61, 171, 181; Severance Bill, 84

Hong Kong, Riots (1967): aftermath of, 14–17, 27, 78–80, 142, 171; China, unrest, relationship to, 11–12, 32, 83; colonial authority, challenge to, 23–26, 80–82, 85, 145–146; prisoners from, 34, 40–42. *See also* Trench; Victoria Harbour, battleship moored in, 13

Hopson, Donald, 40
Hua Guofeng, 159–161
Huang Hua, 141, 154, 172
Hughes, Richard, 43
humanitarian organisations and NGOs, 111, 133. *See also* United Nations
Hunt, Ernest, 64–65

India: Civil Service, 4; exports, 37, 88; governance of, 3–4; Hastings, *see* Hastings, Warren; Indian Survey, 8
Indochina (now South-East Asia), 12–13, 32, 109, 121. *See also* Vietnam
Indonesia: economic matters, 30; Galang Island, 122, 134; Vietnamese refugees, attitude to, 122–126, **124**
International Labour Organization (ILO), 85–86, 92
Italy, 122–123

Japan: Hong Kong, occupation of (1941–1945), 10, 51; Hong Kong, surrender of, 140–141; labour laws, 86; Mass Transit Railway, consortium to build, 90–91; Vietnamese refugees, attitude to, 118, **124**
Ji Pengfei, 148–149
Jiang Qing, 31
Johnson MP, James, 56
Johnson, Lyndon, 111–112

Kaunda, Kenneth, 141
Ke Hua, 128
Kenya, 112
Kerr-Blair, Sir Alastair, 60
Kissinger, Henry, 33
Korea: economic growth, 28; Korean War, 10–13, 28–30

Laos, 30, 121
Lau Siu Kai, 79
Lau, Edmund, 165
Lee, Frederick, 39
Lee Kuan Yew, 128
Liao Chengzhi, 142, 154–157, 165–167
Li Qiang, 153
Li Jusheng, 158–159, 165
Li Ka-shing, 163
Luddington, John, 74
Lugard, Frederick, 5–7

Macao, 122, **124**, 141, 155
MacDonald, Malcolm, 157–158
MacDonnell, Richard, 46–47
MacIntosh, Duncan, 51
MacLehose, Murray: Black, advisor to, 149; corruption, campaign against, 45–46, 54–55, 69–77. *See also* Hong Kong, corruption; Deng, meeting with, 138, 153–161, 167; Denmark, ambassador to, 23, 42; 'difficult' character of, 170, 175, 186. *See also* FCO, unhelpfulness of; England (Joe), attitude to, 86–87; Godber, attitude to, 60–65; *Guidelines for the Governor Designate, Hong Kong*, 55, 149–150; ICAC, *see* Hong Kong, corruption, ICAC; Police Mutiny, handling of, *see* Hong Kong, policing, crime and unrest, Police Mutiny; popularity of, 14; reunification, attitude to, 81–84; Riots, attitude to, 42. *See also* Hong Kong, Riots; social reform, 14–17, 24–26, 43, 54, 78–79, 177. *See also* Hong Kong, policing, crime and unrest; speeches and addresses, 57–59, 62, 92–96, 125, 158; Ten-Year Housing programme, 78, 98, 151–152. *See also* Hong Kong, civil and municipal matters, housing; Vietnam, ambassador to, 23; Vietnamese refugees, attitude to, 119, 122–127, 131–132, 137; 'Who Benefits from Hong Kong?', 89–90
Macmillan, Harold, 39
Macoun, Michael, 56–57, 67–68, 456
Maddocks, Arthur, 41
Malaysia: British military presence in, 39; economic matters, 29–30; Vietnamese refugees, attitude to, 121–122, **124**, 125–126
Malta, 170n1
Mao Zedong: ascension of, 30–31; Cultural Revolution, *see* China, civic and political matters, Cultural Revolution; death, 149–150, 167; Great Leap Forward, *see* China, civic and political matters, Great Leap Forward; Winston Churchill, compared to, 33
McGregor, Jimmy, 73
McLaren, Robin, 153, 161
Mintoff, Dom, 170
Monson, Leslie, 42–43

New China News Agency (NCNA), 40, 154, 158–159, 162–167
newspapers: *Hong Kong Evening News*, 56; *Keung Sheung Yat Po*, 56; *People's Daily*, 24, 141, 149; *South China Morning Post*, 184; *Sunday Times*, 56; sensationalism, accusations of, 67; suspension of, 32; *Wah Kiu Yat Po*, 60; *World in Action*, 87
New Zealand, 22, 30
Nixon, Richard, 15, 33, 173
Norman-Walker, Hugh, 80–81
Northcote, Geoffrey, 50–51
Nova Scotia, 4

O'Keeffe, Laurence, 91
Onn, Hussein, 125
Orr, Ian, 164
Owen, David, 105, 153, 178

Pakistan, 30, 37, 88
Parkinson, Sir Cosmo, 4
Patten, Chris, 1, 106, 170, 175
Perkins, Steele, 50
Philippines: Batan Island, 136; economic matters, 29–30; Vietnamese refugees, attitude to, 121–123, **124**, 136
Powell MP, Enoch, 114
Prendergast, John, 58–59, 64
Prince Philip, 110
Princess Alexandria, 89

Quantrill, William, 159

Index

Queen Elizabeth I: absence of ix; 'displeasure' of, 73, 77, 180; Hong Kong, visit to, 110; images of, ix

Rhodesia (now Zimbabwe), 3
Roberts, Denys, 54, 67, 117
Robinson, William, 47
Royle, Anthony, 57
Rushford, Antony, 152

Sampatkumar, Rajagoplana, 119
Schouten, Peter, 70
Shepherd, Lord Malcolm, 144
Simmons, Joyce, 60
Singapore: anti-corruption laws, 53; British military presence in, 39; economic matters, 29–30; Vietnamese refugees, attitude to, **124**
Song Zhiguang, 158–160
South Africa, 3
Southeast Asia Treaty Organization (SEATO), 30
Soviet Union: China, relationship with, 30–33; influence, fear of, 12, 109, 129; United States, relationship with, 173; Vietnam, relationship with, 109, 120–121
Spanish Empire, 9
Stewart, James, 101–102
Stewart, John, 69, 106
Sutcliff, Charles, 54–55
Sze-yuen Chung, 57–58

Taiwan: British consulate, closing of, 33; China, relationship with, 153–157, 161, 166–168; economic matters, 28; geographical position of, 12; UN membership of (ROC), 15, 33
Tanzania, 113
Thailand: Cambodia, relationship with, 136; economic matters, 29–30; U-Tapao Island, 121; Vietnamese refugees, attitude to, 17, 121–122, **124**, 128
Thatcher, Margaret: Chinese immigrants ('mainlanders'), attitude to, 109; election of, 127; Falklands War, popularity after, 168; land leases (Hong Kong), attitude to, 159, 168, 178. *See also* FCO, unhelpfulness of; social reform (Hong Kong), attitude to, 106; UN conference (Geneva), demand for, 128–131; Vietnamese refugees, attitude to, 127–133, 177
Thornton MP, Edward, 88
Todd, Alistair, 81
Tokyo Economic Summit (1979), 130
Trade Union Congress, 86
Trench, Sir David: British Garrison, attitude to, 39; corruption, campaign against, 16, 52–54, 76, 171; 'difficult' character of, 24, 34–36, 44, 77, 171, 175; labour, attitude to, 92; Riots, attitude to, 27, 31–33, 40–43, 78–79
Tsang, Steve, 49
Tung Chee-Hwa, 170, 183

Uganda, 112–113
United Nations (UN): China, request to no longer regard Hong Kong and Macao as colonial territories, 141, 144–145, 172; China, trade embargo against, 13, 28–30; Chinese membership of, 15, 23, 33, 141; Committee of Twenty-Four, 144; Committee on Decolonization, 141; conference, Geneva (1979), 109, 127–137, **134**, 182; High Commission for Refugees (UNHCR), 115–119, 122, 127, 135; Secretaries General, *see* Waldheim; Taiwanese membership of, 15
United States of America, civic and political matters: American

Revolution, 3–4; anti-imperialism of, 139–140; British ambassador to, 33; China, relationship with, 33–34, 147, 173; Cold War, *see* Cold War; Indochina Migration and Refugee Assistance Act, 112; Shanghai Communiqué (1972), 23, 34; 'special relationship', *see* Cold War, 'special relationship'; Soviet Union, relationship with, 173; Vietnamese refugees, attitude to, 108–119, 124–126, 134–136

United States of America, military matters: Korean War, 10–13; overseas military facilities, *see* Guam, Philippines, Thailand, U-Tapao Island, Wake Island; Vietnam War, 17, 108–110

United States of America, Presidents of, *see* Carter, Johnson (Lyndon), Nixon

Vietnam: ambassador to, 22; China, relationship with, 108–109, 120, 173; Chinese (ethnic) population of, 109, 120–126, 135; Communist regime, 13, 108, 173; Orderly Departure Scheme, 127–129, 135; refugees from ('Boat People'), 17, 106–137, **124**. *See also* Hong Kong, Vietnamese refugees, attitude to; SEATO, 30; Soviet Union, relationship with, 120–121; Vietnam War, 17, 108–110

Wake Island (Micronesia), 121
Waldheim, Kurt, 129
Wang Kuang, 159, 162
Warren, Christopher, 125–126
Weihaiwei, 4–6
Williams, Lady, 80
Williams, Stephanie, 1–2
Wilson, David, 154, 158, 163–167
Wilson, Harold, 35, 79, 85
Wong Chak, 41
Wu, Gordon, 163–165

Yang Shangkun, 156
Youde, Edward, 62, 91, 164, 167
Young, Mark, 51–52, 101
Yuet-Keung Kan, 72–74, 160

Zambia, 141
Zhou Enlai: ascension of; assassination (failed), 12; death of, 149–150; Douglas-Home, meeting with, 148; Kuanda, comments to, 141; Kissinger, meeting with, 33; moderation of, 31; Red Guards, criticism of, 32; reunification, attitude to, 141–142, 148, 157–158
Zhou Nan, 157, 166
Zhu Rongji, 183